THE HANS BLIX IRAQ WAR DIARIES

This diary will take the reader back to the pivotal period at the turn of the millennium, when Hans Blix was the UN chief weapons inspector to Iraq, responsible for extensive investigations into the possible existence of weapons of mass destruction. Blix was required to report to the world what he had – and had not – found, under immense time pressure from the broader political context, where the success of the inspections might avert a US-led war. It sheds new light on the intense diplomacy behind the scenes at the UN headquarters in New York and in capitals around the world, where Blix met with leaders like US president George Bush, UK prime minister Tony Blair and French president Jacques Chirac. The diary is a valuable historical document of events leading up to the Iraq war, but it can also be read as a guide to practical diplomacy with the highest of stakes.

HANS BLIX is Director General Emeritus at the International Atomic Energy Agency. He has a PhD in international law from the University of Cambridge and an LLD from the University of Stockholm. He was Swedish foreign minister from 1978 to 1979, director general of the International Atomic Energy Agency (IAEA) from 1981 to 1997 and chairman of the United Nations Monitoring, Verification and Inspection Commission (UNMOVIC) from 2000 to 2003, tasked with searching for weapons of mass destruction in Iraq. Hans is the author of *Disarming Iraq* (2005) and *A Farewell to Wars* (Cambridge, 2023).

The Hans Blix Iraq War Diaries

2000–2003

HANS BLIX

Shaftesbury Road, Cambridge CB2 8EA, United Kingdom

One Liberty Plaza, 20th Floor, New York, NY 10006, USA

477 Williamstown Road, Port Melbourne, VIC 3207, Australia

314–321, 3rd Floor, Plot 3, Splendor Forum, Jasola District Centre, New Delhi – 110025, India

103 Penang Road, #05–06/07, Visioncrest Commercial, Singapore 238467

Cambridge University Press is part of Cambridge University Press & Assessment, a department of the University of Cambridge.

We share the University's mission to contribute to society through the pursuit of education, learning and research at the highest international levels of excellence.

www.cambridge.org
Information on this title: www.cambridge.org/9781009650199

DOI: 10.1017/9781009650151

© Hans Blix 2025

This publication is in copyright. Subject to statutory exception and to the provisions of relevant collective licensing agreements, no reproduction of any part may take place without the written permission of Cambridge University Press & Assessment.

When citing this work, please include a reference to the DOI 10.1017/9781009650151

First published 2025

A catalogue record for this publication is available from the British Library

A Cataloging-in-Publication data record for this book is available from the Library of Congress

ISBN 978-1-009-65019-9 Hardback
ISBN 978-1-009-65017-5 Paperback

Cambridge University Press & Assessment has no responsibility for the persistence or accuracy of URLs for external or third-party internet websites referred to in this publication and does not guarantee that any content on such websites is, or will remain, accurate or appropriate.

For EU product safety concerns, contact us at Calle de José Abascal, 56, 1°, 28003 Madrid, Spain, or email eugpsr@cambridge.org

Contents

Preface	*page* vii
List of Persons Mentioned	xv
List of Abbreviations	xviii
Year 2000	1
Year 2001	55
Year 2002	102
Year 2003	178
Epilogue	231

Preface

This diary begins with my arrival at the United Nations (UN) headquarters in New York on 28 February 2000 to organize and lead a new unit responsible for finding and eradicating any biological and chemical weapons and missiles that could remain in Iraq. It has been commonplace to refer to me as 'Iraq inspector' or 'chief inspector'. However, as the diary shows, my job was not to inspect on the ground. My expertise is not in biology or chemistry but in international law, and my relevant experience was the sixteen years (1981–1997) I had been the director general of the International Atomic Energy Agency (IAEA). In that capacity, I had been responsible for the operation of the agency's system of safeguards and inspections to verify the peaceful use of nuclear installations. Following the Gulf War of 1991, the IAEA and I had also been mandated by the UN Security Council to run nuclear inspections in Iraq.

The job now given to me by the Security Council was to organize and be executive chairman of the United Nations Monitoring, Verification and Inspection Commission (UNMOVIC) for Iraq and to launch and run its operations. As Iraq accepted the return of inspections only in the autumn of 2002, my work until then focused on organization and diplomacy and that of most staff on the preparation for inspections. Inspectors were employed on a stand-by basis and given training. Results from inspections from 1991 to 1998 and images taken from satellites were analysed.

Actual inspections in Iraq took place from 27 November 2002 until just before the US and its allies launched the Iraq war on 20 March 2003. My diary covers the period of more than two and a half years during which wrangling about getting inspection back in Iraq inched forward, and then the intense period of less than four months of actual inspections before the invasion.

The diary was written in English in the form of letters to my elder son, Mårten, who like my wife lived in Stockholm. The diary covers the period up to June 2003, when, after the Iraq war and the ending of inspections, I returned home.

The texts now published have not been altered other than to correct spelling and other minor linguistic errors. However, many entries and passages not relevant or of marginal interest for understanding the path to the Iraq war and my specific role have been omitted. This applies especially to entries made in the period 2000 to September 2002, when diplomacy about resumed inspections was only in slow motion, and the period after March 2003, when the invasion had taken place. It applies also to many entries relating to family matters. On the other hand, many explanatory comments and notes were added to make the text more understandable. Such additions and clarifications are given in italics. It has not been possible to divide the diary into chapters, but some subtitles have been inserted to signal key content. In the editing process, dates have been inserted in some places to facilitate use of the text for research. Such dates are in italics and placed within brackets. They have been taken from the calendars that I kept at the time.

Entries into the diary were not made daily, and a few were lost, but they give, I believe, an accurate account of the path to the war – as I saw it. They paint a picture of parts of the intense and extensive international discussions that I followed and participated in but also scattered personal reflections not directly related to the Iraq issue and notes on my daily doings and family contacts.

As the diary provides a torrent of notes and observations on matters big and small, I will provide some background to what happened 2000–2003 and call attention to various developments that are described in the diary and which I found particularly significant.

It will be recalled that Iraq attacked and occupied Kuwait in 1990, and a US-led, UN-authorized operation liberated Kuwait in 1991. With the mission of liberation accomplished, Saddam Hussein was left in place, a restraint that was criticized by some in the US, but which was in line with the UN authorization. However, Security Council Resolution 687 of 1991 required that all items relating to biological, chemical and nuclear weapons and certain kinds of long-range missiles were to be declared by Iraq and destroyed. It was left to a new UN body, the United Nations Special Commission (UNSCOM) and to the IAEA to verify the declarations and the destruction and thereafter to monitor the absence of proscribed items. An embargo on the purchase of Iraqi oil was to be maintained until the process was successfully completed. This process was not completed even in 1998, when Iraq refused further inspection. As Iraq had chosen to destroy prohibited material in 1991 without the presence of inspectors, and as its declarations often proved defective, much material was deemed 'unaccounted for'. When, in addition, Iraq on several occasions had refused UNSCOM entry to inspect various sites or 'played cat and mouse' with inspection teams, suspicions had arisen that Iraq was hiding proscribed items. The IAEA did not share such suspicions regarding nuclear items but reported in both 1997 (the Blix report) and 1998 (the ElBaradei report) that the agency had a technically coherent picture of the nuclear programme and that only minor questions remained.

The US, which throughout the 1990s wished to see the ousting of Saddam, insisted on keeping all the disarmament files – including the nuclear – open to a charge of non-fulfilment that would potentially justify armed intervention.

However, the pressure on Iraq weakened. Weapons inspectors from the UN and IAEA were constrained to leave Iraq in 1998, and the sanctions gradually eroded, partly through extensive smuggling of oil, partly through the UN allowing Iraq for humanitarian reasons again to sell increasing quantities of oil under the control of the UN Food for Oil programme.

In 1999, the permanent members of the Security Council did not agree on the way forward. Several, including France and Russia, wanted the now-ineffective UN programme to be gradually phased out. They no longer saw Iraq as a significant threat. The inspections were not only locked out but also discredited by revelations that they had been infiltrated by and served US intelligence. The US, still wanting regime change in Iraq, was not ready to discard sanctions and inspection. A compromise was reached in the Council at the end of 1999 with a resolution – 1284 – that saw the discredited UNSCOM replaced by a new regime – UNMOVIC – that would be truly international and which would focus on resolving 'remaining disarmament issues'. When this was done, inspection and sanctions could be suspended and eventually lifted, and only long-term monitoring would remain.

The Council appointed me chairman to organize and lead the new commission while leaving the IAEA in its old function in the nuclear field. When I arrived in New York to begin my work, many members of the UNSCOM secretariat had left, and my first task was to plan and seek the Security Council's approval of the organization of UNMOVIC. While this had to be done within a relatively short time, there was no urgent pressure for the dispatch of inspectors, as Iraq showed no readiness to accept the new resolution, claiming – rightly, as it had to be recognized in 2003 – that it had no proscribed weapons. Moreover, Iraq's situation was not desperate: it had got rid of inspections that it felt were humiliating and US-infiltrated, and it had succeeded in circumventing and eroding sanctions. It fell to the secretary-general, Kofi Annan, to remind the Iraqi government of the decision of the council to reinstall inspections. The prospect that this decision held out of formally terminated sanctions and of no control of Iraq's imports had some attraction for Iraq. Acceptance of renewed inspections could also reduce the risk of an armed US intervention.

My diary describes how the Iraqi government looked to deflect US armed action by showing growing interest in the UN resolution and readiness to accept the inspections, but also how it sought some assurance that the 'unresolved disarmament issues' would be few and could be handled without interminable intrusive inspection. At the same time, Iraq seems to have asked itself what purpose it would serve to seek freedom from sanctions through acceptance of renewed inspection, if the US would take armed action anyway. The ambivalence on the Iraqi side to inspections had a parallel on the US side. One body of opinion, which manifested itself even as early as 2000, felt it was time for the world's only superpower to abandon interminable UN wrangling and inspections and take – unilaterally, if need be – the action to remove Saddam Hussein that in their view should have been taken in 1991. While not disagreeing with the opinion that it was desirable to remove Saddam Hussein, the other line – championed by Secretary of State Colin Powell – was conscious of the political and human costs of unilateral military action and preferred to push forward on the path that the Security Council had indicated, with the US assenting. A third US opinion felt that continued Iraqi refusal to readmit inspection could be a good thing, as it would justify continued international control of Iraqi imports and incomes and allow them to stop importation of all items on specific lists – 'smart' sanctions.

The UK supported the line – based on Res. 1284 – requiring resumed UN inspections and foreseeing an eventual lifting of sanctions. The British stand probably influenced the US to accept the UN path that was followed in the autumn of 2002 and until March 2003. Tony Blair shared the wish to oust an odious dictator, but for the UK authorization under the UN Charter was important. The calculation was that Security Council approval could be obtained for armed action, either because prohibited weapons would be found or because Iraq rejected or obstructed inspection. There are no signs of speculation that Iraq would cooperate with inspection or that inspections would not uncover any proscribed weapons.

The 9/11 2001 terror attack strengthened US determination to act against 'evil', and while it initially turned with armed force only against the Taliban and Afghanistan and focused on creating a containment of Iraq through a modernized regime of 'smart sanctions', Iraq felt the risk of US armed action increasing. As described in my diary, in the spring and summer of 2002 Iraq had several rounds of talks about acceptance of Res. 1284 and renewed inspection with the UN secretary-general. As the US began to amass troops in the Gulf, the Iraqi government became more open to inspection and UN presence as a way of staving off invasion. In talks with me and with ElBaradei of the IAEA, their representatives showed flexibility, and eventually, in September 2002, Iraq declared that it accepted inspection. The US for its part stiffened its positions. The regime designed by the Security Council in December 1999 (Res. 1284) was seen as in need of sharpening. Ideas about adding national armed units to accompany UN inspection teams began to circulate in Washington, as if they anticipated resistance to inspection and without considering how escorting units from great powers were to act together with UN teams. As I noted in the diary, at an animated discussion in the US State Department, I rejected the idea of transforming UNMOVIC into a hybrid of UN and national units as impractical. I further noted – but did not say at the meeting – that I would have resigned if such a regime had been created. I also deflected suggestions by Colin Powell and Condoleezza Rice that I should have a staff member of US nationality serving near me. I suspected that the suggestion came from US military and intelligence circles that had been used to piggybacking on UNSCOM. I hoped that the civilian policymakers would understand that I was determined not to risk suspicions that UNMOVIC was remote-controlled from Washington.

The first US drafts of what eventually became Security Council Res. 1441 would not have stood a chance of getting a majority. The proposal that eventually was adopted unanimously on 8 November 2002, although toned down and not ostensibly revising Res. 1284 (1999), which had created UNMOVIC, was nevertheless very demanding and threatening. It freed UNMOVIC, which some detractors had branded as weak, from various inspection conditions that UNSCOM had accepted. Iraq was to offer immediate, unimpeded, unconditional and unrestricted access, and any failure would be reported and considered by the Council. Perhaps some of the actors on the US side hoped that Iraq would reject the resolution and withdraw their acceptance of inspections, thereby opening up the possibility of UN-approved or unilateral armed action. However, in vitriolic language, Iraq signalled that it would comply. The resolution was seen as a victory for the UN path of action advocated by Colin Powell.

As inspections began, the benign negligence that US intelligence had shown UNMOVIC until then turned into an overwhelming embrace. I had suggested they were like librarians who were not willing to lend books. Now, UNMOVIC was advised to take a top-down approach – for instance, to go to ministries and search for files telling us where proscribed weapons were located. Iraq would be pressed relentlessly. It was not hard to understand that denials of access would be welcome, as they could serve as grounds for claiming Iraqi non-compliance. We did not follow this approach, which had led to some spectacular results in the early 1990s, but we welcomed and acted on tips about sites that intelligence had reason to suspect held proscribed weapons. In some forty such sites, we did not, however, find any proscribed items. 'Intelligence dossiers' had been made public in 2002 by the US and the UK to convince the public about the existence of concealed weapons. However, they consisted simply of statements that 'intelligence assesses' or 'it is estimated that'. Asked to comment, I used to say they were 'plausible' but not evidence. UNSCOM had similarly prepared a substantial document in which it listed quantities of various weapons that were believed – for instance because of early Iraqi reports or known data on imports – to have once existed, but whose disappearance through consumption or verified destruction had not been satisfactorily explained. UNSCOM did not assert that these weapons existed. They were 'unaccounted for'. UNMOVIC analysed the material to conclude which items should be identified as 'unresolved disarmament issues'. Tony Blair's comment in the introduction to the intelligence dossier that the UK published on Iraqi weapons of mass destruction (later termed the 'dodgy dossier' by critics) that the UK could be reached with such weapons in forty minutes was one of the more unabashed uses of 'intelligence'.

The adoption by the Security Council of Res. 1441 on 9 November 2002, inaugurating a hardened UN path hopefully leading to resolution of 'remaining disarmament issues', did not, as my diary shows, terminate speculations – even predictions – of early invasion. My conversations with Tony Blair showed him to believe that inspections would be a renewed cat-and-mouse game. This proved to be a mistaken speculation. The interaction between UNMOVIC and their Iraqi counterparts was free from significant friction. To our knowledge, we had no agents of US or other national intelligence on our teams, and, as I had pledged, we were demanding but did not humiliate, harass or provoke. The Iraqi side provided inspection teams with unimpeded access – even to Saddam Hussein's palaces. Doors were open, there were no sanctuaries – but up to the end of January 2003 also no serious efforts on the Iraqi part to address the many question marks that formed 'unresolved disarmament issues'. On 27 January 2003, I reported to the Security Council that Iraq appeared to have procedurally accepted disarmament but not actively espoused it. This was my assessment after the initial period of inspections, and it reflected also disappointment that the weapons declaration that Iraq had submitted, many thousands of pages long, had not given much new information and had not solved many issues. The US welcomed the criticism I had delivered. The Iraqis were disappointed but perceived the signal that it was high time to become more actively helpful. They took several initiatives, including ground excavations, to find evidence that anthrax 'unaccounted for' had been destroyed.

Some speculated that while the UN was on the inspection path, the US would feel restrained from taking armed action. Even at the end of January, the US was eager to send participants to UNMOVIC courses for the training of new inspectors. Others were convinced that armed action was coming and US troops in the region increased to over 100,000. On 5 February 2003, the US sent its respected secretary of state, Colin Powell, to the Security Council to present a show of evidence that the US had gathered – and that UNMOVIC evidently did not have – of proscribed weapons in Iraq. As I note in the diary, the show was less than compelling to experts. I also note that on 11 February I told Condoleezza Rice that UNMOVIC was not impressed by this and by other evidence presented by the US, and that we had by then found no WMD at some twenty sites suggested to us by US intelligence. Nevertheless, in the second half of February the US was edging towards the decision to attack. On 14 February, I reported to a packed meeting of the Security Council about both positive developments and remaining problems in the work in Iraq. The report was not welcomed in Washington.

At the same juncture, an idea was born from a sense that if an armed invasion was to be avoided, off-ramp action was needed. As is recorded in my diary, the idea was that a resolution would be passed that would put pressure on Iraq to accelerate the solution of remaining issues: a (small) number of issues could be listed that Iraq would have to help to resolve within a specified time. If completed successfully, another list could be drawn up; but if Iraq failed, the Security Council, it was understood, might authorize armed action. Tony Blair, who was anxious to have Security Council authority for any British participation in armed action, showed interest in this 'benchmark approach', and after my speech in the council on Friday 14 February, I mentioned to Jack Straw, the UK foreign secretary and to Colin Powell, the US secretary of state, that UNMOVIC had completed a document analysing and identifying clusters of 'unresolved disarmament issues'. We could make it public, if this would be of use for the selection of benchmark issues.

Colin Powell asked me to call him on the weekend, and Condoleezza Rice had phoned me already on the Saturday to set up a meeting. In my conversation with Colin Powell on the Sunday, I suggested that benchmark issues could be selected from the

UNMOVIC document and required to be solved, say, by 15 April. Colin Powell said that was too late. In a telephone talk with Tony Blair on Tuesday 20 February, I mentioned one month as a possible deadline. He replied that he thought the US could not wait longer than mid March. Two conclusions may be drawn: one that at the time of these conversations an off-ramp approach was not excluded; the other that a tentative decision existed not to delay armed action later than mid March.

Around 20 February, a US decision seems to have written off the 'benchmark' off-ramp approach. As I noted, on 21 February Condoleezza Rice expressed the hope that I would not declare that Iraq's cooperation had been 'immediate', suggesting that the US planned to justify armed action by claiming that Iraqi tardiness was a breach of Res. 1441. On 24 February, as I also note in the diary, the US representative on the UNMOVIC College of Commissioners declared – to the surprise of other commissioners – that the long-awaited document identifying clusters of unresolved issues was no longer of interest. Solving a few issues was useless, only an Iraqi 'change of heart' was of relevance. The US hardliners had prevailed.

It was clear that many governments felt that the US was not giving the UN path enough time. Iraq had become proactive; long-range missiles had been destroyed as ordered; Iraq was making efforts to find personnel who had taken part in and could testify about the 1991 unilateral destruction of proscribed weapons and material. How long was the 'last opportunity' given to Iraq in Res. 1441 to resolve outstanding issues to be? It could not have been the meaning of the resolution that, after many years without inspections, the resumed inspection should be allowed to run for only a few weeks. Frantic efforts were made by member states such as South Africa, Chile and Canada and by me to prolong inspections by the 'benchmark approach'. The UK, which stood ready to join the US in armed action, searched for a new resolution, in the hope that it could result in some UN authorization of the use of armed force that it saw coming. Iraq sent an eleventh-hour invitation to ElBaradei and me to come to Baghdad, without offering any idea how our presence there could change anything. The many efforts made were of no avail, and on 20 March the UK – and some other states – joined the armed action that the US had been ready to undertake all along without UN authorization.

Journalists asked: Was the invasion a violation of the UN Charter? As chairman of UNMOVIC, I declined to reply, but Kofi Annan gave an affirmative answer, and to follow-up questions he said in plain language that it was 'illegal'. This sparked anger in Washington but much respect in the world, where most international lawyers – including myself – felt that the UK–US legal line, that the licence given by the Security Council in 1990 for the use of armed force to liberate Kuwait could be relied on for a later full-scale invasion, was contrived. The charter requires Security Council approval for the use of force, and the reality was that in March 2003 not only was there no such approval, there was in fact a council majority opposed to the action. The action also disregarded the path and timetable that the council had laid down in Res. 1284 of December 1999. In full conformity with that resolution, which had not been revoked, which had created UNMOVIC, and which had foreseen a peaceful phasing out of sanctions and inspections (but not monitoring), I appeared before the Security Council and, in a surreal turn of events, presented UNMOVIC's work plan of further work on the very day of the invasion.

In the tense months before the invasion I, like many others, had asked what pushed the US to cut the inspection period short. One speculation could be that 9/11 had generated a need for more strikes against 'evil' terrorism than those that had been inflicted on Afghanistan. I could see three other reasons: one could not keep 200,000 men waiting long for battle, especially as the hot season approached; opinion polls showed shrinking US support; and deferment until the autumn would bring the operation unacceptably close to a US congressional election. Perhaps US decision-makers also feared that further inspection, instead of prompting obstruction, would show Iraqi cooperation and undermine the assertions that the country still was hiding proscribed weapons.

Following the invasion, the big question was whether the weapons, which US and UK intelligence and governments claimed to exist but UNMOVIC had only found to be unaccounted for, had been found. Huge US search operations were mounted to comb through Iraq at costs that made UNMOVIC look like a bargain. One factor could be expected to favour the US search. If there were any Iraqi military, researchers, administrators or others who had knowledge of concealed weapons, this was the moment to be rewarded for the information, while a whisper discovered during Saddam's reign would have led to execution. But no one had any revelation to make, and soon David Kay, who led the first US search operation and who had been a loud supporter of the invasion, grabbed the US and world attention that he loved by proclaiming 'we were all wrong!'. Well, he and many others were. The lack of critical thinking in intelligence and government quarters and overdoses of superstate hubris had led the US to an invasion that in Iraq replaced long-lasting tyranny with long-lasting anarchy.

My diary was not written with any thought of future publication but was rather a way of registering for myself what I did, observed and thought. While I had a plethora of human contacts at the UN in New York and in capitals around the world, I lived alone and was more than ever focused on my job. My wife, Eva, remained at her job in Stockholm as ambassador for Arctic and Antarctic issues in the Ministry of Foreign Affairs. We managed to meet from time to time and spoke almost daily over the phone. Our younger son, Göran, and his wife, Bozena, were both at Columbia University, and we often dined together. Our elder son, Mårten, an economist, lived in Stockholm, and it was in the form of letters directed – but not sent – to him that I recorded my days and thoughts.

The notes were in English as I lived and worked in English, and they were given to Mårten after my return to Sweden. During the renewed discussions of the 2003 Iraq war twenty years after it had taken place, he felt – and I agreed – that the notes might contribute to a fuller historical picture of the lead-up to the war and its outbreak.

Persons Mentioned

Per Ahlmark: Deputy Prime Minister of Sweden, 1976–1978
Madeleine Albright: US Secretary of State, 1997–2001
Hosama Amin: Iraqi general in charge of National Monitoring Directorate
Kofi Annan: UN Secretary-General, 1997–2006
Tariq Aziz: Iraqi Deputy Prime Minister and Foreign Minister under President Saddam Hussein
Mohamed ElBaradei: Director General of the IAEA, 1997–2009, succeeding Hans Blix, who had that role 1981–1997
Salwa Barberi: Legal Adviser, UNMOVIC
Paolo Barreto: UNMOVIC staff member
Jacques Baute: Head of IAEA inspections in Iraq
Joseph Biden: US Senator, later US President
Tony Blair: UK Prime Minister, 1997–2007
Göran Blix: younger son of Hans Blix, professor of French literature at Princeton University
Mårten Blix: elder son of Hans Blix, economist, researcher and author
Åke Bovallius: Head of UNMOVIC section on biological weapons
Ewen Buchanan: Public Information Officer, UNMOVIC
George W. Bush: US President, 2001–2009
Richard Butler: Chairman of UNSCOM, 1997–1999
Jim Corcoran: UNMOVIC staff member
Hans Corell: UN Legal Counsel
Richard Cheney: US Vice President, 2001–2009
James Cunningham: Ambassador at US UN mission
Hans Dahlgren: Permanent Representative of Sweden to the UN
Rachel Davies: Head of UNMOVIC section on information, including analysis of Iraqi imports
Thérèse Delpech: French member of UNMOVIC College of Commissioners
Ragida Dergham: Correspondent of Arab English language newspaper *Al Hayat*

Jayanta Dhanapala: UN Undersecretary General for disarmament
Mohamed al-Douri: Permanent Representative of Iraq to the UN
Charles Duelfer: Deputy Chairman of UNSCOM. Later head of US inspections in Iraq
Bob Einhorn: US Assistant Secretary of State for Non-Proliferation
Rolf Ekéus: Chairman of UNSCOM, 1991–1997. Later Swedish Ambassador to Washington
Ed Emerson: Husband of Yirka Emerson
Yirka Emerson: Friend of Hans Blix from studies at Columbia University in the 1950s
Gerard Errera: Ambassador of France
Yuri Fedotov: Russian member of UNMOVIC College of Commissioners
Joschka Fischer: German Foreign Minister, 1998–2005
Dick Gardner: Attorney in New York and professor at Columbia University
Jeremy Greenstock: Permanent Representative of the UK to the UN
Constantin Gryshchenko: Ukrainian Ambassador to Washington, member of UNMOVIC College of Commissioners
Alice Hecht: Head of Administration, UNMOVIC
Sven Hirdman: Swedish Ambassador to Moscow
Andreas Jacovides: Former Cypriot Ambassador to Washington
David Kay: Former IAEA Iraq inspector. In 2003, leader of first US inspections in Iraq
Eva Kettis: Swedish Ambassador, wife of Hans Blix
Gabriele Kraatz-Wadzack: UNMOVIC staff member
Sergey Lavrov: Permanent Representative of Russia to the UN. Later Foreign Minister
Edith Lederer: Associated Press correspondent at the UN
Paul Leventhal: Head of the Nuclear Control Institute, Washington. Critic of IAEA, UNMOVIC
Jean-David Levitte: Permanent Representative of France to the UN
Jessica Matthews: President of the Carnegie Endowment
Gary Milhollin: Founder of the Wisconsin Project on Nuclear Arms Control. Critic of IAEA and UNSCOM
Igor Mitrokhin: Inspector at UNSCOM. Head of missile section at UNMOVIC
Amr Moussa: Secretary General of the Arab League
John Negroponte: Permanent Representative of the US to the UN, 2001–2004
Dimitri Perricos: Head of Operations at UNMOVIC, 2000–2003. Later Chairman (succeeding Hans Blix)
George Papandreou: Foreign Minister of Greece, 1999–2004. Later Prime Minister
Walter Pincus: Correspondent of the *Washington Post*
Olivia Platon: Secretary at UNMOVIC
Colin Powell: US Secretary of State, 2001–2005
Qian Qi Qian: Vice Prime Minister of China, in charge of foreign affairs
Condoleezza Rice: US National Security Adviser, 2001–2005. Later US Secretary of State

List of Persons Mentioned

Scott Ritter: Inspector of UNSCOM
Iqbal Riza: Chef de cabinet of the UN Secretary-General
Amir al-Sa'adi: Iraqi general in charge of relations with UNMOVIC
Naji Sabri: Foreign Minister of Iraq
Mohammed al-Sahhaf: Foreign Minister of Iraq
Åke Sällström: Expert on chemical weapons from Swedish Defense Research Institute (FOA)
Muttosamy Sanmuganathan (Sam): Secretary of the UNMOVIC College of Commissioners
Jarmo Sareva: Finnish diplomat and personal assistant to Hans Blix
Oscar Schachter: Former head of general legal division of UN
James Schlesinger: Former US Secretary of Defense
Pierre Schori: Permanent Representative of Sweden to the UN
Stephen Schwebel: Former President of the International Court of Justice and personal friend to Hans Blix
John Scott: Legal Adviser, UNMOVIC, previously at UNSCOM
William Scott Ritter: Inspector at UNSCOM, author
Benon Sevan: Head of UN Oil for Food programme
Surya Sinha: legal expert at UNMOVIC, previously at IAEA
Olof Skoog: Swedish diplomat and personal assistant to Hans Blix
Torkel Stiernlöf: Swedish diplomat and personal assistant to Hans Blix
Jack Straw: UK Foreign Secretary, 2001–2006
Danilo Turk: Assistant Secretary-General of the UN. Later President of Slovenia
Hubert Védrine: Secretary-General of French foreign ministry
Dominique de Villepin: Foreign Minister of France, 2002–2004
John Wolf: US Assistant Secretary of State, member of UNMOVIC College of Commissioners
Paul Wolfowitz: US Deputy Secretary of Defense, 2001–2005
Ralph Zacklin: Head of general legal division in UN legal department

Abbreviations

BWC	biological weapons convention
CTBT	comprehensive (nuclear) test ban treaty
CWC	chemical weapons convention
FCO	Foreign and Commonwealth Office
FOA	research agency of the Swedish defence forces
IAEA	International Atomic Energy Agency, located in Vienna, Austria
OCHA	Office for the Coordination of Humanitarian Affairs
OIP	Oil for Food Programme
P5	Permanent Members of the UN Security Council: China. France, Russia, UK, US
Res. 1284	UN Security Council Resolution 1284 (1999), adopted 17 December 1999
SIGINT	intelligence obtained through decoding of electronic signals
SIPRI	Stockholm International Peace Research Institute
UAV	unmanned aerial vehicle
UN	United Nations
UNDP	United Nations Development Programme
UNMOVIC	United Nations Monitoring, Verification and Inspection Commission (for Iraq), established through Security Council Res. 1284, 17 December 1999
UNSCOM	United Nations Special Commission (for Iraq), established through Security Council Res. 687, 3 April 1991. Terminated 17 December 1999
WMD	weapons of mass destruction

Year 2000

ARRIVAL IN NEW YORK, END OF FEBRUARY 2000, AND ESTABLISHING
UNMOVIC

Dear Mårten, begun. And this is my first trembling typing on a brand-new Dell computer equipped with Windows 98.

I and *my Swedish assistant,* Torkel Stiernlöf, Dimitri Perricos from Vienna and Åke Sällström from FOA (*Swedish Defence Research Institute*) met at the visitors' entrance of the UN. We were received by the head of UN (*United Nations*) security, my future secretary (Olivia Platon from the Philippines). She has been with the former UNSCOM chairmen, Ekéus and Butler, before me. There was also the head of the UNSCOM/UNMOVIC administration, Mrs Alice Hecht. They escorted us up to the thirty-first floor of the Secretariat building, where UNSCOM has had its premises and where UNMOVIC is now taking over. I walked around and said hello to everybody. I was horrified to see that people almost sat on crates in minuscule areas! It was so crowded. If this is a 'skeleton' staff, how would it be when we are fully staffed?

I had lunch with the under-secretary for disarmament, Jayantha Dhanapala from Sri Lanka, and with the head of UN administration, Joseph Connor, and the chef de cabinet of Kofi Annan, the Pakistani Iqbal Riza. In the afternoon I had half an hour with Kofi Annan, the Secretary-General. He is warm and wise – at least so it seems to me. He is very well versed in the Iraqi issue.

Wednesday 1 March 2000

Starting at UNMOVIC. First, report to the SG (*Secretary-General*) – ten minutes at 9.45. It was supposed to be what they call a 'photo opportunity', but there were no photographers. There was a chat on substance.

Thereafter a meeting with all staff remaining from UNSCOM. Many have left but there are some thirty or so. The professionals have mostly employment contracts and salaries from the governments that have seconded them, and they receive per diems from the UN – some 350 dollars a day. No wonder that some take suggestions from their governments. I told them all that I wanted a clear organizational set-up, with clear lines of command and responsibility. That we would have staff on UN contracts and pay – and UN loyalty. There was no automatic transfer. Candidates from the outside would be invited to compete. There would be as broad a geographic representation as possible. However, the present arrangements would be prolonged for each who so wished at any rate until 15 April, when the Security Council has approved the organizational plan.

After my addressing the staff, I went to see the President of the Security Council, this month the Ambassador of Bangladesh. He appreciated that I promised to keep the non-P5 informed of events. He evidently favoured a conciliatory approach to the Iraqis and underlined that one should try to encourage them to come along ... He did not deviate, however, from the Security Council line that Iraq must not have any weapons of mass destruction and that it must accept unrestricted inspections.

After my talk with the President there was the press conference, which was what I had worried most about. Even if you know what you say and express it reasonably well, you rarely know what is going to come out. However, there is some safety in numbers. They cannot ask too many follow-up questions and there is a certain decorum. I succeeded in planting some lines that I had thought out in advance, like 'Iraq tends to look at inspections as a penalty which it wants to minimize. It should see them as an opportunity which they should maximize.' If Iraq states something about its WMD capacity no one believes them, but if the Commission after extensive investigation and inspection says something it may well be believed and acted upon.

I said that I was fully aware of the terrible situation of the Iraqi people and pointed to the improvements that Res. 1284 brings through easing of imports. The best way, however, was through cooperation with UNMOVIC and a suspension and eventual lifting of sanctions.

I referred to intelligence and said that it was useful but had to be examined critically. There was a good deal of disinformation, too. It *should be* largely a one-way traffic. We could not completely protect ourselves from infiltration (no one could) but if I discovered anyone working for an outside agency, I would fire him ...

The echoes the day after were reasonably good all over. Media will be generally aware of *how we operate*, and twisted allegations may not fly.

Thursday 2 March 2000

I had a visit from the Dutch Ambassador who is also the chairman of the sanctions committee for Iraq. They are on the Security Council, so they are quite important to me. Later, I received US assistant secretary of state Bob Einhorn, who had seen me in Stockholm and whom I know well. He brought an ambassador dealing with Iraq in the US mission (Cunningham?). They offered all kinds of support and cooperation, did not lament that the UNSCOM deputy executive chairman Duelfer had resigned.

Friday 3 March 2000

I got up rather tired because Yirka Emerson (*student friend from my 1955 Columbia University days*) had invited me for theatre and supper the evening before and I had only fallen asleep around 1 a.m. Nevertheless, I gave a 'morning prayer' at the Swedish mission as promised. Mostly people I did not know.

I saw the ambassador of Bahrein as agreed in the Indonesian lounge. I was able to tell him that he was the first ambassador I called on *and* I wanted to tell him quite informally that we were considering what should be our staging area for flights into Baghdad and that Bahrein still seemed very practical and that there was a new building built for the purpose. However, it was not a formal request. He said that Bahrein had been quite embarrassed by the so-called Gateway (*US marine base*) in which UN inspectors were briefed by US–UK–Australia before going into Iraq and – what was even worse – were debriefed as they came out. I told him that I had made it clear that this had to stop. I have the impression that the big boys have simply taken Bahrein for granted and told them what to do. This is not the way to treat anybody if you want to have real cooperation. He said it might be a good idea for me to visit them separately. I agreed but said there might be problems if I travel to the Middle East but do not seek to go to Iraq. We agreed that I could write him an informal letter in which I raise the issue without any request. Before we get to the Security Council with the organizational structure I should have the matter in hand, however.

Next was Hans Dahlgren, ambassador of Sweden. We talked substance for a while. Thereafter my employment conditions.

And work today? I had two very expert journalists from Reuters in my office in the morning. They knew much more about UNSCOM than I do. They also knew the difficult questions. However, I don't think I was snared and we parted in a friendly way. After Reuters I had a TV interview by a young woman from Abu Dhabi. Questions were quite competent and so were the answers – I think.

Only journalists today? No, no. The German ambassador came and offered full cooperation and support. Good. He also hoped that I would rehire a couple of Germans who served UNSCOM and put them on UN contracts. I said I had nothing against rehiring very experienced staff, but they would have to compete with outside applicants. He had no problems with that.

Then came, guess who? Yes, US ambassador Holbrooke, for a courtesy call. It is rumoured that he keeps his hands totally off Iraq because it is not a winner. He is said to leave that millstone around the neck of Mme Albright and to concentrate on things that might make him Secretary of State in a next administration. Whatever the truth of this he was so sleepy that he yawned every two minutes. His questions, like his demeanour, were somewhat brutish. Do you have a budget? Why do the Iraqis not cooperate? When can you send inspectors, if they allow it? By August. OK – first of August or fifteenth? However, he was extremely friendly and supportive. I had his full and enthusiastic support.

At the end of the day, I sat down with my own boys and discussed their new organization and some other matters. And I have now had a plate of New England clam chowder and a couple of cheese sandwiches in my kitchenette. Tomorrow meeting with the staff to discuss what they should do apart from playing computer games. Since no inspections are going out and no inspection reports are coming in there are some limitations on the work. But there is a good deal that can usefully be done even while we are planning the new organization, like procedures for hiring people, programmes for training. Procedures for the analysis of samples, etc.

Tuesday 7 March 2000 at 20.45

Home by eight. Long days and I do not wish them to be otherwise. I have no distractions and need none. I cannot even bring myself to put in motion a search for an apartment.

Today I started with a staff meeting. They were used to 'democratic' Swedish-type 'morning prayers' to which all staff, secretaries and all, were invited. I have never seen the merit in having all clerical staff present during discussions that are uninteresting to most of them. So, I invited the professional staff – as distinct from what in the UN is called general staff. It nevertheless filled the so-called bunker – a security-screened room without window and air. I told them that I was still concentrating on the organizational plan, but I was also conscious of the fact that they need some directives as to what they should do. I mentioned a number of things that I thought would be useful to get done in this transitional period. In the main, however, I suggested that they might themselves know best what might be useful, and they could submit such proposals to me. If, on the other hand, someone did not see anything useful that could be done, perhaps it would be better to leave. No one winced at that. Nor did I receive any resignation. While about two-thirds of the professional staff have already abandoned the organization, the third that remains largely seems interested in staying and several of the states from which they come urge me to keep them. I hope this third is not the least competent. In fact, they are a mixed lot with several extremely experienced whom it would be difficult to replace.

The Chinese ambassador visited me in the morning. He did not have much of a message, except that they would have some candidates. I said that was welcome and asked that they should supply CVs – not just professions and institutions from where they came.

In the afternoon the French ambassador, Dejammet, came. He was 'softer' than the Russians and the Chinese. The result of the sanctions was terrible, and Iraq must be given some way to have them lifted. We must meet them, not just whip them. I said I thought the new resolution opened the road for suspension of sanctions in return for cooperation and progress on key disarmament issues. However, I would not go for cosmetic inspections. I also said my reading of the resolution was that the Security

Council was really united in the view that Iraq must not have weapons of mass destruction and in the view that inspections must be unrestricted.

I think the French have persuaded themselves that it will be impossible to discover all the hidden pieces in Iraq and have concluded that it is better to go over to monitoring to try to ensure that nothing ugly grows up. If the Security Council will decide this, OK, but for the moment the resolution orders us still to look for hidden pieces and I do not wish to delude anyone that everything has been found.

Wednesday 8 March 2000

Yet another day. Three briefings by staff. Rather interesting and probably good for the morale of staff that some interest is shown in what they do. The first briefing was about missiles in Iraq. (I was told that it took five months before Richard Butler agreed to listen to a similar brief...) Most of the missile technology came from the Soviet Union: Scuds. Practically all are accounted for, but little is known about the copies which were produced in Iraq. Later briefing on inspections of sites that are not suspected but which could possibly lend themselves to the production of weapons or parts of weapons. They are mostly identified from satellite photography. Lastly a briefing on the control of Iraq's import. They need licence from the UN sanctions committee *and everything* they import – except that which they buy with the proceeds of smuggled oil – *is* subject to inspection by us or the IAEA. Indeed, a heavy apparatus ...

Thursday 9 March 2000

The days are interesting. An example: the Secretary-General nominated seventeen members to the College of Commissioners that is to 'give me advice and guidance'. An Arab newspaper commented that the SG had not appointed a single member from an Arab country, because the US was opposed to having any Arabs in it. To my knowledge the SG would have liked very much to have a commissioner from an Arab country, but no such country wants to have anyone on the commission, because the whole UNMOVIC is seen as punishing an Arab brother country – Iraq. Nor do these countries want to have any staff in my outfit although we would like to have them. Indeed, it would be useful to have Arab-speaking inspectors! As far as I know the US would have welcomed an Arab representative on the college ...

I had one long briefing today on chemical weapons and one on the use of sensors and air sampling and analysis. They have done a good deal here, but they have not reached the bottom of the barrels.

Monday 13 March 2000

On Friday evening I read various contributions to the organizational plan and felt rather dejected. It is in large measure the English. But also the substance is miserable. Today, Monday evening, I feel a little more hopeful. A few things seem to move forward. On Friday evening I had written a draft letter to the commissioners whom the Secretary-General had appointed to UNMOVIC's (*advisory*) College of Commissioners. I wanted to tell them when I thought that our first meeting should be and – indirectly – that it should not be until the last week in May and certainly not to discuss our organizational plan for which we already have more than ample advice from governments. Today I had the boys reading it and John Scott – the legal adviser – polishing it. I hope that we can send it tomorrow.

Further, I managed to extricate my amended working plan draft from the computer and give it to Scott. So, a first rough draft of our organization is emerging. A lot remains to discuss in it, and some to consult with member states. But, at least, it is on the way, and it is only 13 March. It is due before 15 April.

I had lunch today with Hans Corell, the Swedish legal counsel of the UN. He has some 160 people working for him. Tomorrow he is flying to Cambodia to negotiate about some international presence in Cambodian tribunals which are to try Red Khmer leaders.

Today I also had the visit of the Kuwaiti perm. rep. whom I had met a couple of times as DG (*Director General*). He was enthusiastic about my taking the job (I think genuinely so far . . .). He also had some very good insights into important issues. I asked him why Saddam was holding on to small quantities of chemical and bacteriological weapons. He said he thought it was mainly to threaten minorities in the Iraqi population. He killed a Kurdish village with chemicals, as is well known.

Tuesday 14 March 2000

Sent the commissioners of the UNMOVIC college a letter congratulating them on their appointment, pointing to salient matters in Res. 1284 and proposing end of May as time for a meeting. The implication is that there should not be any meeting before I submit the organizational plan to the Security Council in the middle of April. I cannot see that they could do anything useful with the plan. The P5 and a few others have already advised us on how it should look. And their preferences do not coincide. So, the chance is not great that there would be a consensus in the College . . .

Wednesday 15 March 2000

Tomorrow is one of the great Muslim holidays – the day when Mohammed received the Koran, I am told – and the UN is closed. The UN was already beginning to empty today and I am sure there won't be many people on Friday. I shall go there tomorrow, however. I had Sergey Lavrov, the Russian ambassador, in my office today. He seemed anxious to push for Russians to go into the staff – and for some Russians to be thrown out from the staff.

Saturday 18 March 2000

Spent the Muslim holiday mostly at the office working on the organizational plan with John Scott. We had lunch with Charles Duelfer, the former Deputy Executive Chairman (*of UNSCOM*) who resigned but with whom I have – I think – good relations. He seems a very decent guy, somewhat idealistic basically. He is giving me a good deal of information. Yesterday I learnt that the Senate Foreign Relations Committee is going to have some hearing on our work and that our old enemies (*of the IAEA*), Leventhal and Milhollin, would be there. But also Duelfer – whose presence probably will be to our good.

Tuesday 21 March 2000. *Equinox*

Dimitri (Perricos), John (Scott) and I went over the organizational plan. Dimitri has many good points, really *the* result of good political judgement. He is of great help. John is sure in the writing, in the English. He does have some experience from forty years at the UN. I talked to the Dutch fellow in Chemical. Good if he stays, especially as Horst, the German who is section head, is leaving. We need to have someone left with experience.

Wednesday 22 March 2000 at 23.10

Just back from a dinner in Kofi Annan's house at 3 Sutton Place. It was the 'annual' dinner for the Security Council. I had several useful conversations. I want to cultivate the non-P5, because in some situations it will fall to all outside the group of permanent members to say whether my stand is reasonable. So, I talked to Jamaica, Tunisia and Mali. I also managed to talk to Kofi about our two Russians whom Lavrov insists that we throw out of UNMOVIC. I said that their only sin might have been to be loyal to the UN rather than to Russia and that the issue pained me.

I was a bit puzzled by the meeting to which Kofi had called me at 11.30 today with the Russian representatives and the French. Maybe Kofi feels the general clamour about the suffering of the Iraqis under sanctions is pressing him and wants to push for starting up the inspection machinery as soon as possible so that we may get to suspension of sanction without unnecessary delay. In any case he seems to want us to seek to engage the Iraqis and the French, and the Russians want that, too. I explained I did not think the Iraqis would come along. They felt they were doing fine in their campaign against the sanctions and would like to have them crumble or lifted without accepting any inspections. It was, moreover, perfectly legitimate for them to want to see the organizational plan that we shall submit and judge the UNMOVIC on that basis. I said also that it was not good to come in a position of 'demandeur'. Kofi concluded, fortunately, that there was no hurry to do anything before our organizational plan was out. Lavrov talked about the necessity to get rid of people who were 'notorious' and had taken part in espionage. I said all seemed to want to be pragmatic about old staff. Both Russia and France had each a staff member they wanted to stay in the Commission. There would be no automatic transfer to UN jobs. I had seen no evidence of wrongdoing. It would be awkward to fire people for having been loyal to the UN. I also hoped that the newcomers would be genuinely loyal. Perhaps Kofi had been pressed in Paris a few days ago to call the meeting? In any case, tonight Kofi said to me that the ambassadors had been very impressed with my frankness . . .

Today there were hearings under the Senate Foreign Relations Committee in Washington. No less enemies (*of mine*) *than* Leventhal and Milhollin appeared. There was also Charles Duelfer who suggested that there was not much UNSCOM or UNMOVIC could do if the Security Council was not willing to act. Senator Biden castigated both witnesses, saying essentially that they had no recipes *for* what one should do. They had criticized the US for voting for me in the Security Council. What should they have done? Left the post vacant?

It is now ten to midnight and time to creep to bed. John Scott, Dimitri and I went through the text of the plan this afternoon and polished and modified. It is not so bad. Next step will be to consult Dhanapala. The SG's chef de cabinet, Iqbal, said to me tonight that if Dhanapala had no problems, the SG's office would not even look at it.

Thursday 23 March 2000 at 08.15

Sunny, cool day. Nice. Thought I should note some of the utterances which have come from the Iraqi side. They have rather consistently denounced Res. 1284 and in so doing distanced themselves from UNMOVIC. Until recently Tariq Aziz had been silent, but in an interview in the Guardian the other day he said he would be a fool if he recommended acceptance of this vile text. Asked whether Blix had not given them good marks on the nuclear dossier, he replied that I never stood up for them. The reality was that we said that there remained some questions, that there could never be complete clarity and that it was really the task of the Security Council to determine what residue of uncertainty it would tolerate. Clean bills of health don't exist – whether in medicine or in inspection.

We sent a letter to missions asking their governments' assistance in finding potential candidates with qualifications in biological and chemical weapons and missiles. Torkel and I decided that we should send it – for information – to the Iraqis as a kind of low-key courtesy. Yesterday I had an angry letter from Iraq's resident representative denouncing Resolution 1284 in some detail and ending that they had nothing to do with the commission and sent the letter back . . . OK, pals, I think you are not uninterested in what we do and how we organize ourselves and our letter, though of very minor importance, was nevertheless something you would register. We shall not send you more by mail, troubling you to write further angry letters to us.

You will fish them up in the stream in New York. Last night at Kofi Annan's I told the Tunisian ambassador that the Iraqi apparently had said 'Blix has said it is not a purpose of his commission to humiliate Iraq. Who the hell does Blix think he is, to believe that he can humiliate Iraq?' The Tunisian, who claims they have the ear of the Iraqis, said, well, don't worry, they listen very carefully and your noises have been very good.

Friday 24 March 2000 at 07.40

Yesterday I was at lunch with the Kuwaiti ambassador. Magnificent residence at Beekman place with a view of East River. Met lots of ambassadors from the Arab world. Useful.

I also had a journalist, the so-called Druze missile, who interviewed me at length. She is extremely well informed. Has followed the Iraqi issue since the beginning. There were some risky questions, and I don't know what will come out.

Tuesday 28 March 2000

I have now been here for a month. The room (*at my hotel*) seems more bearable, especially after I got Göran's Senneh Kurd rug. The rug that lay here made my stomach cringe ... However, New York seems dreary to me. I have no longing to explore the 2,000 best restaurants to spend money and get too many calories. I don't need to shop for anything. Theatre once in a while is enjoyable. Remains work, which is really challenging, but the office is horrible, especially when compared to the working environment in Vienna! I must dial seven digits before I can begin to dial a telephone number!

Had dinner Friday night with Dick Gardner (*New York attorney and professor at Columbia University*) at the Century Club, which is for writing people. Dick says he is very close to Vice President Gore. I hope he will be rewarded. This time it is Richard Holbrooke who is in the limelight. Saw him yesterday with Jeremy Greenstock (perm. rep. of UK) in the SG's office. We talked Iraq and Jeremy stressed the need for saving institutional memory and not losing valuable old staff at UNMOVIC. It was a useful counterweight to Lavrov's and Levitte's pressure last week. I think the SG realizes that tossing out the two Russians is not that simple ...

Yesterday we finalized the organizational plan, and I gave a copy to Dhanapala who is to see it on behalf of the SG, who is to be consulted about it according to the resolution.

Tomorrow I shall have a chat with Ambassador Chowdouri, Bangladeshi President of the SC until Saturday. I shall describe our organizational plan without giving him the document.

Saturday 1 April 2000. Subject: Iraq

This morning, I have been reading two chapters about Kofi Annan and his handling of the Iraq problems in William Shawcross' Deliver Us from Evil (Simon and Schuster, 2000). First-class writing. The *first chapter is* about the so-called palace crisis early in 1998, when Annan went to Iraq and reached a memorandum of understanding with Saddam Hussein about the rights of UNSCOM to inspect 'presidential sites'; the other *chapter is* about the crisis in November 1998 when the US threatened to bomb, and Annan helped to avert the threat by getting Iraq to back down. Both chapters show Annan with a lot of stamina, diplomatic skill, much realism and also a wish to avoid violence. Reading this I feel stimulated to put down some ideas.

It remains very important to seek to have a consensus among the P5 – and preferably the whole SC. Annan did not go to Baghdad in Feb. 98 until he had consensus on main *points* in the SC. The British helped bring it about and he stuck to it.

All the P5 seem determined that UNMOVIC must have unrestricted rights of access. However, three – China, Russia and France – seem sceptical of very tough inspections. Or is it only demonstrative, harassing or provocative inspections they oppose?

Looked at overall it would seem difficult for Iraq to acquire a substantial capacity and to become a major military factor again. However, biological and chemical weapons require little space and with a few missiles with 600 km capacity or a few pilotless planes such weapons could create fear and even bring substantial injury before massive retaliation set in. The political impact of a continuity or revival of Iraq's programme would be even worse. If the world fails to keep WMDs out of the hands of Iraq, despite control of Iraq's oil revenues and export controls, despite the most draconian inspection regime ever designed and despite US and UK bombing threats, how could we hope to dissuade other states – like Iran? But one also needs to look at the situation from Iraq's *perspective*. We must assume that Iran and Syria and Israel have C (*chemical*) weapons, that Israel has nuclear weapons and that Iran is moving toward nuclear capacity. Does not all this simply lead to the conclusion that the Middle East peace process is vital to reduce the perceived need for such weapons and the creation of a zone free of weapons of mass destruction with stiff verification. Of course, it will take time, but even a not too fragile movement in this direction might be helpful. Perhaps one should talk more about the zone and the Iraq control regime as a learning process?

What can I do to stimulate consensus among the P5? The most evident is to build UNMOVIC to become a dispassionate, independent, genuinely international body. Do not testify to more than we see. Give *an accurate idea of* what we do not know. Do it all in calm accurate descriptions. Have the right mix of people. Now is the chance to redress the balance. We want competent Chinese, Poles, Turks, Indians, Latinos. Inspection teams should not have a majority of Anglo-Saxons. Nor should the leading positions be dominated by any one group. Yet there must be competence! I doubt that independence, measured language and objectivity will persuade Iraq to 'come clean', but it is of some importance to them and it is also of importance to make UNMOVIC acceptable to all the P5 and to other members of the UN.

Kofi Annan comes across as wanting to engage Iraq in dialogue. Query whether he has been disappointed in his efforts. I certainly don't think the present juncture is the right moment for any determined effort. It would only be met by an upbeat Iraq demanding the termination of international financial control and effective inspection. However, while direct dialogue with them would be hopeless today, the public dialogue goes on all the time. When I am interviewed, I am aware that what they print is read by Iraq. The same goes for Kofi Annan and for the US. And we read what the Iraqis are saying ... This must be used very consciously.

An important point is probably that Iraq must get the feeling that sanctions really can be lifted or suspended. They may not believe that this is the case, having heard US politicians say that sanctions will not be lifted until Saddam goes. Certainly, it is difficult for the US to affirm loudly that, yes, indeed, they are ready to lift sanctions if Iraq fulfils its obligations. But a bit more explicit US support for the suspension concept might be possible and desirable. The US could distinguish the cases of lifting and of suspension. After all, suspension would allow a reintroduction, if Iraq stopped cooperating! Another matter is that sanctions today really mean not many restrictions on needed food imports, but rather financial controls of what is imported. If smuggling continues on a large or increasing scale, the financial controls become less meaningful. Combined with restrictions on the monitoring and inspection, the road to a revival of weapons programmes would be there. It would seem important that the US gets Iran to help stop traffic through Iranian waters of oil tankers. Perhaps also Turkey to clamp down on oil trucks. Pressure on Jordan would also be important – perhaps more difficult.

Assuming that it may be quite some time before Iraq admits UNMOVIC, that time should be used well. If we are not on the ground, we must energetically make use of other sources to remain expert on what Iraq does. How? Open media should be studied. Leads like the – perhaps dubious – one about a missile factory in Sudan needs to be studied closely. We should get more satellite imagery. Hence, we need personnel who can read such imagery. Would we have need of U2 and Mirages (*aircraft*) as well? We need to be fed by intelligence services in East and West. In particular information about procurement by Iraq should not be all that sensitive. So, we need the intelligence expert on board. Study of our own documents concerning export/import would also be important. We have the heavy pile of data (*from the time of UNSCOM*) to comb through.

While we should not rush to expand our staff as soon as the SC has approved the organizational plan, we should recruit to have a balanced core of managers and we should lose no time in setting up the training course for a balanced inspectorate. Perhaps twenty-four to thirty-six participants? It would give us the roster of inspectors trained by us that we need if Iraq suddenly accepts inspection. Location: state of New York. Time: July. Length: six weeks. Teachers: our own staff and past staff.

Earlier staff in Baghdad and Bahrein. Perhaps also some diplomats from the US, UK, Russia and France to illustrate the differences . . .

A vital task already set in motion is the compilation of remaining disarmament questions. This task is now before the sections. The UN Doc. S/1999/94 is there but we need crisper lists. They should be subject to the critical scrutiny of the fresh personnel that comes in. The subsequent much more difficult task will be to decide which are the key disarmament issues. This should be left for later to me and a few collaborators. After our own views have been formed, perhaps we would call in government experts to discuss it with us . . . to avoid quarrel when we submit them to the SC.

Perhaps it would be good that Iraq *gets to know* our demands before we go in rather than discussing them when we have gone in (if we go in). They must know that it is not a crippled UMOVIC that comes, but one with full powers and rights, but also one which can be expected to be truly international. We should also be ready to act on the MOU (*memorandum of understanding*) *concerning* inspections at some presidential sites – and tell them so in advance. The procedure for such inspections is not all that cumbersome. Iraq should be put on notice that this will happen – but not when. This will also be a deterrent for them. Presidential sites are not immune . . .

Sunday 2 April 2000

We finished our draft on the organizational plan for UNMOVIC this week and it has the support of the undersecretary for disarmament, Dhanapala. In the coming week I shall consult with the Canadian ambassador who is this month's president of the Security Council as to how we shall submit it. Copies must go in English to all the members of the Council at the same time as they go to the translators, because the text invariably leaks when the translators get it. Scandalous, but you have to count on it!

This Sunday morning, I had a meeting with the deputy minister of defence of Israel (*Mr Snee*). He was in transit from California to Israel. He apologized for asking to see me on a Sunday. We had a good talk. He sought to impress upon me how important they felt UNMOVIC's work was. They would help us with information and fully accepted that it was a one-way traffic. We are not in the trading business. He thought Saddam's highest priority was to keep power for his tribe and family. The power and standing of Iraq were only the second priority. I said, if so, did he really need WMDs? To keep his own population under control, biological, chemical and nuclear weapons were hardly needed. I also stressed the long-term vision of a zone free of WMDs. He said for Israel the criterion was first comprehensive peace. I commented that (*Shimon*) Peres had said to me that democracy, too, was needed. Mr Snee denied there was such a requirement. He agreed that a rapprochement between the US and Iran and a peace between Israel and Syria would make Iraq less dangerous. For the present time they saw in Iraq the greatest danger to Israel.

Chemical and biological weapons did not cause enormous injuries by themselves, but they were terror weapons that would scare people.

Tonight, I am going to the theatre with Torkel. And tomorrow I shall have lunch with Richard Butler – my predecessor. I shall also go through with section heads the various names of applicants and the various names they have suggested from previous inspectors. We need to get a flying start on recruitment of a core team. As for inspectors we can limit ourselves to recruitment to a training course. We need also to focus on the sources we have to assess what is happening in Iraq. OK, there are no inspectors, but satellites are in the sky, suppliers submit export licences, intelligence goes on. Newspapers publish reports. Use what we have.

Saturday 8 April 2000

It has been a fairly lively week. On Monday I had lunch with Richard Butler (*former chairman of UNSCOM*) at an excellent restaurant on 42 E 20 Street: Gramercy Tavern. He has just finished his book. He goes on lots of speaking trips all over the US and apparently makes lots of money from it. He loves publicity and being in the limelight. Indeed, this was one of the reasons why he became impossible. He reported to media before the Security Council ... On the analysis of Iraq, we don't have any differences. He was too close to the US. Russia, France China and others felt ignored. It got so far that Lavrov, the Russian ambassador, refused to be in the Security Council so long as Butler was there. Butler does not have many friends at home in Australia, either. Perhaps he is too noisy, too crusading? After our lunch I walked up the twenty-five streets to the UN to get some exercise.

We had promised to give the Canadian President of the Security Council the organizational report before lunch on Thursday. As had been predicted, the report was spread further the very moment that we handed it over. In the same afternoon Reuters and AP (*Associated Press*) had descriptions of it. And an Israeli delegate was seen to be carrying it only an hour after we had seen the Canadian! Well, people seem to be used to this. The main thing was that media did not have it before we gave to the President of the Council. At our end there was no leakage.

The Russian ambassador, Lavrov, visited me only hours before the report was given. He seemed rather relaxed. I told him that I was thinking of placing Mr Zhukov on the post as External Relations officer in my own office. This seemed to cheer him up a good deal. He also knew that we have asked four Russians to come for interviews. Even without having read the report he congratulated me on it. However, it is nevertheless likely that he will say some negative things about it in the council to please the Iraqis who so far will have nothing to do with Res. 1284. The Chinese ambassador visited me yesterday and he had nothing negative to say, although he had read the report. This is encouraging. He, too, knew that we are asking four Chinese *candidates* for interviews ... I also made it clear to him that the job of activity evaluator in my office could be Chinese ... The French ambassador is coming on Monday. Naturally we are also calling some French *candidates* for interviews ... The Brits, Canadians and Americans seem quite pleased with the report. Hope they don't show it too much ... Well, if it sails through without much creaking it will be because we have stuck very faithfully to the balance that was struck in Res. 1284.

Next week I shall concentrate on preparing for the meeting in the Security Council. I must have a short introduction. I am also beginning to think about the meeting of the College of Commissioners which is scheduled for 23 and 24 May. This could be used as an occasion for me to elaborate a bit on how inspections are to be conducted and send Iraq signals that I do not feel bound by Ekéus' 'modalities' of inspection of 'sensitive sites' and that I feel the SG's memorandum of understanding regarding inspection of presidential sites is not only binding but alive and operative. Butler said to me that inspection of such sites is now a dead issue. I wonder.

If I were to lay out the text to the College, I should probably also explain the view that inspections are, as I have said publicly, an 'opportunity', not a 'penalty'. So far Iraq has not seen it that way and certainly not used it that way. However, taking them at their word that they have nothing more, maximum cooperation with inspection would be a way they could try to convince us and the world. Grudging cooperation will not. When they complain that the burden of proof has been placed on them to show that there is nothing and hold that the inspectors should prove there is something or else acquit them, I think they are smartly trying a parallel that is false. An accused is presumed innocent until proven guilty and he can stay silent and let the prosecution do its job. There is no presumption that Iraq does not have any more weapons of mass destruction unless we prove the opposite! It should be in their interest to convince the Security Council and the world that nothing remains. Convincing the inspectors is the shortest way to do this. Thus, Iraq should facilitate their work. Inspections are more credible if there is no notice or minimal notice. Thus, such inspections are in their interest. On the other hand, there is no need for the UN demonstratively to display inspection power. Just do it in an unobtrusive manner. We can probably without much loss of effectiveness avoid flying over Baghdad if such flights are seen as insulting. The no-notice or short-notice technique is used in the IAEA and in the CWC (*Additional Protocol for safeguarding inspections under the Chemical Weapons Convention*). Thus, it is not a concept invented to humiliate Iraq.

Thursday 13 April 2000. Family Events

The week has been good for the family! On Monday 10 April Göran had his oral for the PhD and got an A+. He phoned me in the evening, and I was happy to join Göran and Bozena for an Indian dinner at Dawat on 58 St. His exam had taken two hours and gone very well all the way through. Wonderful. He has now six months to prepare a plan for his dissertation which will deal not only with Balzac but the period and particularly what Göran calls 'l'ecriture visualiste' (*visualist writing*).

Yesterday, Mårten called me and told me that a reorganization in the Riksbank (*Swedish central bank*) might give him a job as director of a division in the Economic Department. Not bad at thirty-one. He is now about to fly to Cairo and then on to Sharm El Sheikh and a week of diving in the Red Sea.

ORGANIZATIONAL PLAN IN THE SECURITY COUNCIL

Today I presented my organizational plan for UNMOVIC in the Security Council and with some grumbling and blurring the plan was approved. All the members of the Council spoke. Lavrov, the Russian, spoke first and in greatest detail and with most questions. He had a good deal of praise first, then fired off some critical remarks. What he really wanted to do, I think, was to lay the ground for reservations. Unless the implementation proved to be to his satisfaction, he did not know whether the plan was good ... In particular, he wanted to see that UNMOVIC really proved to be new, i.e. got rid of the old staff he did not like (but kept the Russian they did like). He was supported by the Chinese on this point. Otherwise, the Chinese *representative* was mild and positive. The French *representative* was very warm (perhaps they felt they owed it to me, having been the ones who nominated me ...) and raised mainly the question of Amman rather than Bahrein as field office. I suspect this goes back to some Iraqi objection. It is easier for Iraq to force land travel if we are in Amman. If they refuse flights from Bahrein, it means rejecting inspections. Other members of the Council were friendly in tone, but the Malaysian thought a non-P5 member of the College should have chaired the college.

Richard Holbrooke, the famous US ambassador, came late – really when I was delivering the last page of my introduction. He was inscribed as the first speaker but asked the Russian to speak before him. Lavrov said he would be glad to do so if Holbrooke did not have his script ready ... After some squabbling Lavrov spoke (at length) and then Holbrooke spoke (very briefly). Almost immediately thereafter Holbrooke left. I guess I should take it as a compliment that he came and delivered the speech himself. However, it is questionable whether one can look at such diva-like conduct as a courtesy ... ?

So now my first – and lowest – threshold has been crossed and I can turn to seriously look at the selection of staff. Some twelve candidates have been invited for interviews, four Russians, four Chinese, four French. We shall invite more people. I want Dimitri Perricos also to see them. Simultaneously we shall begin to organize the first meeting of the College of Commissioners, which is to take place 23 and 24 May, in time for us to let the first quarterly report pass through it.

Tomorrow I am invited by the Japanese ambassador for lunch at Lutece, a famous French lunch place.

SATURDAY 15 APRIL 2000 AT 16.00

The Japanese ambassador, Mr Saitcho, proved to be very interesting. He felt there was a difference in mentality between the Asians and the Europeans. Buddhism tells you that there are things you do not understand. Europeans think they can understand and fix everything. To be sure we also discussed Iraq and the ambassador promised me that they would try to look for Japanese experts on B and C and M (*missiles*).

Moscow came out with an official statement on our organizational plan. It is much harsher than what Lavrov delivered. Clearly Russia is embarrassed by the fact that two of the most competent inspectors are the two Russians from UNSCOM, Smidovich and Mitrokhin. They must have promised the Iraqi that these two will be thrown out. A second motivation behind the Russian statement I see in a wish to preserve the freedom to criticize in the future. Russia never gave its blessing to the organization. If conflicts arise, they would have wanted to have a conciliation mechanism in UNMOVIC and political advisers to help avert the problems. Such mechanisms together with a 'collegiate management structure' (they cannot very well talk about veto and consensus) could also have been used to stall and paralyse UNMOVIC.

The proposals for the five political advisers call to mind the old proposals for a 'troika' in the Secretariat. It is almost surprising that such proposals can be tabled!

What remains effective is the requirement that reports to the SC shall go for advice through the College of Commissioners. Here judgements can be shot at. OK, there is also a chance to get to some rapprochement before clashes occur in the SC. I think the non-P5 members of the Council may well turn out to be important.

I can very well understand that Iraq will not declare where it stands until it sees more of the new Commission: what staff it will have, what regulations it will have regarding inspections, etc. But it does not seem reasonable for members of the Council to demand that at this stage. They have only instructed me to present an organizational plan, and they should approve that. However, it all leads me to the conclusion that we can hardly wait until the presentation of our work programme to explain how we shall go about inspections (modalities, presidential sites, sample takings, U 2, etc.). Iraq will not give its acceptance until these things are known and the Russians are now serving us notice that they even have reservations about the organization(*al plan*) until they have seen it.

So, I am now thinking of using the occasion of the meeting of the College of Commissioners to present positions on a number of crucial points. My thought is that it would be better to present Iraq with a number of these things upfront before they are asked to make up their minds. If they thereafter say OK to inspections, they should know what is coming and contradicting our positions would be more difficult.

Thursday 27 April 2000

Monday morning. Easter Monday. Was not a holiday here – but it is at home. Up a quarter past four to put Eva in a car for Kennedy airport at five! Horrible. Attended opening of NPT (*Non-Proliferation Treaty*) review conference. Listened to Kofi Annan. Good speech. He saw me in the audience and sent for me after his speech. He had met the Iraqi foreign minister at the non-aligned meeting in Havana. Later in the day he sent me the transcript from the meeting. I said to Kofi that I thought I ought to be upfront with my views how inspections should be conducted, so that the Iraqis would know and could take it or leave it – but not negotiate it. He seemed to agree. This is now foremost in my mind. To make a policy speech at the meeting of our College of Commissioners.

Tuesday. More interviews. A very good Russian woman chemist. We were all enthusiastic. Lunch with Mohamed ElBaradei who had spoken at the NPT review conference.

In the afternoon I interviewed Lieutenant General McIver, a New Zealander, whom I want to make our intelligence officer.

Today more interviews, then visit by Celso Amorim, earlier perm. rep. of Brazil in NY, earlier foreign minister of Brazil, now ambassador in Geneva. He chaired the famous Iraq panels for the Security Council before UNMOVIC was set up. I said we had tried to follow their ideas almost completely. I asked him why he did not take the Chairmanship that I have. Having spent all his life on peace and disarmament he had not said no. But it became clear to him that one perm member of the SC would not accept him (presumably the US). When he learnt about it, he refused to let his name go forward.

Tonight, buffet dinner for Nordic NPT delegations at Hans Dahlgren. Talked a lot to Hans. He said that Butler had been too talkative, too media hungry, too preaching. It did not go well down in the Council. UNSCOM had also not been very popular. He could compare the reports of the IAEA and those of UNSCOM. The agency's reports were matter of fact. Dry. This suited the council much better.

Sunday 7 May 2000. Stockholm

Home for a long weekend. Left New York Thursday afternoon. Had had lunch with a 'false beard' (*intelligence agent*). My luncheon companion told me that my Russian paid staff member was an officer in their intelligence service. Nice of them to ask priority for him in the hiring of new staff. Here they preach about the necessity of making UNMOVIC a UN body and about the spy scandals of the past and push *me to hire* one of the same kind! (if the information I got was correct.) No illusions.

Thursday 11 May 2000, New York

Swedish crown princess here. She is writing a study about UNSCOM and UNMOVIC! I asked Bovallius (from FOA) to join us and *we* gave her a one-hour briefing. Asked good questions of her own. We talked from 11.00 to 13.00. Thereafter I hosted a luncheon for her plus her two security guards. It was nice and we had a fine table in the delegates' dining room. Excellent view of East River.

Saturday 13 May 2000

The days in the office melt away. Much is administration and information ... On Friday the three section heads for inspection of biological and chemical weapons and missiles, Gabriele Kraatz-Wadzack, Igor Mitrokhin and Nikita Smidovich came with their reports on 'unresolved disarmament issues' – a hot issue. It is excellent that they have worked on this with their knowledge of history. We shall have had a flying start ...

The training course is also taking concrete shape. I have signed letters to all instructors inviting them – and promising no payment except travel and per diem ... The course is in Nikita's hands, and he is very effective. ...

In a conversation between Knutsson (*assistant to Secretary-General Kofi Annan*) and the Iraqi ambassador, the impression was gained that the most important point for the Iraqis was how we define 'unresolved disarmament issues'. I am not surprised. Their tactic at the moment is to say that Res. 1284 is absurd and that they will have nothing to do with it. At the same time, they are making it known what would be their price for accepting it: not too many unresolved disarmament issues, stopping the US/UK bombing, stopping US no-fly zones, termination of sanctions, throwing out Smidovich and Mitrokhin. The eternal bazaar ...

Friday 19 May 2000

Yesterday I saw Kofi Annan and briefed him on Iraq. I asked him at least to refrain from siding with the Russians on their demand for the removing of Smidovich and Mitrokhin. He promised this and said he would advise the Russians not to make such a fuss about the matter. Torkel Stiernlof reported to me that the Russian counsellor says the Russians feel I am treating them badly. I did not accept their idea for a political advisory committee (of the P5) inside the secretariat. Now I am also not accepting their Middle East Desk officer, 'Kalmukhavov' or something. Moscow had already placed him here! They now have no post for him ... It is outrageous! They believe that international posts belong to them and that they can do what they want with these posts! The counsellor had also said that they had wanted to help me. As things stood, they had given up. I would have to run my own race. OK. Fine! I don't doubt they have some influence on the Iraqis, but I don't think they will accept inspection for my blue eyes or for Russian persuasion.

Monday 22 May 2000

Tomorrow (*first*) meeting with College of Commissioners for UNMOVIC. Worked long on an introductory speech. Interesting to see if Russians will be militant. They appear more and more as spokesmen for the Iraqis.

THE COLLEGE OF COMMISSIONERS

Friday 26 May 2000

Tuesday and Wednesday I had the first meeting of the College of Commissioners. About eighteen of them, including P5. I think the French (Thérèse Delpech) and the Ukrainian ambassador to Washington, Gryshchenko, being in the middle and rather independent, might be very helpful to show what is reasonable. The chemistry of the group was good. In the best case it could prove to be a place where agreements could be worked out between P5 states.

I had a long – partly academic – speech laying the basis for more practical arguments. The cause célèbre of the Commission was when Nikita Smidovich had done his presentation of the 'training programme'; the Russian member, Fedotov, took the floor and asked Nikita whether he felt it was 'appropriate for him to run a training course' ...

Saturday 27 May 2000

It is Saturday and I have a long weekend ahead of me. Monday is Memorial Day, and the UN joins the US in taking it off from work. I plan to push ahead reading Richard Butler's book *The Greatest Threat*, which has just appeared and in which he curses Saddam Hussain, Tariq Aziz and other Iraqis, but has also harsh judgements of the permanent five members of the Security Council and of Kofi Annan. It will be interesting to see if he has any self-criticism ... I have no doubt about Richard's idealism and intense drive to eliminate weapons of mass destruction. Nor am I unaware that on several crucial occasions he has succeeded in pulling very unwilling rabbits out of the hat. He did so at one of the NPT review conferences (1985 I think), *and* did it again to bring the CTBT (comprehensive test ban treaty) before the General Assembly despite Indian opposition. That manoeuvre cost Australia a seat on the Security Council for a time, but – the CTBT is there.

Tonight, I shall have dinner with Steve and Louise Schwebel. Steve went into retirement February this year, having been a superb President of the International Court of Justice for a number of years. We are coming full circle. We first met in 1954 or '55, when Steve worked at White and Case and I was at Columbia Law School. We had lots of fun together in New York. Then we met again in the General Assembly of 1961, where I was a – rather young – Swedish delegate in the Sixth (legal) Committee and Steve assisted the US delegate, whoever that was. After the end of the assembly, we went together to St Croix, Christiansted, for swimming and sipping rum and orange juice.

For the first time in a long while I feel rather relaxed. There were three milestones for me in coming here. First, the press conference after I had presented myself to the Secretary-General. And the meeting with the remaining UNSCOM personnel. The second was forty-five days after that, when I was to present the organizational plan for UNMOVIC to the Security Council. On the whole, it was warmly endorsed. Only the Russians had significant reservations, though, I must say, they sounded in part a bit contrived. One of the more curious Russian suggestions has been that we should have a unit that would rush in and help solve frictions and conflicts between UNMOVIC and Iraq. Within UNMOVIC we would then have a unit that should solve our own conflicts! Would it mediate between the Chairman and Iraq? Would it be manned by someone Russian or French or American ... ?

Another weird idea from the Russians was that we should have a five-man-strong group of political advisers. My immediate reaction was that on any difficult issue arising the chances were that five advisers from the P5 would disagree. We would simply import into UNMOVIC the differences existing among the P5. Or was the group meant to substitute for the Chairman? If so, we would import the veto and the paralysis of the Security Council. On p. 101 of R. Butler's book *The Greatest Threat* I find that in November 1997 a message from Saddam Hussein to the SG of the UN suggested that *there should* be a deputy executive chairman appointed for each of the five permanent members *of the Security Council to undertake specifically with the Executive Chairman the responsibility of decision-making and the direction of activities of the Commission.* Thus, the idea was to disarm the chairman and – if necessary to paralyse.

When this idea, the origin of which I have now seen, did not materialize in my organizational plan – no one else had bought it – Lavrov suggested that we should strengthen the legal adviser's office ... An unusual idea to come from Russia ... the more so as they did not have any candidate for that office. Well, I am now trying to recruit Surya Sinha, Indian. He would be loyal and has a good name from the IAEA.

Now, the third milestone was the meeting of the College of Commissioners – some eighteen of them. One from each of the P5, one from each of the world's regions and one for each of the weapons types we are after (biological, chemical and missiles). Plus a few extra. I worked long and hard on a speech for the College. For several reasons. One was that I wanted to share my thinking about the opportunities and limitations of inspection with the commissioners. However, I also reckoned that the speech – despite the private character of our meetings – would get to the Iraqis and that it would be good if they learnt upfront how I saw inspections. The speech was a difficult one to write. Also, on some points I found that if I declared very clearly where I stood, the comment from the Iraqis, Russians and perhaps others would be that I was totally hardline and even worse than my predecessors ... So rather than proclaiming where

I stood on a couple of points, I asked the commissioners for advice. This worked well. The meeting was very lively and good. The chemistry was rather good. We have Bob Einhorn, assistant secretary for non-proliferation from the State Department; hard but reasonable and experienced. Fedotov from the Russian MoFA (*Ministry of Foreign Affairs*): a solid and experienced fellow, said to be hard-line. Then Thérèse Delpech, head of international affairs at the Commisariat à l'Energie Atomique. She was not the choice of the Quai d'Orsai (*French Foreign Ministry*) but was her own – and Kofi Annan's – choice. She is forceful and independent, and she was very helpful. She told me she wanted to work *for* me. I replied I wanted her to work *with* me. Amb. Gryshchenko (from the Ukraine's embassy in Washington) was also most helpful and independent. British Mr Shulte (from their ministry of defence) was able and also helpful. Two Latinos (an Argentinian named Heineken and a Brazilian microbiologist named Monteleone Neto). A German professor biologist named Boehm, an Indian nuclear scientist, Dr Prasad (formerly with IAEA), a Nigerian named Abidion, a Senegalese named Sheikh Sylla, a Canadian military and former UNSCOM commissioner (Clemenson), a Finnish professor and former UNSCOM commissioner and a Japanese *diplomat* (Kazuhara, formerly accredited to the IAEA).

I suppose the function originally imagined for the College was that it should guard against the Executive Chairman doing some wild things. For Ekéus the commission was always a rubber stamp. After Butler (and to some extent Ekéus) it would be there to restrain. My conclusion is that in the best case it could be of great help. Differences between the US and Russia could be dealt with here directly or with the help of other commissioners or me. It could be a place for negotiations rather than one where the chairman was taken to task.

THE 'MODALITIES' PAPER

During this first session we had a discussion about the so-called modalities. It was an instruction that Ekéus issued in 1996 for his chief inspectors after a meeting with Tariq Aziz during which they signed a joint statement. The instruction regarded inspections of 'sensitive sites' and stipulated that if stopped the inspectors should await the arrival of a senior Iraqi official to help smooth the inspection. They should enter with only four persons. I expressed the view that these unilateral points were not legally binding (as an agreement) upon UNMOVIC. On the other hand, I said it was understandable that Iraq, just as any other country, would be particularly sensitive to inspections in institutions like military headquarters, police buildings, etc. Thérèse suggested that we should go through the cases in which it had – or had not – been applied. I shall let John Scott and Ewen Buchanan do that.

The atmosphere in the College was good and pleasant at this first meeting. My guidelines for procedure, including no voting and no records, were approved. And the meetings are closed, so no one should be tempted to play for the gallery.

A summary will be made without attributions. Each member can, of course, relate to the public his or her own statements.

Only on one point were the discussions disagreeable. For a long time, the Russians have been requesting that I should get rid of the two Russians I have on board, Nikita Smidovich and Igor Mitrokhin. They had told me this already in Stockholm, when I jokingly countered that it would be paradoxical to fire staff for having been loyal to the UN ... All I hear from others is that the two were excellent, very loyal to the UN (did not follow Moscow instructions). Moreover, they were on UN contracts because the Russians had never wanted to pay for them. So, I have resisted any idea of ouster and have also brought Kofi Annan to my line *of thinking*. After all this is an issue touching UN integrity. My guess is that the Iraqis have said to the Russians that 'two Russians are the worst inspectors we have' and Moscow has promised that they should be eliminated.

Before the meeting of the College, we had – somewhat imprudently – indicated that the Commissioners would get certain briefings. *Inter alia* that Nikita Smidovich would brief about the training programme. When this became known in Moscow, Lavrov, who was there, was asked to convey to me the Moscow expectation that Nikita would not take part ... In my telephone conversation with him I did not, of course, promise any such thing and I let Nikita read his brief to the College. When he was through after five minutes the Russian Commissioner, Fedotov, asked for the floor and said to Nikita: 'Do you think that with your background you are the right person to be responsible for running this course?' Arms went up so Nikita did not need to answer. I think the Ukrainian ambassador came first with warm praise for Nikita. But then a lot of the other commissioners, including Thérèse, the Brazilian and the Chinese, supported Nikita. Either the Russians now let the matter drop, having understood that they are isolated and that I have some good reasons for not going along. Or I shall get some tough comments in the Security Council, when it looks at the first quarterly report. Considering that Lavrov, himself, feels he has been humiliated in the issue, I suspect he will come back ...

Our quarterly report to the Council has now been transmitted by the Secretary-General, who was generous to write in his transmittal: 'UNMOVIC has made a good start under the leadership of its very capable and experienced new Executive Chairman, Dr. Hans Blix. In order for UNMOVIC to become operational, it is essential for Iraq to start cooperating with the Commission.' Considering that he did not have to write any such thing and that the precedent of doing it could be a nuisance, I think it was very sweet of him. I wonder if Ekéus and Butler were not too jealous of their total independence.

Monday 29 May 2000

This is the evening of Memorial Day (the day to remember those who fell in wars for the US), the last day of my three-day weekend. I have spent much time reading

Butler's book. Staffing is complicated. You want a good geographical distribution and high professional qualifications. And you must have a balance between divisions and inside divisions. Perricos was there today, and we sat between ten and two thirty. His energy is limitless, and his judgement is good.

On Wednesday morning I shall have a staff meeting. The some ten staff who have government contracts are getting nervous. The staff paid by the UN have contracts that expire at the end of June, and they have only been promised that they can compete with outsiders. Now that we probably have most of the applications that we shall get from outsiders we must make choices soon. I think the staff is reasonably relaxed with me, while at the start it was probably sceptical and worried. Smidovich and Mitrokhin are probably relieved that I am not dumping them under some political pressure but regarding the matter as one of UN integrity. I think all will be glad to see some order. Butler and Scott Ritter are probably not missed.

Wednesday 31 May

I took Swissair at Kennedy (*airport*) in the evening to arrive *in* Geneva the next morning, Ascension Day. Eva, who had arrived the evening before, met me. Glorious warm weather. What a difference to be together. So many lovely flowers whose names I don't know in English. And we heard the cuckoo and 'marmots'. Lovely feeling of spring.

In the evening (of 4 June) I took Air France to Paris and caught a bus to Porte Maillot and a taxi to a small hotel – Hotel de France, 102 Bd Latour Maubourg, near Invalides. It was a hotel discovered by Alice Hecht and used by both Ekéus and Butler. Amazingly cheap. 490 francs. Less than a hundred dollars. A drab room but perfectly functional.

Monday 5 June. Paris

Meeting at 11.30 with the Foreign Minister, Vedrine. Gerard Errera was there plus a number of others. I found them surprisingly firm against Iraq. Their public posture is perceived *to be* softer. I warned against showing any anxiety and urgency for a dialogue and agreement with Iraq. The Iraqis will only raise the price if they see you eager. It is no different from buying a rug in the bazaar. I asked about possible assistance *provided through* Mirage photo flights. I said the Iraqis surely did not like any overhead watching, but probably disliked French less than American, because the French could not be suspected of identifying targets for bombing.

After lunch, to the ministry of defence and the strategic affair unit, where there was a round table for me to address. And to answer questions. Lots of military. I guess they sized me up. At the end, a visit to the minister of defence, Richard, who evidently liked to speak English (and did it very well). I asked him whether we could have French satellite pictures and French intelligence. Although the resolution of the French satellite pictures is less than the American, it would be good to have a source outside the US.

Tuesday 6 June in New York

After a shower at the apartment and leaving laundry with the Korean laundry I went to the office and met the French counselor who briefed me about the next day's meeting with the Security Council. He foresaw no great problems and, indeed, it turned out to be an easy affair. Lavrov had a long off-the-cuff statement with various reservations, but nothing harsh. He pleads for dialogue with Iraq. Well, if the Council does not want to sell out Res. 1284 I think it should not show eagerness. In any case it was a relief to have the Council meeting over. On Thursday (8 *June*) I had a long talk with Olof Skoog, who has been Hans Dahlgren's assistant and who Torkel recommended me to take on as executive assistant. He knows all other delegations and seems bright and effective. So, I offered him the job.

Saturday 10 June 2000

Two weeks have passed. It is now decidedly summer. 25–30°C. The last few days of May I had lots of people to interview. I find it interesting to talk to people and try to size them up. It is as much a matter of watching their demeanour as assessing the answers. It is also good that I am not the only one to interview candidates. Dimitri, Rachel Davies and Alice Hecht sitting together have another, often longer and more thorough go. So far, our conclusions have been remarkably similar.

Sunday 11 June 2000

Whitsun was as warm as the preceding days – over +30°C. Mårten and I had a huge pizza with Göran and Bo on Broadway. I bought a book about the Iraq conflict and found in the text the same erroneous statements that have come several times before and that originate – in all likelihood – from David Kay. What makes me indignant is to see that one political writer after another gladly swallows these things without checking. It is instructive to compare the source pages in Richard Butler's book with those of the political writers. Richard's are almost only official letters and UN documents. I would seriously quarrel with the judgements he offers in some places but not often with descriptions of events or statements made. The political writers seem to practise a genre between fiction and history.

Wednesday 14 June

Assad of Syria has died. In the longer run I think it improves the outlook, as the younger have grown up with Israel next door and are used to it and as they are better educated and more outward looking. Whether this would be true of Saddam's sons is another question.

15 June 2000. New York

Today, some things cleared. For a long while I had thought of *candidates for the job as legal adviser*. Among the candidates there was a Sudanese woman who had served in the preparation of the referendum in Western Sahara. She stated a diplomatic background in the UN but also a PhD in international law from Oxford. And, as important, fluent Arabic. She was said to be bright and a good writer, wrote stories and poetry. Not that we need stories, but I thought if she liked writing stories it means she likes writing and has a feeling for words and language. Not bad for a lawyer. So, I decided I would phone her in Oxford and ask whether she was interested. Yes, indeed! She had been pushed out of the Sudanese diplomatic service when the fundamentalists came in and lived in exile – and comfortably – in Oxford. She came today. Lively, bright, charming, articulate, knew lots of international lawyers, had served in the Sixth Committee, did not feel the sanctions on Iraq were immoral and would be delighted to serve and work hard. So, we hired her.

Friday 16 June

Had an interesting talk this afternoon with Ambassador Buallay of Bahrein, where we want to have our relay station for trips into Iraq. I said that the Iraqi position was not to accept Resolution 1284 of Dec. '99 as the way out of the impasse reached after the collapse of UNSCOM. In my assessment a solution might grow during the summer and autumn. It was unlikely that this would come together before the US presidential election, but it could happen in December. By that time UNMOVIC should be ready to go in. Ambassador Buallay seemed to agree: the situation staying static seemed unlikely. The US/UK were under pressure to stop bombing and ease sanctions. Iraq was under pressure to accept inspection and wanted less financial control (*by the international community*) over its oil proceeds. Standing still was unlikely. *Time may be ripe* for change.

I had a short talk with Nikita Zhukov today, telling him that I want him to be fully and usefully engaged. He will have the position of Adviser on External Relations. I suggested that he could continue doing what he has been specializing in, namely, watching Iraq, the leadership's composition and attitudes. If he wanted to report something he thought sensitive, it might be wiser to give it to me orally. We always risked that a written brief could go astray. I took it for granted that he would brief me on Russian positions. He seemed gladly to agree to my suggestions and said he thought no one was interested in much action at present. Russia was certainly interested in an easing of restrictions on the export to Iraq. For Russia these exports were of great importance to keep a variety of enterprises going. The grumbling in the Security Council was more lip service.

On Saturday 17 June something unlikely happened. Before going home for Midsummer and to Berlin I felt I had to do something about my apartment situation, so I phoned the Swedish broker who was known to the Swedish mission and told him what my wishes were. He contacted me the morning after, and we went to see the flat. It has the location I wanted: some twenty blocks' walk from the UN. It has a lofty view. The rent is quite decent – 3,500 dollars per month. But the brokers' fees were terrible: over 7,000 dollars or 17 per cent of one year's rent. We signed the contract on Thursday 22 June, the same day I left for Stockholm.

Friday 23 June, arrival in Stockholm and you (Mårten) met me in your beautiful little toy, the BMW with map and electronic guide. How wonderful to see trees and green fields again ... And nice to be driven well and prudently. You met me at Arlanda and took me to Gräsö (*the Blix family island compound*) where Eva had already arrived the evening before. The weather was fine. Eva went jogging every day and took a dip in the +14°C water. I, too, went in twice. In the afternoon, we dressed a midsummer's pole with leaves and flowers and danced around it singing 'Vi gaa oever daggstaenkta berg ...' 'Smaa grodorna ...' etc.

Back to Stockholm on the Tuesday (*27 June*) after Midsummer. Göran and Bo arrived (*in Stockholm*) on my (*seventy-second*) birthday, Wednesday 28 June. We all went to Wedholms Fisk restaurant and had a good birthday celebration.

Stockholm 2 July 2000

On Saturday 1 July we attended the wedding between Lisa Kettis (*Eva's niece*) and Anders Martin Lööf. Some 120 people. First at Övergarn church – lovely, medieval. The wedding reception and dinner was at Kraegga Vaerdshus. Fantastic view of Lake Malar and huge dinner in a barn.

On Tuesday (4 July) I go to Berlin for a Chernobyl pledging conference and for the Chernobyl Shelter Fund Assembly. Then a visit to the German foreign ministry and thereafter to New York and my new apartment at 200 East 61 Street. Apt 30 F. Exciting!

Excellent talk in German foreign ministry with state secretary Ischinger and the head of disarmament and UN desk. They promised continued strong support.

Flight to New York. Moving into 200 East 61 St Apt 30 F

Kind reception by the doorman at 200 East 61 Street. Strange to come into a new apartment, make the bed, find the lamps. Göran and Bo came with stuff they had kept for me and they helped me take stuff I had stored at the UN. Feel better now. Have *filled the refrigerator* and have left laundry at the Korean laundry across the street. Tomorrow I must work on my lecture for the training course.

Sunday 9 July 2000

Feeling better today. Slept until seven and had a leisurely morning. Wrote notes for my welcoming the people at the training course on Tuesday. Walked around the closest blocks to see what stores there are. It would be nice to get the TV going too, but I don't see how. The *New York Times* has come, however, which is nice.

Tuesday 11 July

UNMOVIC's first training course began today, organized by Nikita Smidovich. Some forty-four participants from eighteen countries. The course will last a little over four weeks and members of our old staff are also taking part. I opened the course today and gave a long lecture on the role of international inspection, zeroing in on UNSCOM. Rolf Ekéus has been invited to speak tomorrow. I invited Rolf for lunch yesterday. He was clearly hurt by Barbara Crosette's article in the *New York Times*, in which she suggested that Butler had come on board an already-sinking UNSCOM ship. Yet I think it was true.

Friday 14 July. Bastille Day

It is evening. I sat in my drawing room tonight and watched dusk coming. I think it was Astrid Lindgren who used the expression 'hålla skymning' – 'celebrate dusk'? There is something very special about 'les heures bleues' – the blue hours. The span between the end of the toiling day and the restful night. The moment of relaxation, of détente. Watching dusk setting from my drawing room is not a bad way to decelerate. Watching how the airplanes rise in the sky above La Guardia. Watching one helicopter after another buzzing over Manhattan. Watching how the rather ugly desert of stone houses is transformed into a cosier mass of black with a thousand lights indicating life and warmth.

On Tuesday I shall go to Washington and see Pickering (Undersecretary for Political Affairs) and Holum (Undersecretary for Disarmament). I bring with me Perricos, chiefly to show Washington that he has a strong position on my staff. On Wednesday I fly to London, and I shall see both foreign minister and defence minister. I'll do that alone. I am struggling with a paper on UNMOVIC's 'operating procedures'. I know in the main how I want to modify the 'modalities', but I think it would be unwise to spell it out in the document that comes in advance of the (*College*) meeting. The Russians might show it to the Iraqis and would be bound to get negative reactions which they (*the Russians*) would feel they would have to register. Better to come with these points orally and stimulate a discussion, hopefully to get support. I prefer neutral formulations that do not openly assume non-cooperation.

I meet more observers who somewhat doubt that Iraq will ever let UNMOVIC in. Well, it is by no means certain. In the global bazaar they will press for much greater financial and trade freedom and for as little inspection as they can get away with. If it looks too meagre to them, they will hold off and hope that the other side will budge. All I can do is try to look impartial and reasonable. I think the risk is small that the US and UK would go along with pressures on me to go for 'light' inspection. And I would rather go home. Cosmetic inspection is worse than none.

Tuesday 25 July at 08.45

In half an hour Dimitri Perricos is coming. We shall take the shuttle plane to Washington, where we shall see a lot of people, notably Tom Pickering – the undersecretary for political affairs – and John Holum – the undersecretary for disarmament affairs.

The last few days have been focused on the new discussion paper on 'operation procedures' for the College of Commissioners. There is a balance to be struck between firmness and unwillingness to concede any rights and the need to look reasonable, not fanatic, not imbued with a crusading spirit. The organization and manning of the commission, all must have this balance. Not that we have much hope that the Iraqis will change their ways and be sweet and helpful, but we should at least avoid putting them in a belligerent mood straight away. They cannot very well think that the Security Council would modify 1284, but they would try to keep and read as much as possible into the 'modalities' paper of 1996 and stick to whatever other concessions they have seen on air operations, etc.

Early tomorrow I am taking a day flight to London to have a full day with the British FCO and Defence Ministry on Thursday. Then on to Stockholm on Friday.

Tuesday 1 August 2000. At Rosten

Last Tuesday (25 July) I and Dimitri Perricos were in Washington – a rather full day. It began with a luncheon in Georgetown. The talk was much about the just-failed negotiations between the Israelis (Ehud Barak) and the Palestinians (Yasser Arafat). Jerusalem was the *stumbling block*. I cannot help reflecting that as soon as people are convinced (by religion) that something is the command of God, it becomes very difficult to walk away from.

In the State Department was Tom Pickering, Undersecretary for Political Affairs, former Ambassador to Moscow, former UN Ambassador. He is really remarkable! Of course, he was in New York during much of the Iraqi affair, but he had many other matters before him and I am amazed that he seemed to know all Iraqi resolutions by number and by salient points. He seemed like a bit of a hardliner. Perhaps he did not want me to go away with the impression that the US was conciliant on any point re: Iraq. Yet he said he was not quite sure that UNMOVIC would ever get in. A hint that on-*the*-ground inspection was not indispensable, but toughness was. I would agree that no concessions should be made in the manner *in which* inspections are to be carried out – in order to get the Iraqis accept inspections. Pickering also agreed with my instinct not to travel to Iraq. Good!

Day flight to London on 26 July. Thursday 27 first meeting with the Defence Minister, Mr Hoon. Very well briefed. We agreed that a new *situation* was arising, when, at the end of August, UNMOVIC would be able to mount an inspection.

On to the FCO, where I had a short chat with the minister of state, Hain – who had seen me in New York at the time of the NPT review conference. He was the one who surprised me by asking if I should not go to Iraq. I could sense that he was pained by all the public pressure on 'sanctions' and felt that somehow, if we showed our interest in going in, the burden was more clearly on the Iraqis for not moving things forward. I explained I was sceptical. He asked why and I said Iraq would believe that I would not like to leave Baghdad empty-handed and would use this as a leverage. I should have said that if I were to go to Baghdad it would look as if I came to ask for something. I don't. They should want inspections because that is the way they could have some trade and economic restrictions suspended.

I next saw the Foreign Secretary, Robin Cook, wrinkled but agile like a squirrel and tough-minded. I told him that I thought the political level had a role to play in explaining to the public that Iraq actually can sell as much oil as they want and that there are no restrictions on their purchase of food and medicines. Restrictions regarded weapons and dual-use items. If they accepted inspection, the import of dual-use articles would be easier. In the evening I saw people from the intelligence side.

And on Friday 28 July, I went to Stockholm and off to Öregrund and Rosten. We bathed both yesterday and today and it was really warm in the sun. Today, I chopped a lot of wood and Eva has been mowing the lawns. Tomorrow the BBC is going to call me at eleven. I also talked to Dimitri in New York.

Sunday 6 August 2000. Eva's Birthday

A lovely day. No presents but I gave Eva breakfast and some roses at bedside. We picked blueberries. We walked around to the old boathouse place. The sheep were there. Fifteen of them. Last night we all had crayfish on the lawn that used to be the potato field. A new venture. Hardly any mosquitos. Göran phoned Eva from New York and Mårten from Canouan (*in the Caribbean, where he was diving*). Yesterday Eva and I (*here at the Baltic Sea*) took the aluminium boat to the islands. We saw a black adder and a heron and visited our old wild strawberry peninsula. Some *tracks in swamps* between the islands are mystifying. Rather narrow. No droppings. Hare? Fox? Hardly elk? We have sometimes seen elk walking between the islands in the past, but it was long ago. The sea eagles fly quite often over Rosten. Eva has been interviewed both in the Goteborgsposten and Svenska Dagbladet in connection with her birthday. Nice articles and very nice pictures of her.

Thursday 10 August 2000 at 21.10

Still light but you can feel the autumn is coming. It is only around 16 degrees (*Celsius*) in the daytime and 17 in the water. We had an excellent pike for dinner, given to us by Erik (*nephew*) yesterday. The eagles are visible rather often. Their sound is a pathetic squeak, incongruent with the majestic silhouette in the sky. Dimitri Perricos has phoned me every day from New York. The impression is that things are moving somewhat. The Iraqis are showing interest in Resolution 1284. They are looking for assurances on lots of things and trying to bargain for a number of things ... There might be meetings in New York in connection with the UN celebration of the millennium early in September. It seems Tariq Aziz is coming.

On Monday, I shall go back to New York and there will be a heavy week ahead of the meeting of the College of Commissioners and my visit to Washington, where I shall meet both the Secretary of State, Madeleine Albright, and the White House Security Adviser, Sandy Berger. My new executive assistant, Olof Skoog, will accompany me.

Saturday 19 August 2000. New York

It has been a busy and frugal week. Soup and iced tea for dinner. Every evening at home reading and writing. Wednesday morning, I had the whole professional staff together and briefed them on how I look upon the current situation in which the world seems to be talking about the lifting of sanctions, while governments (including the Russian) seem to stick to the need for inspection and armament control in Iraq and the Iraqis themselves seem to be checking what kind of arrangements they might have under Res. 1284. It seems pretty clear that Tariq Aziz on his visit in Moscow was told that they would have to accept 1284. The point that interests them most is probably what kind of financial controls there would be under para. 33 of Res. 1284 if there were a suspension of restrictions.

Tonight I have been reading the chapter about UNSCOM in a new biography of Richard Butler. With Scott Ritter, the CIA and espionage it is a horribly complex picture one gets – whether true or not.

Sunday 20 August 2000 at 23.00

Got up early this morning. *Took a* one-hour walk in Central Park. Marvellous weather. In the afternoon I have worked on speeches for the College of Commissioners, mainly on the so-called 'modalities' of inspection. Difficult subject to tackle. But the document which shows how the modalities were applied in 1996–1998 is quite interesting. No abstract report but concrete narrative.

Eva is back in Stockholm. She has a long travelling season ahead of her: Rovaniemi, the Hague, London, Alaska, Tasmania and New Zealand. Then Christmas (*with the family*) in Colorado. Hope she gets her fill of the travel so that we can confine ourselves to Europe when I return ... I am preparing for a trip to China and perhaps Malaysia and Bahrein in October.

Saturday 26 August 2000. New York

The past week lots of things happened. Visit to Washington Tue. 22. Went with my new executive assistant, Olof Skoog, to Washington. He has a sharp mind, diplomatic feeling, energy and is low-key in behaviour. I think he will be fine. Olof knows a lot of people in the various missions after several years in NY. This is an asset. He can scout and be a messenger. He is cautious.

MEETING WITH US SECRETARY OF STATE MADELEINE ALBRIGHT ON 22 AUGUST 2000

Madeleine Albright received me beaming in the door of her office. It is interesting how you sit at high-level meetings in different countries. In China you sit next to each other – with a small table between you. You do not face each other. It can have some advantages not to have to stare the other in the eye all the time, but on the whole I find it a bit awkward. In Japan – and many other places – you sit at an angle. This is the most common and I find it the best. You have easy eye contact, but you do not seem evasive if you do not keep staring at your partner. Often you are, of course, right across from each other over a table, often with collaborators at your side and on the side of your interlocutor. Here you have a feeling more of a negotiation, very business-like. Mrs Albright and I sat in easy chairs right opposite each other and rather far from each other in front of a large fireplace. In front of the fireplace and some distance from it was a large sofa on which there were several officials. There was also a second row of officials behind the sofa. As in all these meetings you have to speak fast, not get sidetracked and not get stuck on some issue, taking time from other issues. We did rather well. She recalled earlier meetings, notably when I came to the Security Council and presented the North Korean case. She also recalled our meeting in Vienna. First of all, she assured me of full US support for my work and praised what I had done so far. She was interested in hearing me explain what I thought might move the Iraqis to accept Res. 1284. (I explained I thought the financial alleviations to be offered under para. 33 was the most important factor.) I also said I thought *that in a package of elements leading to acceptance and implementation, there would somehow figure the ending of bombing*. She remarked that there could be no quid pro quo. She said people speculated that the US could not act during the election campaign. This was wrong. They were ready at any moment to act.

I cited to Mrs Albright my earlier statement that Iraq tended to see inspections as a penalty but should see them as an opportunity to get rid of sanctions. The US grabbed this idea, adapted it to their earlier talk about 'Saddam in his box' and stated that Res. 1284 was not a penalty box for Saddam, but an opportunity box. She assured me that the US was ready to act in accordance with the resolutions (687 and 1284). Thus, she distanced herself from the position that removal of Saddam was a condition for lifting or alleviating sanctions.

MEETING WITH THE NATIONAL SECURITY ADVISER, SANDY BERGER

After a sandwich lunch in Robert Einhorn's office, we move to the White House to meet the National Security Adviser, Sandy Berger. I met Sandy Berger once or twice during the IAEA period and we both recognized each other. He was equally full of praise. (I hope they temper it publicly. Kisses of death are not desirable.) The talk was more relaxed. One important point we discussed was whether the Executive Chairman should take it upon himself to report squarely that 'Iraq has cooperated in all respects and progress has been made on key disarmament issues' or should choose a narrative way: in the past period Iraq did this and did that, provided much cooperation on this, but less on that, progress was made on this issue but not at all on another one. In this way it would be for the Security Council to judge whether the conduct attained the level meant by the Council in the resolution. Berger did not seem to have thought about my option to pass the buck to the Council. He said that it was because of the enormous responsibility placed on the Chairman that they had been so particular about who they got as Chairman. He elaborated a bit on my outstanding record from the IAEA. It was, indeed, very flattering. At the same time, the responsibility could be awesome.

MEETING OF THE COLLEGE OF COMMISSIONERS, 23 AND 24 AUGUST 2000

On Wednesday and Thursday, we had the College of Commissioners. It was a very rewarding session. The P5 representatives (Einhorn, Fedotov, Shulte, Delpech and Cong) are disciplined, knowledgeable and cooperative. Shulte (UK) is the sharpest in tone. It is good to have someone out on one side to balance what may be out on another side. It makes my job to keep balance easier. Several of the non-P5 are also most useful. The Ukrainian (*ambassador to Washington*) Gryshchenko is very smart and seeks to keep a balance. The Brazilian (Monteleone) and Argentinian (Heineken) have the great advantage that they have participated in inspections and thus do not come with *innocent* blue eyes. The non-diplomatic members will need more time to understand that the commission cannot make agreements with Iraq modifying the conditions set by the Security Council.

The main theme was 'operating procedures'. There was complete frankness in talking about the fact that Iraq is an oppressive, totalitarian state, that Iraq has consistently tried to hide and now has had two years to refine their methods of hiding. On the question whether UNMOVIC can demand access to private sites, it was said that in an ordinary democratic state, you do not barge into private residences. Yet all agreed that the rules laid down allow us to go in, that the Iraqis use private residences for hiding files. Thérèse Delpech reminded us that the most important document collection of all in Iraq was at the 'chicken farm' – a private property.

We also had a good discussion about the interview modalities. It was agreed that any Iraqi presence during interviews was an intimidation and a videotaping for Iraq would be equally intimidating. Gryshchenko urged that there should be clearer rules for the Chief Inspectors on how to behave and perhaps special training for them. Too much had been left to their personalities. Shulte stressed that you must give them discretion. On the definition of 'sensitive sites', I insisted that an Iraqi designation was not conclusive. If it was considered 'frivolous', it could be rejected. I also had support for the view that UNMOVIC's inspector, alone, should determine how many inspectors should go in, but decide on numbers that were commensurate with the size and complexity of the site.

We had disseminated a rather fat document describing the experience of UNSCOM in the application of the Ekéus 'sensitive site' modalities and of the subsequent Butler additions. Our paper gave a very fresh picture from the field and impressed all. It was *instructive* reading. Of course, I would not be surprised if Iraq comes out with rebuttals and their own descriptions. Our document is restricted but it is likely to leak. One feature that does not immediately strike you when you read it, is that in no one case of these inspections did the teams find anything. Also, it is not shown that in very many cases it was Scott Ritter who was the chief inspector. What is not described in the reports is the SIGINT – electronic surveillance – that appears to have been part of these inspections. According to the book about Butler, an inspection vehicle carried equipment registering Iraqi radio traffic, noting increased traffic as inspectors approached. It seems that the US succeeded in breaking the Iraqi codes but did not tell UNSCOM what was radioed. For my part I have reached the conclusion that electronic surveillance is too deep waters for UNMOVIC. Query whether the Security Council would have authorized it. Another special matter was that these inspections mostly touched military installations, preferably the Republican Guard. Thus, a mapping of their installations was made. With the close relations to the US the maps could later be used for bombing.

The only minor difference in the College *was* how we described our current readiness. The moment we are ready, it is clear that the absence of inspections is due to Iraqi defiance of the resolution 1284 and the questions media then love to ask is 'what is the Security Council – US – Russia – France – going to do about that . . .?' Well, we reached a sufficiently fuzzy text on the matter . . .

Tuesday 29 August

On the Sunday I walked up to Göran's and Bo's apartment by seven in the evening. They were to come at 7.50 by train, but the train was a bit delayed. The cat was pleased to have me in the house. She had pulled out a couple of books, one of which was about selecting the right wines. Civilized cat . . . They had had a nice weekend far upstate in New York. Eva phoned from Rovaniemi where she is attending a meeting of parliamentarians. She was very pleased. Beautiful and useful.

Dagens Nyheter (*a main newspaper in Stockholm*) last week (Thursday?) had a nasty article about UNMOVIC and me. It says that the inspectors we have recruited were not 'the best in the branch'. There were a number of misinterpretations and errors. I first suspected the Kay/Ahlmark source, but Ewen Buchanan guessed it was Ekéus (who had lectured the training course and seen some participants). I sent a letter to DN correcting some of the things in the article. One of the Editors in Chief contacted me and said they would take an abbreviated letter – but there would, of course, be some comment attached to it. Normal. A newspaper will hardly ever concede it was wrong. Nevertheless, it might be good that a lot of people I know will see that I refute the criticism.

AN INSPECTION USING SIGINT?

Saturday 2 September 2000

Reuters made a TV interview with me on Tuesday 29, and it was OK. Still, I was amazed by some things. What really turned him on was my statement that we would not use SIGINT – electronic eavesdropping. I said I did not know what exactly UNSCOM had done, but there were long descriptions of such activities in a recent biography about Butler. I said I was not sure whether such activities were in line with what the Security Council had authorized. (Having read the OMV – *Ongoing Monitoring and Verification* – plan resolution I think one could probably defend the activity although the Council seems never to have focused on the issue.) Yet I felt this was too complex an activity for UMOVIC. The Reuters man (very experienced old hand) said I might be criticized for this position. So far there has been no negative comment. It might come – as examples of a 'softer' UNMOVIC. Nevertheless, I am convinced I did the right thing. There are no records of this activity in the UNSCOM archives! Nor does UNSCOM seem to have learnt anything which it could use in reports to the Security Council. The operation seems to have been under US/UK management – but under UNSCOM auspices! Piggybacking. Not so nice. We are authorized for inspection and monitoring – not espionage.

On Thursday (31 August), Kofi Annan asked me to see him. He was not sure whether he would be able to see Tariq Aziz during the millennium summit. Nevertheless, he asked me what I thought he should say. I said he might intimate his view that what still remained of the sanctions would not go away but for Iraq accepting 1284. That UNMOVIC was an opportunity. I am still inclined to think there will be a package.

President Clinton yesterday gave a major speech at Georgetown University, declaring that he would not go ahead with any deployment of national missile defence. He gave diplomacy, deterrence and defence as the US means to protect itself and the peace. One feature that struck me was the continued emphasis on proliferation of weapons of mass destruction. Curious that he did not directly refer to

North Korea, Iraq, Iran and Libya. How can one avoid feeling the relevance of success/failure in the case of preventing Iraq from keeping or acquiring such weapons? If we fail in that case, how shall we fare in others?

Tuesday 5 September

I have been reading Ken Alibek's Biohazard about the Soviet (and Russian) programme for biological weapons. Horrendous! They were said to aim especially for bacteria and viruses for which there were no vaccines. He says he had heard that 'several' Russian biological scientists had gone to Iraq and North Korea. He also reports on efforts to export large fermentation vessels from Russia to Iraq in 1995! Thus, indicating that Iraq even at that time had further ambitions in the biological weapons field and Russia was prepared to ignore the need for exporting only under the oil for food programme!

Today the UN millennium celebration started at a ceremony during which the Japanese peace bell would be rung. Kofi Annan gave a good speech and pushed a pole against the bell three times. Nice ring. Film and photo. On the way out he grabbed me, and he said Barak (Israel) had expressed concern about what Iraq *could be planning*. I said to Kofi that *one idea often ignored was the zone free of weapons of mass destruction referred to in Resolutions 687 and 1284*. Most people seem to think this is so distant and hypothetical as to be meaningless. I said I admitted it might be distant but not redundant. All countries consider their long-term strategic security. Iraq could hardly ignore the military capacity of Iran, Syria and Israel. Iranian missile, nuclear, chemical or biological capacity was bound to constitute incentives for Iraq to have such capacity. Efforts to prevent Iraq from getting such capacity must be coupled with efforts to prevent the emergence or (in the case of Israel) indefinite retention of such capacity. Kofi agreed that the regional aspect was very important. A package that would bring Iraq to accept 1284 should have some passing reference to a zone free of weapons of mass destruction.

MILLENNIUM SUMMIT AT THE UN

Wednesday 6 September

Today was the big millennium summit at the UN. First Ave was blocked between 49 St and 42 and I had a hard time walking down 2nd Ave for all the policemen and police cars! However, I came down shortly after seven to join a breakfast 'for foreign ministers'. I sat down with the Irish foreign minister. She said there was a strong pressure in Ireland about the lifting of sanctions. I met Maurice Strong. Maurice said the millennium summit was his idea (in a report about reform at the UN) and that was why he was invited. He talked most about his current pet project: the University of Peace in Costa Rica.

In the morning, I watched and listened to the General Assembly on the TV in my room. I have now been through the various texts and feel somewhat disappointed. Even Blair was not more than passable. Chirac was empty. Putin was specific but hardly eloquent. IAEA was the only organization he mentioned besides the UN! I was invited to the Secretary-General's luncheon with the heads of state, this time held in the big delegates' lounge. Sat between the foreign ministers of Burma and of Turkmenistan. Clinton's speech of thanks at the lunch was excellent. He cited somebody stating that we are what the world made us, and in some cases worse (I wonder if he had himself in mind). In the case of Kofi Annan, he was also what the world made him, but even better. He also said that some people would characterize Annan as an 'idealist' and added: 'good for you'. I liked that comment, because it reveals that Clinton, too, thinks that 'idealism' is positive. After the luncheon, in the general chaos reigning I did see some people. Amr Moussa, the current foreign minister of Egypt, caught me. He said they tried to tell the Iraqis how excellent I was but did not get a positive response. 'They have problems with you.' Well, they have problems with all who do not support them, like Meguid, me and Kofi Annan.

I met President Mbeki of South Africa. He said they had some influence on Iraq and promised that they would help UNMOVIC if they could; Tariq Aziz was talking to Dhanapala as I came past. He saw me at two metres' distance, and I could sense how he wanted to avoid showing a sign of recognition; I also kept a straight face, not wanting to embarrass him.

I had a hard time moving against the current (with most guests going toward the Trusteeship Chamber for the photo). At one point I was in a spot between Clinton and Putin, stuck in the crowd. I did not try to take the opportunity to shake hands. Why should I? This, after all, is not tourism. Castro was also nearby, but, again, I did not approach him, though he might have recognized me. I had no business to transact. Tariq Aziz was there, looking somewhat frozen out, but I did not approach. Well, what a show!

Thursday 7 September

The show is soon over and next week the regular General Assembly begins. But today it was still in full swing! Tariq Aziz spoke a bit about US hegemony, but it was not venomous. He stressed respect for the Charter principles of 'sovereign equality' but somehow managed to forget to mention the ban on aggression. I went to Senegal's reception for Arafat. I walked up to him and explained who I was and told him we had met in Algiers many years ago (at the celebration of Algeria's fifteenth (?) anniversary). He looked expired. He has led a rough life and his current predicament cannot be easy – settling totally with Israel or letting it slip on account of Jerusalem.

The Norwegian ambassador came up to me and asked if I wanted to be introduced to the King of Norway. I followed the ambassador and was introduced to King Harald. I said I had a good Norwegian name – Blix – and added that my family had come from Norway at some stage during the sixteenth century, when it fled from the Danish tax men (*fogdarna*). Then we talked Iraq and I said I hoped Norway would get onto the Security Council. The King asked whether the job with Iraq was very difficult, and I answered that so long as we are not inside Iraq it was rather easy. We all laughed at that. With the King was also Jens Stoltenberg, the Norwegian prime minister (*later Secretary-General of NATO*) who is the son of my old colleague Thorvald Stoltenberg.

At five I left to go to the reception of President Clinton at the Metropolitan Museum. I walked up from 42 St, to 81! The checkpoint to get a pass for the reception was easy but I had to walk through almost the whole bottom floor of the Metropolitan to come to the reception. Endless rows of Greek sculptures and – as I neared the reception – endless rows of Egyptian mummies. Also, endless numbers of White House guides who urged you on. Eventually I landed in a beautiful huge room with water and a fountain and an Egyptian temple. Lots of people.

I ran into Dick Gardner, who told me that he would be a delegate to the coming General Assembly. I met Holbrooke and his charming and intelligent wife – who has written one book about Carl XIV Johan Bernadotte and one about Raoul Wallenberg. I had a short chat with Amr Moussa (foreign minister, Egypt). I also talked with the nice Israeli ambassador – who is an expert on French literature – and we agreed I should send him an official letter asking that they take up contact with my intelligence man, McIver. The loudspeaker kept announcing arrivals. The only ones who were missing were the hosts – Bill and Hillary Clinton.

Saturday 9 September at 08.15

A footnote to the Clintons' reception at the Metropolitan Museum: Prime Minister Persson reported to the Swedish UN mission that he had, indeed, shaken hands with the President – after first standing in line for this memorable event for one and a half hours! He did not seem to have resented it, but he marvelled that President Putin of Russia had put up with the same treatment!! Horrible: I couldn't see Clinton standing in line at the Kremlin?!

Yesterday, Friday 8 September, I had morning coffee with Mr William Morris and Mr Burhan Al-Chalabi of the Next Century Foundation. We met at the Crown Plaza hotel, because it is impossible to get visitors into the UN building during the Summit. We had a long talk. Al-Chalabi, who seems to have contacts with Tariq Aziz, clearly was sympathetic to a variety of Iraqi views, while Morris seemed to look for compromises everywhere. Al-Chalabi said that a great problem was that Iraq did not have confidence in the UN after the UNSCOM debacles. An effort was needed to sell Res. 1284 to Iraq and he seemed to think I should be part of it. I commented that a root problem was that Iraq needed to create confidence in the world that it was ridding itself of weapons of mass destruction. At the suggestion that it had seemed that very little was left, I said that there seemed to be a general view that by the end of

1998 the nuclear file had the fewest question marks and that the biological one had numerous ones. It was true that there would always be a residue of uncertainty (this was now generally admitted). It was a political question how much uncertainty the Security Council would tolerate. Perhaps it would have been wise to say in 1998 that the nuclear file was acceptable and to urge that other files needed to be brought to the same level. It was a fact, regrettably, that panels of experts, both UNSCOM and non-UNSCOM, had agreed that there were many contradictions and question marks in the biological file.

Who has the burden of proof of existence or non-existence of WMD? I brought up the arguments about the 'burden of proof' and said I thought it was misleading. True, there would always be a residue, which not even Iraq could eliminate. However, they had all the personnel under their authority and could turn to them for clarifications and they had all the archives. It was easier for Iraq to reach for the bottom of the barrel than for UNMOVIC to do so. Further, it was misleading to say that UNMOVIC had the burden of proof and that Iraq should be 'acquitted' if UNMOVIC did not prove there remained *some*thing. 'Acquittal' in criminal law was based on the idea of a presumed innocence in the absence of evidence to the contrary. Here, however, there was a need for confidence that Iraq had no more WMD and confidence would not arise from any presumptions but from laborious and credible demonstration of a long-standing programme.

We discussed the concept of 'cooperation' and I said it did not easily lend itself to definition. However, we would not ask Iraq for things that were undoable. We are reasonable people and will act reasonably.

We also talked about the concepts of 'unresolved disarmament questions' and 'key disarmament issues'. Which were they? I said that the 'key disarmament issues' would have to be defined by us in the work programme that we were to present to the Security Council sixty days after having begun work in Iraq. As the programme is subject to the approval of the Council, we cannot predict the list of issues and Iraq cannot know it until after it has opened up under Res. 1284. As to 'unresolved disarmament questions', this was something we had already begun to work on. We could not have started earlier because we wanted to have new staff on board to look at the issue with fresh eyes.

What was meant by 'begun work in Iraq' in Res. 1284? Our interlocutors insisted that a dialogue with Iraq was needed and implied that I should help to sell Res. 1284 to the Iraqi government. I said that was not my job. My door was open at all times, however. But I was sure they did not want to come. Indeed, how could they? Their rejection of 1284 would begin to look undermined if it became known that they talked to me – even though it might only be about interpretations of 1284. What about private meetings? What about presidential palaces? They had been inspected and there was nothing in them. What would be the use of inspecting again? I explained that it was very important that there were no sanctuaries.

I *said I thought* what UNMOVIC stood for and would do, would gradually become clear as the organization was built up. The structure became known last spring when we submitted our report to the Security Council. The recruitment and staffing are now known in large measure. *I* had said all along that we needed both fresh eyes and institutional memory. On one point I had made it public that I would refrain from an activity which UNSCOM reportedly undertook, namely SIGINT. I would not authorize electronic eavesdropping. I considered it too difficult for us and I was not quite sure that the Security Council resolutions were meant to authorize it.

Our interlocutors said there would be a need for something face-saving. I said I can see that. The most important point, presumably, was what kind of financial arrangements would *follow a* suspension *of sanctions*. There was not much talk about that problem. I could also see that some other points would be of importance. All these items were outside the purview of the Executive Chairman – and also of the Secretary-General. What I could do was to continue building up the organization as it was contemplated by the Security Council and the Amorim report. It was not only to list 'unresolved disarmament issues'. We had to put together a new 'inspectors' handbook'. Certainly, we would use a lot of UNSCOM procedures, where these had worked well. No need for change for the sake of change.

Stockholm. Sunday 17 September 2000

Landed in Vienna last Wednesday. Stayed at the Country Inn Hotel on Wagramer Strasse. On Thursday we interviewed a number of Jordanian candidates for inspection jobs in UNMOVIC. Jordan is the only Arab country that has nominated. Perhaps we should try to approach Morocco. My old friend Ben Moussa (who was ambassador in Vienna) seems to be head of the international organizations department in Rabat. Had a long talk with Mohamed ElBaradei. He seems somewhat soft – sanctions cannot go on forever ... However, I think he appreciated that I want to share with him what rules we want to follow in inspections. It was an amiable talk, especially when we talked about our children and our wives.

Friday 22 September 2000. Back in the New NY Apartment

Dinner on tuna fish salad. Not yet managed to work the TV. At least I can now use the microwave oven. Presented UNMOVIC's second quarterly report in the Security Council this morning and it went very well. OK, we are in the easy phase. Build-up and no confrontations with Iraq yet. However, everything related to Iraq can be inflamed and avoiding that seems to be a feat. All in the Council praised our 'professionalism'. Must stand in some contrast to the 'amateurism' of the past?

Today in the Security Council I was impressed that all members pronounced themselves in favour of implementation of Res. 1284. The French, who staunchly stated that Iraq should not believe there was any way out of sanctions except 1284, pleaded nevertheless for some 'clarifications' of the resolution. The US (Cunningham) said any amendments to 1284 were out of the question. Iraq knew perfectly well what it had to do. Tunisia pleaded for a dialogue, and suggested the Secretary-General might be the intermediary. The Russians explained that Iraq would be deaf to 1284 until some central issues were solved: the bombing of Iraq was illegal and must end. They must also feel convinced that there really could be suspension. So long as someone talked about overthrowing the government or supporting internal revolt, one could not expect Iraq to come around.

I was asked to comment at the end and said that one ambition of UNMOVIC was to help maintain agreement in the Security Council. When the Council was united it was strong. The College of Commissioners was an instrument which could be used to attaining consensus. I said that while Iraq was negative to Res. 1284, at the same time it showed interest in it. We had seen the close interpretation of the Res. presented at the Kuala Lumpur conference. Some Iraqi concerns regarded paragraphs which related to UMOVIC, e.g. what was meant by 'cooperation?' And what by 'key disarmament issues?' While we could not clarify which were the 'key DA issues', as this would be done much later and be subject to decision by SC, 'the unresolved DA issues' were a matter we were already working on and results would be coming within months. 'Cooperation' did not easily lend itself to definition, but we had said that we would not ask anything which was not 'doable'. However, we reserved to ourselves to judge whether something was doable. Iraq should also see that we tried to build up a respectable UN body and we had said that we would not do anything to 'harass', 'humiliate' or 'provoke'. However, again we would not leave it to Iraq to determine if something was 'harassing'. They might well consider the whole inspection system 'harassment'.

It is a relief to have this Council meeting behind us – even though I fully realize that we are now in the easy phase. In Stockholm the press asked me when I thought we would be able to go to Iraq. I replied that many people thought it would not be before the US election and that might be a good guess. It was interesting – but not really surprising – that the Russian (it was Gatilov, not Lavrov) did not say anything about the recruitment of personnel. Not a word about Nikita Smidovich and Igor Mitrokhin, whom they wanted me to fire earlier.

I take it that unpleasant issue is set to rest, and I have excellent use for Nikita and Igor, as they are very knowledgeable.

POSSIBLE ELEMENTS IN A DIALOGUE WITH IRAQ

Saturday 23 September

Gloomy weather. Grey and drizzling. I have noted possible elements in a dialogue with Iraq – whoever will undertake it. Not me. They may be good to have for memory and for me to print if I want to make use of them.

Tuesday 26 September 2000

Yesterday I sent a printout of the *'catalogue'* paper to Kofi Annan. Today I discussed the subject of a 'package' with Jeremy Greenstock, the UK ambassador. He thought it was important to get a dialogue going about the implementation of Res. 1284. Otherwise, the resolution might be drowned in all the talk about the lifting of sanctions. He did not say how the dialogue should be promoted. He did not think that Kofi Annan would move, because he has burnt his fingers twice on Iraq. Nor did he expect that I would take initiatives. I explained that I declare myself ready and happy to receive Iraqis and discuss the contents of the resolution. But even without such visits, our interpretation of it is gradually becoming known to Iraq through our communications with our College of Commissioners and our action in recruitment, etc. I said I did not like the idea – advanced by UK minister Hain – of going to Baghdad, because it would look like a 'position de demandeur'. If they did not wish to see me here during the General Assembly, why should I rush down there? We could meet in NY – or in Geneva. I had the feeling that the Brits would not mind if we made a bit more noise to remind people that UNMOVIC is there. But not too much. Ragida Dergham, the NY commentator of the Al Hayat, has written two long articles in which she deplores the lack of dialogue and criticizes all sides and suggests action by all – including Kofi and me. Interesting that she urges a 'give and take', a mechanism and a memorandum of understanding. Precisely the things that Tariq Aziz stress in his talk with the UK Next Century Foundation.

Thursday 28 September

Today I had lunch with Ragida Dergham – the 'Druze missile' – and Ewen Buchanan. She continued to search *the horizon* for initiatives at a dialogue. Tried to assert that the sanctions pressure was lost. Iraq was the only state that had big oil reserves and the world needs to deal with the Iraqis. Even very moderate Iraqis had been very disappointed in her first interview with me, in particular when I had said that I could not predict in what terms I would report to the Security Council about Iraqi cooperation with UNMOVIC. I replied that under Res. 687 it was clearly the Council which 'determined' whether Iraq had been freed of its WMDs. Under Res. 1284, too, members of the Council might disagree with my characterization of the cooperation and veto a suspension.

She tried to imply that the inspection of presidential sites must be laid aside. I said the resolution talked about 'unrestricted' access and the MOU of Kofi Annan had confirmed that this also meant presidential sites and had, indeed, laid down a special procedure. How could one then forget them? Another matter was how often one would need to inspect them. I talked about the need for strategic equilibrium and the need to keep the long-term goal of a zone free of weapons of mass destruction alive. She agreed but did not seem to be very impressed. At a Swiss dinner tonight for the Harvard Law School I had a chance to see Kofi Annan momentarily. He had read my paper about (a catalogue *of*) elements in an Iraq package, and we should talk about it when he and I are back after next week's travels. The Russian ambassador, Lavrov, said he was glad to see me. He had planned to visit me, but this place was even better. He said that the Iraqis really were interested in clarifying a number of things about 1284. They had referred to Boutros Ghali's MOU in connection with Oil for Food. It had taken six months to negotiate, but it had stuck. The Russians had said that 1284 was a different matter. The Iraqis' first question was not the financial arrangements after suspension. I said that I was at all times ready to discuss – but not to make agreements. Moreover, Iraq would gradually see how we interpreted the resolution. I also made statements that should interest them. I had said that we would never have the aim of harassing, humiliating or provoking them, and I had said we would not go for electronic eavesdropping. Lavrov said *that these things should be appreciated by Iraq*.

Wednesday 4 October 2000. Stockholm

Left New York last Friday (29 *September*) and arrived rather tired on Saturday. Eva and I did some shopping and we went to Mårten for a drink before dinner. At seven when darkness has fallen the view from Mårten's twenty-second floor of the city and its lights is uplifting. When I compare the view from my thirtieth floor in New York what strikes me is greater homogeneity of the cityscape in Stockholm. Houses are generally six floors here, while in New York you have a great variety – from six to sixty.

On Sunday the weather was still glorious early autumn. We took the car and went to Angarn lake with sandwiches and tea in the rucksack. We walked all around the lake, about two and a half hours. There were still lots of migratory birds. Thousands of geese flew up and seemed to try unsuccessfully to form a V. There were also a few herons and lots of lapwings and ducks that I could not identify. Some ornithologists with huge field glasses or cameras and a few Sunday walkers. What a privilege to have a place like this within twenty-five minutes of our parking space.

Yesterday, Tuesday, I gave a talk about Iraq and UNMOVIC at SIPRI. Rolf Ekéus turned up and sat through it. After the meeting he told me that there had been attempts between the US and France – Pickering and Errera – to come to relations, but it just got worse. They had moved the talks to a lower level and had asked Ekéus to act as a 'moderator'. He would go to Paris in October for this purpose. Tomorrow (5 *October*) I shall brief the King at four o'clock and then get the car and drive alone to Gräsö (*the Blix family summer place*). And on Friday we have the year 2000 asado (*barbecue*).

Sunday 8 October 2000. New York

Back in New York again. Now eight o'clock in the evening with my body at two in the morning.

The briefing of the King (*on 5 October*) took thirty to forty minutes. I arrived before he did and was received by the Marshall of the Court. The *King was just* back from the Olympics in Australia. I had prepared some points. However, I quickly understood that he preferred a conversation, and I delivered what I had had in mind in this manner. At the end I mentioned to him that I had briefed his daughter – Crown Princess Victoria – and that she was very alert. The sofa in the audience chamber is horrible. He sits in one corner and the briefer in the other. Perhaps it is deliberate?

From the King, I went to our garage and took out the car. Made it to the eight o'clock ferry. At Rosten, they had left the lights on at the garage and the cart was there, so I could move up with all my gear.

I work hard (*on Friday morning* 6 October) to make a huge fire with logs to get adequate *glowing charcoals* for the grilling of the lamb. It was lovely to be out among trees again. The grass was tall and between my feeding the fire with logs I used the lawnmower and cut the grass on the 'lagårdsplan' (*lawn*) and in front of our house. A bit chaotic, as usual, but all participants get plenty of meat and gratin and salad, cheese and cake. I had written some rhymes which I read at the dessert and *other family members* similarly presented some verses. I like that. Keeping up the tradition of a little effort at an intellectual content – and not just food and drink. After the misty and rainy Friday the night was delightfully starlit. At Gräsö you really see it. We did not leave until the afternoon on Saturday and made the four o'clock ferry. Nice evening in Stockholm. The flight today was uneventful. Far from a full plane. Eva should be at Anchorage now, staying overnight before she catches the plane for Barrow. I hope she got to see the same marvellous sight of Greenland as I did today. We flew over the highest mountains, some 4,000 metres, along the southern coast. Could see the glaciers emptying into the sea. Magnificent sunshine. Snow, ice, not a single soul, not a ski track.

Saturday 14 October 2000. New York

An uneventful but nevertheless tiring week. Several briefings of groups: Norwegian and Danish parliamentarians. Also – closer to the operational scene – briefing of the ambassadors of the Gulf Council (Saudi, Oman, Bahrein, Kuwait, United Arab Emirates). The week has been dominated by the violence in Israel, Gaza and the West Bank. Iraq is positioning itself as the vanguard of the Palestine cause. It hopes to be accepted into the brotherhood and to get it more firmly on its side for a quashing of the sanctions. While more planes are landing in Baghdad there is little to suggest that the sanctions which mostly regard oil, could collapse. I therefore think that the Iraqi interest in 1284 and efforts to get commitments to as much as possible for an acceptance of the resolution will continue.

Eva has attended a meeting of the Arctic Council in Barrow, Alaska this week. She phoned me on a miserable line two or three days ago. They were not allowed to go outside the hotel for the risk of polar bears. An exotic conference place!

Saw the second debate between Bush and Gore this week. It was extremely polite. Both had evidently been admonished not to be aggressive. So, it was on the dull side ... Gore does not show one iota of a sense of humour. But he does show commitment. He stands for something. Whether Bush has any convictions of his own is doubtful. I have the feeling that he just floats along with what the Republican mainstream may wish and tries to avoid being stuck with some extreme position.

Sunday 15 October 2000

Still nice sunny, mild autumn weather. I have a lot of homework to do. Only managed to write a plan for the UNMOVIC handbook yesterday to replace the more militarily sounding 'standard operating procedures'. Query whether guidelines should be in injunction paragraph form or in narrative.

Eva spoke to me from Seattle yesterday midday. She was to take a look at the city before the evening plane to Copenhagen where she had to change. I hope she succeeded in getting an upgrade to business with her bonus coupons. In an hour we should be able to talk on the phone again. It really makes you feel how small the globe is getting when you ponder a call yesterday to the west coast of America and one this afternoon to the eastern part of Western Europe! I told Göran that I had read some rhymes at the asado celebration. We are not very good at being solemn with each other. The verses allow you to insert solemn praise in a form that marks that you are stepping out of the usual. Adding humour and poor rhymes makes it easier. To give a solemn prose speech of praise is much more difficult.

Tuesday 31 October 2000

Back here (*in New York*) today after a twelve-day trip around the world.

I left NY on Friday 20 October by direct flight to Tokyo. Nearly fourteen hours. Next morning departure for flight to Beijing. Sen Pang and Olof Skoog met me at the new airport and took me to town. Stayed at the Hilton. The mobile phone did not work in China, nor in Japan! I used the ordinary phone and reached Eva in Hobart, Tasmania. She had been rather tired, having flown in one go Stockholm–London–Singapore–Brisbane–Hobart.

Here is what I noted while in Beijing (*22–24 October*): the new terminal is built in current cosmopolitan style. No Chinese flavour. Along the road from the airport to town now lots of high-rising apartment houses. I remember in the past there were endless rows of tents for people who had lost their homes in a big earthquake. On the main roads there used to be thousands of cyclists. No longer. They seem to have a lane of their own. The Hilton, where I am staying, is excellent. Rooms in good taste. I marvel that they serve FRENCH butter and ENGLISH marmalade. We went to the Beijing opera and saw something rather boring about the eight immortals. Only in the last act did one get the mixture of acrobatics and theatre that I remembered as exciting. Most of the audience were tourists. They say it is a dying art. Too slow for the young. I remember from 1964, when Eva and I were in Canton (*Guangzhou*), that we went to an amusement park. A show of some uplifting Communist theme about good social conduct had few spectators but the show about an emperor and his many concubines, all in glittering clothes, had a large enthusiastic crowd. No more. Neither draws a crowd now.

The talks were very successful. The Chinese had been furious with Butler but became quite supportive. Said Tariq Aziz was to come before end of year. Felt sympathy with Iraq but wanted implementation of 1284. My long acquaintance with Qian Quiqian helped but the talks with the vice foreign minister Wang were also very good. The scheduled talk with the foreign minister fell out of the programme because he was taken by meetings with Chirac who was there after the European–Asian talks in Seoul. On the last morning they had arranged for me to have acupuncture – at the hotel. A mild professor came with an interpreter. He examined my legs, made me bend them and concluded that the nerve was damaged on the left leg (correct). Needles were stuck on the back of my left leg. Like mosquito bites. An electric current was led through the leg, apparently to stimulate the nerves. No pain really. He also did 'cupping', which consisted in a small cup being applied to create an underpressure on various spots. Reminded me a bit of the past Swedish practice of letting blood – but there was no blood lost in this case. Seemed more doubtful than acupuncture but did not do any harm. We went to a Taoist temple for some sight-seeing. Rather dull. Scattered women prayed to a variety of deities. Monks strolled around. The most remarkable feature were signs in English where the division of words was completely unconventional, like Gr-acious, d-ivine, etc.

On Tuesday 24 October on to Tokyo. Stayed at the New Otani. Room 16 F in the Tower. Lovely view of gardens. Much cheaper than Okura and others. Sushi bar one of the best in Tokyo. Felt like a cat that had had its fill of raw fish. Talks at defence agency. Japan wants to contribute to UN peacekeeping operations and to us, as well. Talk with a vice foreign minister (member of parliament). Interview with NHK television.

On Thursday 26 October

Singapore Airlines from Narita to Singapore. First Class. Never seen one like that before. Each chair separate and a kind of wall on one side – even when you were in the middle. Like a little compartment to yourself. We stayed at the Westin Plaza because the Foreign Ministry was in the same complex. Superb. Refined taste everywhere.

Discreet colours. Soft touch. Good restaurant. We went to Raffles to have a Singapore sling. Sat in their courtyard which has a strong colonial touch with huge fans and buildings with the hotel rooms and arcades surrounding the yard. Talk with the foreign minister, Mr Jayakuma, a law professor. Round-table discussion with desk officers. I think we might get a staff member from their terrorist defence agency.

Saturday 28 October. Kuala Lumpur

We had planned it so that we would have talks in Singapore on the Friday when Muslim Kuala Lumpur is closed. And talks in KL on Saturday. It turned out the Malaysians work only half a day on the Saturday. Tried in vain to phone Noramly bin Muslim (who was DDG (*Deputy Director General*) for technical assistance in IAEA before Qian came). The present head of the Malaysian Nuclear Agency got wind of my presence and came over for a chat

Hotel Shangri La was rather old and mediocre. The centre of KL is now a modern agglomeration of Asian skyscrapers, including the famous highest in the world twin tower. No longer the picturesque open market where we bought copied luxury good many years ago. Now a city not for strolling but for moving by car. Talk with the permanent secretary in the foreign ministry. Thereafter, talk with Mr Halim, former ambassador in Vienna and now the Secretary of the Government and as such the most senior civil servant in the country. The mobile phone worked well both in Singapore and Kuala Lumpur. Talked to Eva in Hobart, Tasmania and Mårten in Stockholm.

On Sunday 29 October we went from Kuala Lumpur to Bahrein via Bangkok. It took the whole day to go from KL to Bahrein with a change at Bangkok's old airport. We were met by friendly foreign ministry head of UN bureau (former perm. rep. NY), UNDP res. rep., Abdul Gader (nice and competent Sudanese) and UNSCOM rep. Patulis. Taken to Holiday Inn where I was given suite of three large rooms for the price of eighty dollars. UNSCOM was a huge customer, and the hotel is a warm supporter of inspections in Iraq. In any case it was good. Security guard. The city – an island – has some 500,000 inhabitants. Lives on oil and a lot of Saudi tourists, who come to enjoy the more liberal climate (drinks) and to play golf. Lots of hotels. On the Monday the programme was full and well organized. UN res. rep. had done good job. He had warned against any media appearance, as relations with Iraq are sensitive and Bahrein does not wish to be seen to be too energetic in going after Iraq. The agreement about our field office is nothing they want to advertise too much. Talk with the Foreign Minister. He was rather firm on the need for inspections in Iraq – as indeed they were in their speech in the GA of the UN. He seemed genuinely positive towards accepting a field office of UNMOVIC – on the understanding that it was fully independent from the US. I assured him there would be no more Gateway.

Tuesday 31 October. Bahrein–New York

Departure by Gulf Air around two in the morning for London. Slept a good deal. Arrival in London very early in the morning. United Airlines lounge. Talked to Eva on the mobile. She was still in Tasmania. Then off to New York. Went to the office for a while in the afternoon.

Thursday 2 November

New York. Talk with SG Kofi Annan. He is going to the Gulf, and I briefed him on my views as to which chips are relevant in any possible future deal under which Iraq would accept inspection – no bombing, no-fly zones, non-intervention, air traffic, financial arrangements in connection with suspension of sanctions, etc. All outside UNMOVIC and outside SG ambit as well. Within UNMOVIC and 1284 sphere: definitions of 'cooperation', 'key disarmament issues', timetable, etc.

Friday 3 November. New York

Departure by Swissair for Geneva in the evening.

Monday 6 November from Geneva to Paris. No time to go to hotel but directly to Quai d'Orsay and talk with M. Paganon, head of UN bureau. Thereafter (Ambassador) Errera and then on to Ministry of Defence and a round table headed by M. Brichambeau, nice Conseiller d'Etat, former legal adviser of foreign ministry. Lots of friends in common. The French attitude is helpful. Staying Hotel de France, like last time. Really very modest. Amazing. You get a nice dinner almost anywhere here. No diners, dumps. But we learnt brasseries are where you go for decent food at low prices.

Tuesday 7 November

Over one hour car ride past St Cloud and beyond Versailles to the Thomson campus, where our training course (for sixty participants) took place. A long lecture which was partly designed to contain responses to questions we know the Iraqis are posing. As the lecture is not a restricted document it will get around. In fact, we had sent it to the French and Russians last Friday and to all other members of the Security Council. I think the lecture went down well. Reception in the evening in the Armed Services Club. All the participants. I have hardly felt Paris so lovely before although the weather was foggy, drizzling, cool. The long perspectives, the houses of the same height, the homogeneity, gave a harmonious solid stable impression. Not an eighty-storey tower next to a brownstone house. Testimony to a strong central power able to enforce town planning.

Wednesday 8 November. Paris–Moscow

Met at Sheremetova by Nikita Zhukov. Staying at the ARBAT hotel – near the foreign ministry Stalinist skyscraper. This was the hotel where Morris Rosen and I stayed in 1986 when we came for the Chernobyl accident. It was then reserved for the Central Committee. Old style but OK and not expensive.

Thursday 9 November. Moscow

No programme in the morning. We walked to the Pushkin Gallery which was only fifteen minutes away. Marvellous van Goghs and Gauguins and Monets. I was particularly taken by two van Goghs, one is the prison yard with grey-blue prisoners getting their daily walk. Around them you see the high walls of the prison. An enclosure. The other is a lovely light green picture of fields. I loved a Monet painting of a rock at sea with marvellous blue waves around it. (Later seen at the Metropolitan the same rock but not the wonderful blue water of the Moscow painting.) Lunch with Sven Hirdman, Swedish ambassador and old friend. The Embassy is splendid and Sven most knowledgeable and capable. Meeting with Minatom minister Adamov, who told us about the Russian ideas for a new type of reactor which had a closed fuel cycle, hardly any waste, nearly inherent safety and proliferation-proof. How the world would get to it, he did not say. I congratulated him on their inventiveness. Few other countries devote much thinking to the nuclear future. I said perhaps the greens would go along with some *new line in nuclear*. It might save their faces. But the thing has to be sold. Putin's sudden proposal in the General Assembly was not the best way. I recommended the G8 as a better forum.

In the evening the Institute for Chemical Analysis headed by Professor Petronin, father of our *staff member* Mrs Svetlana Outkina. Briefing about their capacity for analysis of samples of chemical weapons. Twenty million dollars lab donated by the US. Fine. 'Refreshments' after. Turned out to be lots of vodka and some bread, cucumber, tomatoes, etc. Many toasts and our host sang for us. Anton, husband of Svetlana, interpreted into good American. He was the head of one department. So, the whole family has benefited first from the build-up of the Russian chemical weapons programme and now from the dismantling of the whole thing. Not bad. They seem most knowledgeable. The old labs were in decrepit buildings. It really looked 1920. Actually part of it had been a brandy distillery long ago.

Friday 10 November. Moscow

Round table in the foreign ministry. Vice minister Ordzhonikidze, Ambassador Lavrov et al. A somewhat arrogant and flippant beginning, but it got nicer and friendlier. Much *talk* about the suffering of the Iraqis and the illegality of US/UK bombing and no-fly zones. Lunch in the ministry mansion. Lively discussion.

Lavrov said everybody cheats under disarmament agreements. I protested. Talk with foreign minister Ivanov. More serious. And listening. He is off to Baghdad on Monday. Somehow it seems a strange time to persuade the Iraqis to accept Res. 1284 when they are high on the conflict in the Middle East and seem to believe they can get the sanctions to crumble by themselves. Snow and ice. Traffic chaos. The car took us directly from the talks to the airport. I nearly missed the plane. Total absence of traffic discipline but our driver – from the UN ILO (*International Labor Organization*) – was excellent.

Saturday 11 November. Stockholm

Wonderful to be home in our apartment. Walk in Lill-Jansskogen.

Monday 13 November. Back in New York

At the office in the afternoon. Plenty to complete on documents for the College of Commissioners. I am appalled how indifferent – or unaware – the technical people are about fuzzy language. Eva phoned from Christchurch. Her hiking tour around the South Island of New Zealand had been marvellous. Mostly excellent weather and fantastic views. Now waiting to fly to the Antarctic. I am happy for her.

Saturday 18 November, New York

I hope Eva is now underway! She phoned me this morning, again from Christchurch. They had left by a Hercules jet yesterday and flown about four hours and had one and a half hours left when they turned around. 'White-out' at the landing place. So, they made eight hours of flying – in very uncomfortable seats – and got back to the starting point after midnight. She will hang on for two days more but thereafter she will have to abandon the trip. She cannot be away indefinitely from her office in Stockholm.

Today, at Metropolitan Museum *and* an hour and a half on the twentieth-century European painters – van Gogh, Monet, Cezanne. It is their paintings that catch the astronomical prices at auctions. Why is that? They please the eye. They give us nature as we like to have it – and don't always get. Sunny. Colourful. Not much of the dark side of reality. I love it, too. There is one painting at the Met which I always like to return to. Lepage's painting of Jeanne d'Arc. I am unsure of the symbolism of the painting. The woman looks like a beautiful young peasant. The remarkable thing is that the picture appears to be three-dimensional. She stands in the foreground and there is clear space between her and the background! I know no other painting that creates such a strong feeling of depth. Two weeks ago in Moscow at the Pushkin gallery I saw another large painting by Lepage and the same woman. The three-dimensional effect was there, too, but not at all as strong.

The vote counting in Florida in the US presidential election is still going on. By now people – and I too – are tired of watching all the turns. Yet I certainly think that all votes should be checked if there is reason to believe that there have been significant errors.

Thursday 23 November. Thanksgiving

I and Olof Skoog saw the SG as scheduled. He confirmed what we had assumed, namely, that the Iraqis suggested a free (no preconditions) dialogue with the UN, while the SG would be bound by all UN resolutions. He said such a dialogue had occurred earlier with them (I think on the oil for food). He was aware what points interested them and that most of these concerned matters he could not deliver. Nevertheless, he has a task force on Iraq headed by Dhanapala (undersecretary for disarmament), which could explore matters with Iraq. The Iraqis did not want him to be accompanied by Vorontsov (dealing under Res. 1284 with missing Kuwaitis) or me. I said I thought it was probably an advantage that I was not involved. It is far better that these matters be discussed internally in UNMOVIC and in the College of Commissioners (with the P5 and others).

A point that is puzzling is why the Iraqis seem eager to get into a dialogue at the present time. My guess is that while there will be sympathy in public opinion in many countries (not just Arab ones) for a speedy timetable, there will be no great support for great leniency on inspections. Our position should be that we will do a 'professional inspection job'.

Why are the Russians so eager? They complain that they lose a lot of export opportunities. However, they are not doing badly under the oil for food. Perhaps the Russians are eager just because they want to be seen by the Iraqis as their most loyal friends. Why are the British so eager? They have not been sufficiently energetic in explaining that Iraq can import a lot for today's oil proceeds. Perhaps all have an interest in sounding eager while none is eager? Well, I think the Iraqis want to get out of the financial control even though these controls allow them to put the blame on the US for all the shortcomings in the country. They are proud and feel good about the public support they have in the Arab world (*for a lifting of sanctions*) and the financial controls remain a humiliation. However, they may not be likely to get a free hand on these resources even in the case of a suspension.

For UNMOVIC there are no problematic choices at the present time. We should simply prepare for action without much noise. Seek consensus in the College on timetables and inspection rules and build up staff and logistics. We have concentrated on experts on the various weapons. We shall need interpreters, communications people, logistics people. We should probably plan for specialized training courses for such people. Perhaps also to have a separate roster for them.

Saturday 25 November 2000

Eva phoned from Christchurch and Auckland. She had spent three days at the New Zealand base in the Antarctic. One day was fine and they made several helicopter tours. The other two were windy and they could not go out. The American base was three kilometres away. She flew back on an American plane. Ten hours and no toilet (for women). Going back now through Los Angeles. Should phone me this afternoon.

Sunday 26 November 2000

Rain all last night and still grey and steady rain. I had hoped Eva would phone from Los Angeles or Seattle, but she might have tried in vain when I was out. Mårten phoned to inquire when she would arrive in Stockholm. He planned to meet her.

Sunday Night. 26 November 2000

Sweet Mårten went to Arlanda and waited for four planes from Copenhagen and gave up. I was mistaken. Eva came from Los Angeles to London and from London to Stockholm, arriving around 8 p.m. She was tired but not exhausted. Had slept a good deal over the Pacific. Nice she is safely back.

Jimmy Wang (*friend ever since student days at Columbia University in the mid 1950s*) phoned tonight from Washington. Jimmy and Chungling (*his wife*) are coming to New York 10 to 15 or 16 Dec. I suggested they stay to 16 and we could all have dinner on 15, which is the day Eva arrives. Dear Mårten, it was nice to have you here. I hope you will have a nice week in Belize.

The past week has been a lively one on the Iraqi issue. We had the College of Commissioners here from Monday to Wednesday. The atmosphere and chemistry are still good. However, there is a big risk that we shall lose the US member, Robert Einhorn, assistant secretary for non-proliferation. With a new administration he will have to tender his resignation. The subject that interested us most was that of a 'timetable' once Iraq accepts inspections again.

On Tuesday I shall go to Washington and meet relevant Americans (Pickering, Einhorn, Welch, Gary Samore et al.) at a luncheon with Jan Eliasson (Swedish ambassador). Perhaps they cannot say much about what the US administration will do, but I can certainly express a few opinions. A worrisome feature is that many seem innocently (?) to assume that if Iraq just accepts Res. 1284 and inspection, the suspension of sanctions will happen automatically in six, seven, nine or ten months. I have warned against the assumption that accepting the resolution is like stepping on the first step of an escalator which takes you automatically to the floor of suspension. They have to cooperate in all respects with us and the IAEA for 120 days and make progress on key disarmament tasks. I can easily see that we shall be under pressure to testify positively after those 120 days. But I can also see that Iraq will be under some pressure to behave well to us during those days. I have some difficulty in understanding the Russians and the French trying so hard to accommodate Iraqi wishes: to get a premature definition of 'key disarmament tasks' and to define 'cooperation'. They will tell you that they are very unsure that Iraq will accept the resolution otherwise. It is true that the Iraqi regime does not suffer much under the sanctions, but I think it is pretty clear that it is bargaining in the bazaar. It does not show itself *to be* anxious. Nor should the other side. It has long been *evident* that Iraq wants to go by Res. 1284. They just want to squeeze out as many advantages as they can from that step. An important point hardly discussed is whether a suspension – or, indeed, lifting – of sanctions would lead to better conditions for the Iraqi civilian population. People seem to urge the lifting of sanctions which are already gone! After all Iraq can now sell as much oil as it can pump and buy as much food and other humanitarian items as it wants. What guarantees are there that they would not, if they were free to use oil proceeds as they like, acquire more dual-use articles to help their armament production?

After the visit in Washington we – Olof Skoog and I – shall take the train back to NY and then fly to Paris in the evening. Give a closure speech to the trainees at our course in Paris and fly home to Stockholm for the weekend. Sunday family dinner (Mårten should be back from Belize that afternoon). Monday to Oslo to brief them (they will be in the Security Council as of Jan. 2001 and chair the sanctions committee). Then back to Stockholm Monday evening and a brief breakfast with Torval Stoltenberg Tuesday morning before we go back to NY.

Tuesday 12 December 2000

Back from Stockholm this afternoon. Skoog and I took the train to Washington last Tuesday (5 Dec.). Went to the magnificent (*Swedish*) residence which Boheman (former Swedish Washington ambassador) once bought (for $160,000). Jan (*Eliasson*) had invited Mr Rydell and Gary Samore (both from the Security Adviser's office). Rydell has handled Iraq. Gary is known to me for several years from IAEA matters. Bob Einhorn and David Welch were also there. The luncheon began with an introduction by me and then comments from our American colleagues. It was clear that they did not like the SG's initiative to start a dialogue with Iraq. (I said there was a risk that an Iraqi wish list might get a lot of publicity and support from France and Russia.) Einhorn cautioned me not to emphasize a zone free from weapons of mass destruction in such a way that Iraq could use it as a condition for their own disarmament. I said I talked about the zone as a follow-up to the disarmament in Iraq. The resolutions talk about this work in Iraq as a step toward a zone.

Wednesday morning 6 December back to New York by the metroliner. We went directly to the office in icy hard wind. In the evening Skoog and I left by Air France for Paris. A late plane. We arrived late lunchtime in Paris Thursday 7 Dec. and were met by Alice Hecht and car and driver. We slept a few hours in the afternoon. In the evening, a walk in the neighbourhood. We had an excellent chateaubriand at a somewhat touristic little place. All meat was advertised as 'Argentinian' to calm people against the 'mad cow' fear which now grips France.

Friday 8 December

By car to a lovely castle owned by Thomson industries in the Versailles region. Conclusion of training course. Speech by me. Certificates handed over. Before all this a walking tour through the marvellously restored castle. Very tasteful. Wonderful textiles. I think my pep talk was useful. The participants get the feeling that we attach importance to their training. Directly to the airport and SAS to Stockholm. Not much time at home. Going to a British performance of HAMLET at the City Theatre. Excellent performance. Usually Hamlet is made an elegant, melancholy and beautiful prince. This time the chief actor, a forty-year-old overweight actor, had taken seriously the words of the queen that Hamlet was pale and fat and the information of the grave digger that he was thirty (forty?) and that Hamlet was born the same year as he. Actually, the kind of philosophical, theological monologues and discussions that Hamlet engages in fit better this more mature character than an elegant young prince. The actors articulated so well that the difficult Shakespearean language became easier. But there are so many philosophical lines and thoughts which one does not have the time to digest. They flow through the air. One should read the play slowly.

Saturday 16 December. New York. Eva Is Here

The US has now got its President – Bush – by a majority of one vote in the Supreme Court. Today Bush announced Colin Powell as his Secretary of State and the latter made a good speech of acceptance, apparently without reading a script. It was balanced and judicious. Saddam was to be contained or, if need be, confronted. Weapons of mass destruction were still in focus. The US needed its military forces but also its diplomats and both need their resources. Not a word about the UN. Eva arrived yesterday. Makes me happy. My landlady, Mrs Garcia, sent another TV set today. The superintendent was here and connected the right cables. God bless him and I gave him twenty bucks. Now the TV works.

Thursday 21 December

The past days have been dominated by my cold, by presentation of the third UNMOVIC report to the Security Council and the consolation that Eva has been here. The UNMOVIC Christmas – season's – party was on Tuesday. I had to act as Santa Claus and distribute packages.

Today we took a cab to the Metropolitan (*Museum*) to see the special exhibition on the Scythians. Gold and other pieces from fourth century BC. Remarkably beautiful! Amazing that a nomadic people could produce such art. And evidence of much contact with the Persian and Greek civilizations. Mårten is arriving tomorrow, Friday. God willing and United Airlines flying we are off on Saturday to spend Christmas skiing at Vail, Colorado.

26 December 2000. Vail, Second Day of Christmas

So, here we are. Bright sunshine. White snow. Splendid. Four magpies hopping around in the pine outside the house and a small squirrel evading them. The house is spacious.

It serves us all well and is a new experience. The open fireplace works well. We enjoyed it last night. I have stayed indoors, fitted the necessary notes into my 2001 calendar, read the draft UNMOVIC manual which is in need of much more work.

Year 2001

Wednesday 3 January 2001

New York. I am again alone in New York. George W. Bush has now announced all members of his cabinet. It looks terrifyingly conservative. But for the most part it also seems competent. The environment friends who voted for Nader ought to have second thoughts when they see what environmental records several of the cabinet members have!

Sunday 7 January 2001

Stayed 'at home' almost all day on Saturday. Spent much time putting new applications for jobs into my long, computerized list of potential staff. Went to the Metropolitan Museum after my lunch yoghurt. Chose the Greek, Cypriot and Islamic sections. I wonder what the Greek sculptures would look like if they had retained their colours. While their shapes are refined, they do look a bit anaemic. What I like best in the Islamic department is the room from a Damascus house. The calm, the harmonious colours, the fine proportions, the slow running of water. There is a lovely serenity and taste in it.

Wednesday 10 January 2001

A busy social week and rather quiet at the office. Tuesday lunch with the Ambassador of Singapore, Mr Mahbubani, current President of the Security Council. He was accompanied by two lady counsellors, both very capable. He told me that the majority of his professional staff was female. Not bad! I don't think that Iraq is his main priority, but I tried my best to convey information and whet his appetite. After the lunch – at the Perigord – he took me down by his car to the UN and gave me a book he has recently published Can Asians Think? It appears he criticizes the West for hubris and preaching democracy and human rights to the Asian societies. The latter also developed hubris during the march of the Asian miracle beginning with Japan and continuing with the 'tigers' (Korea, Taiwan, Hong Kong and Singapore). The economic collapse taught them a lesson. What he seems to be aiming at – and one can easily agree with – is that Asia has no reason to swallow the Western pattern lock, stock and barrel. If the Asians can preserve their family cohesion, fine. But do we really preach anything opposed to that? I don't think the West really preaches Westminster-type democracy but rather pluralism and tolerance. The real subjects of criticism are countries like Burma (*Myanmar*) and DPRK (*North Korea*). In his book, Mahbubani stresses the population development which in 2050 will give a heavy preponderance to the developing countries. If they have caught up, they will dominate the economic picture. If they have not caught up, there will be a very heavy pressure on immigration to the Western states. He takes the same view as I have expressed: the Mediterranean is no greater barrier to illegal immigration than the Rio Grande was for the US. Europe is already getting its *flow of refugees* and animosity to immigrants is even greater in Europe than in the US.

Friday 19 January 2001. New York

Leaving in a few minutes for Newark and Stockholm. Rainy and a few degrees.

Saturday 20 January. Stockholm

Clear sky and a few degrees below freezing. The plane was half an hour early. Eva has been skating at Norrviken today. I took an hour's walk in Lill-Jansskogen. Today is the inauguration of G. W. Bush in Washington. American TV reported that the various ceremonies would cost together some 35 million dollars!

HOW CAN IRAQ BE INDUCED TO ACCEPT RES. 1284 AND INSPECTION?

Sunday 21 January 2001

Last Friday Sir Jeremy Greenstock, permanent representative of the UK, visited me in view of my trip to London and meeting with Minister Hain in the Foreign Ministry. He told me (and Olof Skoog) that the British had had long talks with the incoming administration in Washington and tried to influence it. The current internal British view was that the 'sanctions' were eroding and that this was not good for the authority of the Security Council. Saddam was comfortable with the current situation. He got enough money from smuggling. The Brits hoped that the 'comprehensive dialogue' of the SG would soften up the situation. When I pressed Jeremy on what could be given, he did not signal much (while Hain in interviews seemed to have said that anything was negotiable). I asked if they would amend Res. 1284 – which Jeremy denied. I said that the French seemed to have suggested that the P5 could try to define 'key remaining disarmament issues', and Jeremy said this had not got off the ground, but he did not endorse my suggestion that consensus on this list could be reached in our College of Commissioners. Rather he seemed to think it inevitable that there would be fighting about it. He did not seem to think that an ending of the bombing and no-fly zones was high on the *Iraqi agenda*. Even my suggestion that liberal attitudes to export of dual-use items could be offered in return for inspectors on the ground watching the items did not evoke any spontaneous affirmation. I rather got the impression that they focused on the 'key disarmament issues'. If the list is short – and the Security Council can ensure that – the process leading to suspension could be facilitated. I warned against seeing an Iraqi acceptance of inspections as a step onto an escalator that automatically leads to suspension of sanctions. The criteria were 'cooperation in all respects' and 'progress' on the key disarmament issues. Sir Jeremy agreed. He also affirmed that Res. 1284 could not be changed (but maybe it can be added to . . .). He did not seem to think it would be unrealistic that the Iraqis might reject all acceptance of 1284 but nevertheless accept inspection. This is an option Olof and I have conjectured about.

Friday 2 February 2001. New York

London was stimulating. Had a round table at the FCO. Saw also some intelligence people. And the foreign minister of Oman and some of his European ambassadors. They would have liked to hear me send some soft signal as to how I would use UNMOVIC's authority. I told them, however, that I could not give any discount on resolutions of the SC. But I also said, as usual, that we did not see it as our task to harass, humiliate or provoke Iraq. And that UNMOVIC was very different from UNSCOM in structure and composition. I also had dinner with a minister of state of Kuwait at the residence of the Kuwaiti ambassador. It was not as dry as in Kuwait . . .

Saturday 3 February 2001

It has been a heavy week. What we call an ox week (*oxvecka*) – when you pull hard with all your muscles. Next week we must send our documents to the College of Commissioners for the meeting to be held in Vienna. While the 'UNMOVIC handbook' is shaping up rather nicely after long work and the recent return of John Scott, the inventory of 'unresolved disarmament issues' is in critical condition even two days before we must freeze it.

The new US Secretary of State, Colin Powell, is coming here to see the SG on 14 Feb. I have been alerted that he might want to see me as well

Friday 9 February 2001 at 19.25

Tired. Long week. I did have heavy work, especially on the UNMOVIC handbook. We settled it on Monday. Over twenty chapters. It still needs overhaul to avoid much overlapping, but it contains a lot of guidance. The worst part was the reporting on our efforts to list 'unresolved disarmament issues'.

Had a talk with the Secretary General yesterday. The 'comprehensive dialogue' is to start on 26 Feb., the first day I am back from Vienna, and they are preparing for it. We are certainly not in the talks, but we have also not been asked to take part in the preparation, which is led by Dhanapala. I have not insisted but simply said we want to be kept briefed all the time.

Saturday 10 February 2001

I read that Senator Alan Cranston died at the age of eighty-six. I met him several times. He was a great *proponent* of non-proliferation and of IAEA's role in control. I must quote a Chinese saying that Cranston was reported to have carried in his wallet for years:

> A leader is best when people barely know that he exists, less good when they obey and acclaim him, worse when they fear and despise him. Fail to honour people and they fail to honor you. But of a good leader, when his work is done, his aim fulfilled, they will all say, 'We did this ourselves'.

NEW US ADMINISTRATION. COLIN POWELL VISITS UN. SMART SANCTIONS

Monday 12 February 2001

The new Secretary of State, General Colin Powell, visited the SG . Although they discussed Iraq (among other subjects) I was not asked to join. I have understood that there are actors in Washington who are not so certain that they really want inspectors back. They fear that inspections might give sweet marks to the Iraqis, reporting that they have found nothing, and that Iraq cooperated beautifully. This could make it more difficult for the US to bomb . . . This is not the official line. Rather, that line is supportive of Res. 1284 including inspection. But I can see that before Washington puts 1284 in focus, it will want to have concluded its internal deliberation.

So far, a number of lines have been clarified in Washington:

> They want to make the economic sanctions more effective but direct them more narrowly at weapons and items of use for making weapons, less at items that are needed for the Iraqi population. There are undoubtedly things they can do on this score. Drop a number of the vetoes that the US has been applying to chlorine, etc. It will be popular and a conciliatory gesture to the moderate Arabs.
>
> They seek to put the spotlight on the risk that Iraq has and may be producing weapons of mass destruction and that these are a direct danger to the states in

the Middle East – not primarily to the United States. I think this is a laudable effort, but not an easy one. Usually, the Arabs say that whatever Iraq may have left, Iraq is today not a military threat. Reservation being made for the possibility that Iraq might have enough to threaten a terror attack with a couple of missiles and a couple of biological weapons, the Arab objection may be right. However, it is clear, at the same time, that should Iraq succeed in redeveloping a programme in nuclear, chemical or biological weapons, it would be a colossal blow to the world consensus against proliferation of these weapons.

They (the US) want to tighten the sanctions that should remain. Bush has been saying again and again that the sanctions are like a Swiss cheese. I guess they want to have an American cheddar. It will not be easy though. At present one out of ten trucks coming from Jordan takes a line where their cargo is checked because it is licensed by the UN (under Oil for Food) and the exporters cannot get paid unless the UN checks the goods. However, nine out of the ten trucks go directly in and no one knows what they contain. To get Jordan to tighten control will not be easy, as the country is so dependent upon Iraq economically. A good deal of oil is smuggled by truck to Turkey with good profits for Kurds and Turks and non-controlled money for Iraq. As the US needs the air bases in Turkey and generally good relations with the Turks they have tolerated this traffic. It will be difficult to stop it. At the same time there is little consistency if they do not stop it. There is similar smuggling from Iraq through Iranian territorial waters and for the US to get the Iranians to stop it won't be easy. Colin Powell will need to be very articulate about the need to prevent Saddam from developing the ABC (*Atomic, Biological, Chemical*) weapons. The Iranians may not be confident about success and may say to themselves that, just in case, it is best that they, too, get these weapons. And Iraqi awareness of this will be an incentive for them to try to get the ABC clandestinely ... Potentially the most serious breach in the sanctions is the newly repaired Syrian pipeline for oil. Syria is poor and this is a god-sent income. For Iraq it is, again, uncontrolled money.

There is no doubt that the US would prefer to see that the 'comprehensive dialogue' that Kofi Annan begins on Monday (26 Feb.) will just peter out without any meaningful conclusions. I think he will be careful not to come out with any conclusions as to what should be the next step. He knows that the US will want to be the prime mover on the stage and that it has the power. It may be enough for him to be seen to move in a humanitarian direction.

Friday 16 February

I was visited by Jim Cunningham, acting US permanent representative. We had a long talk. He assured me that the US stood fully behind the Res. 1284 and UNMOVIC. (He said nothing about those in Washington who are not so hot on international inspections.)

I did not know that the US was bombing a number of radar posts the very same day. This I learnt on CNN the same evening. President Bush was interviewed at the ranch of President Fox in Mexico. He said it was 'a routine operation planned by the military', but rushed to add 'and I authorized it . . . '. The reactions have varied. In the Arab world people have burnt US flags: in the Palestinian areas, marches in the streets with big portraits of Saddam. Saddam has been rushing forward to espouse the anti-Israeli sentiments and to fan the conflict; he wants an escalation while the other Arab leaders want a de-escalation. He is closer to people's sentiment. And he can fan the anti-American sentiment – and get support for a lifting of sanctions.

The reasons for the US bombing are easy to identify. First and foremost, the purpose was to knock out a number of radar posts which were becoming dangerous to US/UK planes. They cannot take the risk of having one of their planes shot down (especially not when Colin Powell is travelling in the region!).

Secondly, they felt it was not a bad idea to send the signal that this US administration is not meek and not be fiddled with. Maybe it also indicates that inspection is not the first priority, but their own air control is the first weapon against Iraqi WMD.

Thirdly it was a bit of a pre-salute for Colin Powell going to the region . . .

Went to Vienna on Saturday 17 Feb. to open the third basic training course and give the opening lecture and to chair the fourth meeting of the College of Commissioners (our policy-guiding group).

The UNMOVIC training course had fifty-two participants. Very good spread. Thinnest recruitment on missiles. Nikita Smidovich is a very effective manager. My lecture on Monday was a little more theoretical – on non-proliferation and verification – than the one in Paris, but it contained a number of sentences addressed to the Iraqis and messages about how we intend to run UNMOVIC. I went into the SG's 'comprehensive dialogue' but just to give them a flavour of what is going on and make them feel that they are part of the events. A central message was (almost uncomfortably) similar to that of Colin Powell, namely, that the Iraqi issue was very much the question of spread of WMD. If the world and the UN fail in Iraq, then where do we stand? The idea which I have tried to peddle quietly is that if the Russians and Chinese really are eager to avoid the US missile shield being built they should give maximum help to defuse the cases which have triggered and are pushing the US, namely, the three (*Iraq, Iran and North Korea*), including Iraq.

The College of Commissioners met for two days. The chief items were a draft UNMOVIC handbook and a first paper on the identification of 'unresolved disarmament issues'. We had a rather good discussion, and several members were very positive about our texts. I think Fedotov makes a mistake if he thinks that they can limit the rights of UNMOVIC. I am sure the Iraqis have asked them to try. On the other hand, I am trying to make UNMOVIC appear more respectable and reasonable by confirming that there are limits we have to observe, that we are not to 'harass, humiliate or provoke' and that our jobs are only to look for WMD, etc.

The paper on 'unresolved disarmament issues' received a lot of criticisms from many members of the College.

It strikes me often that in the choice of heads of international organizations attention is hardly ever paid to their managerial ability. Yet, if you are the boss of 2,000 people – or even 45, as I am now – it is central that you can manage your forces. The selection is rather by rotation among countries and continents or diplomatic skill. This is important but far from enough. Of course, the same is usually true of ministers in cabinets. But they often have civil services who know something about organizations. In the international sphere the top layer of the staff is frequently selected on the same poor geographical, political basis as the heads.

Tuesday 27 February 2001. Back in NY. SG Dialogue with Iraqis

The Iraqi foreign minister, Sahaf, plus the legal adviser (undersecretary) Al Quasi and a few Iraqi ambassadors have been here yesterday and today for a comprehensive dialogue with the Secretary General. The events are intriguing and I am not sure of their meaning. The expectations were played down by everybody – Iraqis as well as the UN – before the talks. The exit comments today by the Iraqi foreign minister were that this was a *dialogue*, i.e. they had not just been talked to (as in the Security Council?) but there had been a two-way traffic. They had been listened to and they expected the SG to convey their grievances to the Security Council. He said they would come back in two weeks and bring feedback from Baghdad. So it sounded rather upbeat ... Yet, when I talked to Dhanapala as we were leaving the Secretariat tonight, he gave the impression that the whole thing had been a rather tedious affair with long speeches by the Iraqis listing all their grievances and mostly listening by the UN side. My interpretation is that the Iraqis are eager to move out of the current situation, while the SG has to be cautious not to promise anything, as the power lies in the SC and the hands of the Council's individual members. Also, what the Iraqis want seems very far from what the Council would give: lifting of sanctions *and* inspection. Sahaf talks about a ten-year long *aggression* – sanctions – against Iraq. This is not likely to draw agreement in the Council. While Russians and French may wish to lift sanctions they will insist on inspections. And while they may feel that UNSCOM exaggerated Iraq's cheating they will not agree that Iraq has fulfilled all its disarmament obligations.

Iraq is pouring scorn on Colin Powell and his efforts to build agreement around 'smart sanctions' – by which he means sanctions concentrated on items from which Iraq could make weapons of mass destruction – and readiness to drop sanctions on other items which are needed by the Iraqi population. Clearly the Russians will not go along with the US when the Iraqis decry it. But it will be very interesting to see if the French will support Powell's push. They might say, as some Arabs did, that it goes in the right direction ...

I suspect that the most difficult part of Powell's proposal is that which envisages effective enforcement of the slimmed sanctions. Another difficulty lies in bringing inspections back. Sahaf stated that Iraq would not accept inspections even if sanctions were completely lifted. It could imply that they are ready to live with what remains of sanctions rather than accept inspection. It could also be bluster at the beginning of the bargaining in the bazaar. They are also saying that they would accept 'monitoring' only if other states in the Middle East – notably Israel – accepted the same monitoring. This may be a politically smart line, as most people in the Middle East feel that Israel should do away with its nuclear weapons.

Sahaf was asked whether he would not meet Blix and replied that he certainly would not. Why not? Blix and UNMOVIC are only a 'detail' of Resolution 1284, which they reject. Well, what else could he say? He could not politely regret the inability to meet. Nor would he express scorn – as he did about Powell. Yes, he could have said that I was a 'part' of the resolution. But what the hell ...

Kofi Annan has now requested me to be a member of the group that prepares for the meetings with Iraq. I imagine that the group will convene before the next Iraqi visit here.

HAGGLING ABOUT IMPLEMENTATION OF RES. 1284

Wednesday 28 February 2001

The SG reported about the talks with Iraq today at an informal meeting of the Security Council. I have a feeling that the Iraqis are very anxious to get into some process. During the US presidential campaign there was no point in talking to anyone. There were informal contacts with the British through the Century Foundation and through Oman in the Gulf state group. The US was not interested. Now there is a US that at least listens. But the distance between positions is enormous. Iraq now says it is willing to 'cooperate' with the UN provided that the no-fly zones are abandoned, sanctions are lifted (not just suspended), territorial integrity respected (non-intervention) and monitoring is applied equally to states in the Middle East, especially Israel.

It seems out of question that the new Bush administration should give up no-fly zones. Clearly, these – and the bombing they lead to – are unpopular in the Arab world and a weakness is that they are not based in any UN resolutions.

'Sanctions' will be transformed into an export ban covering WMD and items that can help Iraq build WMD. This transformation may stave off the drive to go further and abolish 'sanctions' altogether. Perhaps it could be seen as damage limitation. The difficult part is not to 'slim' or 'concentrate' the sanctions. The difficult part will be to enforce what is left. Will Jordan and Turkey really control what goes from them into Iraq? Along their long borders?

A system of monitoring will not be set up to cover the whole of the Middle East. The resolution certainly does not require it. Rather it views the control system for Iraq as a step toward a zone free of weapons of mass destruction.

One may assume that in any discussions among the P5 Russia and France and China will support Iraq's demand for an end to the no-fly zones. They will agree with the US and UK, however, that Iraq has not fully done away with its WMD and that Iraq must accept inspection. The prestige of the Council will hardly allow that 1284 be lifted or modified. At the most there could be an additional resolution or a MOU. But that is unlikely. The reason for the French and Russian abstentions have been said to be that some terms have been 'unclear'. True, what financial and operational regime will be set up in conjunction with a suspension of sanctions is not defined in the resolution. Unlikely that it will be done in advance.

It might well be that the Iraqi regime feels it can live with the sanctions, such as they are, and even more easily the slimmer sanctions that may come, and is not willing to accept inspection for an uncertain prospect of a suspension.

How long will the bazaar haggling go on? Sahaf came out yesterday and talked about a new meeting in two weeks – which I interpreted as a sign of anxiety on the Iraqi part. However, today the SG's office said the next meeting would be end of April or early May. Sounds wiser. Policy formulation in Washington will take time. So will talks among the P5. And the Iraqis will need time to cool down and see where the new US policies and measures will land. So UNMOVIC will have more time to prepare itself. A blessing in disguise ...

Friday 2 March 2001

This morning the Financial Times had on the first page an article about our progress report on 'unresolved disarmament issues'. It was used to support the hardliners, saying that the new commission was finding that there remained a lot of weapons of mass destruction in Iraq. It fits well into what surely is some orchestration of information by the US, UK and Germany to show that Iraq remains very dangerous. An anonymous French spokesman was reported as commenting that UNMOVIC seemed no different from UNSCOM. In a television interview that AP (*Associated Press*) made with me later in the day I was asked whether I thought the article about our thinking would make it less or more likely that Iraq would accept inspection. I replied that we did not really consider that aspect. We were asked to provide a professional inquiry and assessment. We do not tailor that.

The Russian counsellor, Gatilov, visited me today. Gatilov said the Russians were very eager to re-establish consensus in the Security Council. This will be particularly difficult on the 'no-fly zones' and bombing. I cannot see that Colin Powell could retreat from the air operations, when he is already being criticized by the hawkish side for slimming sanctions (to what might be sustainable!). Yet the no-fly zones are unpopular in the Middle East and Russia, France and China criticize them as being without UN authorization.

I mentioned to Gatilov a number of points on which the Council might move forward, e.g. the slimming of sanctions could occur immediately, perhaps without any formal action in the Council. If and when inspectors go in again the export of dual-use items could be permitted provided the inspectors could check that the items were used for peaceful purposes. Domestic air traffic could be given the green light. International air traffic could be authorized provided checking occurred at the foreign point of departure and in Iraq.

There could also be confirmation that the members considered implementation of the resolutions in Iraq as steps toward a zone free of weapons of mass destruction.

I said I doubted they would get anywhere with the no-fly zone item.

Gatilov had some fancy interpretations of Resolution 1284, notably, that there should be a suspension of sanctions as soon as inspectors came back.

I pointed out to Gatilov that the document the Iraqis had submitted to the Secretary-General on disarmament laid out a large number of grievances against UNSCOM. When you looked at these you would be struck by the fact that UNMOVIC is not open to the same criticism:

> Iraq criticizes the lopsidedness of UNSCOM. UNMOVIC has no American deputy chairman and no preponderance of American staff. It seeks to be a bona fide UN organ.
>
> UNSCOM spent inordinate efforts on proving a 'concealment mechanism'. UNMOVIC has no section for this purpose. (I believe we can take for granted that the mechanism exists. We do not need to expend such big efforts to prove it ...)
>
> UNSCOM devoted itself to electronic eavesdropping. I have declared that UNMOVIC will not use such techniques – even if they are permissible under SC resolutions.

Sunday 4 March 2001

Watched CNN tonight: 'the Reagan years in pictures'. There is a bit of a Reagan revival. The programme helped me to better understand his popularity. He did have a very charming smile and a nice presence. He built his political career on two issues: anti-communism and lower taxes. He started as a poor boy and a Democrat but changed into a conservative Republican when he earned much money and saw how much of it went into taxes. Unlike Bush he was able to speak eloquently by himself. Reagan was a poor academic student and hardly grasped a fraction of the policies he dealt with. But he did have character and was a very decent person. It came through. Carter was intelligent and certainly had character. Perhaps he was too complicated – and puritan. He comes across as an idealistic and not very practical person. Bush senior gives the impression of an intellectual and high civil servant but at the same time as someone without very strong political convictions of his own. His son, W. Bush, seems much less intellectual, more of a nice likeable chap, and also without strong convictions of his own. Clinton is impressive intellectually. Quick-witted, a lot of intellectual intuition, ability to articulate and to empathize. But often lacking in basic judgement or overpowered by impulses not restrained by a sufficiently strong moral code.

Tuesday 6 March 2001

Introducing our report in the Security Council at 10. A relatively mild affair. The Russian (Lavrov) complained a bit about the paper on 'unresolved disarmament issues' which leaked to the Financial Times. The French ambassador (*Levitte*) asked whether UNMOVIC could not give a sort of preliminary enumeration of 'key remaining disarmament tasks', thereby helping in the comprehensive approach to the Iraqi issue. I regretted the leak and said we do not seek press coverage but also do not hide from the press. The discussion about UDI (*Unresolved Disarmament Issues*) had been lively, some criticism, good suggestions that we shall take to heart. I said it could be good if we were able to solve some issues in our College rather than having them surface in the Council. They adjourned the meeting at 11.00 for the Council to listen to Lord Robertson, Secretary General of NATO, in another room. They came back shortly after 12.00 to continue on Iraq. We were ready by 13.00. Tonight, I said they had me for appetizer and dessert and NATO as a main course ...

Thursday 8 March 2001

It is becoming ever more evident that Secretary Colin Powell is the moderate voice in US foreign policy. The other day he intimated that the US perhaps should pick up where the Clinton administration left off on the DPRK issue. However, in the end it was declared that the US would take some time out ...

Tuesday 13 March 2001

Lunch at my desk. Same every day: lemon yoghurt, apple, tea and croissant. Reading press clippings meanwhile. Today interesting to see that Saddam urges that the Amman Arab summit not touch the Iraqi issue but focus on Palestine. The Iraqi issue is 'better' treated bilaterally ... Which, I suppose means that they do not feel confident as to the outcome of a collective discussion. There would be no denunciation of Colin Powell's switch to 'smart sanctions'. Saddam even threatened that voicing support for the initiative would be regarded as a 'hostile act'!

I had a meeting with Group Bovallius, which has the task of identifying 'unresolved disarmament issues'. I am not at all sure that Bovallius and his boss

Diamantidis have succeeded in describing how we want to go about this job and what methods we will use. Later in the day Svetlana Outkina came up to my office and said she wanted to take advantage of my saying that my door is open. She had several interesting things to say. She felt that in many cases UNSCOM inspectors had not been technically very clever on the chemical side. She thought that we could benefit from attending some seminars arranged by OPCW (*Organisation for the Prohibition of Chemical Weapons*). They were open to observers. Yes, why not?

Directly after this meeting, I had a meeting with the 'senior staff' group. We always begin with some discussion of the current political environment: Washington, Middle East, etc. I think all like to feel they are part of the latest analysis. I asked Sen Pang whether it was plausible that the Chinese military had in fact been active in Iraq on a commercial basis to install fibre optics. He replied in the affirmative. The military had long conducted their own business to make money. Still did. But for some time, the government had now instructed them to abandon this, and they were instead to get more in the budget. Olof (*Skoog*) later talked to Pang who told him that China had been in touch with Baghdad after Powell's proposal on smart sanctions. Beijing felt that Baghdad was now softening and wanted a solution. Olof and I agreed this still looked very problematic. The biggest issue was perhaps the 'no-fly zones', and the bombings connected with them. On this the Americans would not yield much. Some adjustment but not more. The philosophy in Washington was 'containment' and for this inspection might not be indispensable but bombing to pieces if something appeared suspicious. Such action could, indeed, be made more difficult if inspectors were there and just reported that everything was dandy!

ON UNMOVIC'S REPLACING UNSCOM AND ON THE COLLEGE OF COMMISSIONERS

New York. Thursday 12 April 2001. Easter. Is UNMOVIC 'Softer' Than UNSCOM?

So, it is Easter. I have three days to write a keynote speech on multilateral control regimes for non-proliferation, to be given at Monterey outside San Francisco in about ten days. They expect a lot of people from various US departments, so I shall have a chance to give a profile and face to UNMOVIC. There is an assumption in some parts of the US establishment that UNMOVIC is softer than UNSCOM. I sensed concern that the more broadly recruited UNMOVIC would not have the same bite as UNSCOM. The image of the new UNMOVIC being softer was probably cultivated by the bitter and disappointed UNSCOM staff at the time when the Security Council abolished UNSCOM and created UNMOVIC. They felt insulted and abandoned. They had been too good, too effective. They were victims of the Russians, French and developing countries who wanted softer inspections.

The reality was that UNSCOM carried itself the seeds of its own destruction. When it was based on voluntary contributions of staff and equipment it was doomed to become too dependent upon the West. A list of chief inspectors shows no other nationalities than the industrialized West plus two Russians (Smidovich and Mitrokhin) who had emancipated themselves from Moscow. When, in addition, *the Commission's inspectors* got a reputation for cowboyism, it was revealed that its links to the Israeli intelligence were very close and it was suspected that the CIA was able to piggyback and get whatever intelligence it wanted about targets, it became too much. UNSCOM lost legitimacy as a UN organization. The Security Council dropped the damaged structure and established a new one with the same rights and duties, but with a broad UN recruitment and cooperative management (Resolution S/RES/1284 (1999) para. 6).

With financing now coming from Oil for Food it became possible to recruit from all over. The criticism we meet of UNMOVIC is that the College is said to reduce the freedom to act forcefully. This remains to be seen. The P5 each have one national in the College among fourteen others. The chairman must let his reports to the Security Council go for consultation to the College, but he is not obliged to have them endorsed by any consensus. There is no voting and if the commissioners are divided – as they might be on a politicized issue – the chairman can follow his own judgement. In the best case the college would be used by the P5 for quiet efforts to reach consensus. The other matter alleged to point to softness is the broad geographic recruitment. OK, UNSCOM had very smart people, but their Western appearance damaged their credibility. They were suspected of bias. Moreover, it is questionable whether you need PhDs in every corner. You may well have some steady infantrymen among the inspectors. Another matter is that you need very good and well-trained brains in the detective work that the Commission is driven to in the absence of Iraqi cooperation. I hope we shall have enough of that kind though at the moment I am not convinced ...

In Oslo Monday 19 March to interview some candidates, to give a seminar and to meet the foreign minister. I think one must say that Norway in the last few years has been very active and successful in the peacemaking area, first in the Middle East and at present in Sri Lanka. I was asked recently whether I thought that Sweden's neutrality had something to do with the use of lots of Swedes in international mediating tasks. Considering that Norway is a member of NATO I wonder whether it is not the small-state status plus an ambition that has led to these tasks. We are so small that we cannot be suspected to have any axe to grind and we have well-trained internationally experienced people.

Tuesday and Wednesday (*20 and 21 March*) in Brussels. Invited by the permanent foreign affairs committee of the council of ministers. There was a working luncheon, the idea being that the others lunched while I worked to enlighten them about the Iraqi issue and UNMOVIC. Very useful. We probably need to present ourselves in many capitals. Since there are no confrontations, we do not get much publicity and we have to make ourselves known – at least in the political circles.

From Brussels to Munich on 22 March to visit the Bundesnachrichtendienst – which is about to move to Berlin. Royal treatment and interesting briefings. They are down to earth. Credible. I am glad I made the visit.

Vienna to give final speeches to our third training course. Invited Nikita Smidovich, Franz Kolar, Gabriele Kraatz-Wadzack, Alice Hecht and Brian Mullady (*UNMOVIC staff*) for dinner at a genuinely Austrian restaurant in Hietzing. Good.

Friday 23 March 2001

Meeting with Mohamed ElBaradei at the IAEA. Nice chat. He is pessimistic about getting into Iraq. The West has lost the propaganda battle in the Arab world. He has just been recommended for a second term, so he seems relieved.

Monday 26 March 2001

Quai d'Orsay and Ministry of Defence. M. Pagano and M. Brichambeau. I must say that the French have changed a lot. Much more cosmopolitan. They address you immediately in English. (Assume you are a barbarian . . . No, I think they even cherish showing how good they are at handling everything in English . . .) But they were also very direct in their discussion. No arrogance whatever. They were not optimistic about Iraqi will to come along. There is a sharp difference between the military and the diplomats. The military judge Iraq and Saddam Hussein a much greater danger than do the people in the foreign ministry. The military have no doubt that the Iraqis are rearming themselves. The diplomats seem to be intent on finding some way out – inevitably involving concessions to the Iraqis . . .

28 March 2001

I had lunch with Oscar Schachter. He is now eighty and still teaching international law at Columbia. He was head of the general legal division in the UN Secretariat during Hammarskjöld's tenure and he is a great admirer of H–skjold. I told him a lot about UNMOVIC and UNSCOM. I think he tried to get Columbia to give me an honorary doctorate but did not succeed.

MEETINGS WITH CONDOLEEZZA RICE AND COLIN POWELL

Washington. 3–4 April 2001

Went down by train to avoid any risks of delays at La Guardia. Travelled with Olof Skoog and Dimitri Perricos.

Gave first a lunch talk on non-proliferation at the Monterey Institute's Washington branch, invited by Larry Scheinman. There were lots of knowledgeable people: Sandy Spector, Linda Gallini, Bob Einhorn. I think it went well. Then off to the White House. We were somewhat late. However, Condoleezza was also late. The net result was that we had only twenty minutes. She is very attentive, sure but unassuming. I briefed her at machine-gun pace. She assured me of US support for the Commission, while making it clear that they would not make any concessions to get the commission into Iraq. She also made the point that it was important that the inspectors were well trained. I think the background of that is that some critics in the US feel that with a broader geographical spread of inspectors, the quality may go down.

The meeting with Colin Powell was preceded by a meeting with a Polish diplomat who had been taking care of US interests in Baghdad for some six years. He reported that the regime felt high now, but time was probably not on its side. The two main pillars of the regime – the military and the security forces – are war-weary.

The talk with Colin Powell was less hectic than the one with Condoleezza. He looked trim and youthful and was knowledgeable on the subject. He explained their aim to concentrate and consolidate the sanctions. He made the same remarks as Condoleezza about the inspectors. We did not discuss the no-fly zones. I made the point that Russia and China probably are willing go an extra mile to avoid US unilateralism. I made a plea (as I had done with Condoleezza) for US intelligence. Bob Einhorn explained to me that the restraint they have shown is general.

Saturday 14 April 2001. Easter

My lecture for Monterey moves only slowly. I have to work a lot on it today. I have got stuck – as often – on the introduction.

Tuesday 24 April 2001. New York

Just back from San Francisco. An interesting weekend. Indeed, a break from the routine in New York. Stayed with my Cambridge seminar mate Arthur Albrecht on Saturday and went to the Centre on Proliferation Studies at Monterey for a conference on Monday. Back to chronology.

I had thought that the three free Easter days would suffice for my writing the keynote speech I was to deliver at Monterey on multilateral organizations and regimes against proliferation. As often I had great difficulty with the opening. I want to approach a subject from a broad perspective and it usually entails lots of abstractions that are difficult to formulate. Then I began with the substance – which is much easier to write – and found, as usual, that there was much more of it than I could pack into a forty-minute lecture. So, in the end I am driven to discard much of the laboriously written introduction ...

Fortunately, not too much work piled up in the office. I saw the Secretary-General on the Easter Monday and he told me about the Arab summit at Amman. The Iraqis really shot themselves in the foot by asking too much. Kofi does not want to meet the Iraqis for a continued 'comprehensive dialogue' until the Security Council comes up with some response and they will not do that until they have talked through the US ideas about smart sanctions.

Wednesday 25 April 2001

A tiresome day. Slept not so well. Left laundry in the morning. Had an exit meeting with the external auditors. In principle I favour external auditing. Someone looking from the outside, really intent on helping. But the experts on administration seem all steeped in the same form. You must have medium- and long-term plans with benchmarks and goals for every unit and performance reports every so often. I remember that in the IAEA I said there has to be some damned balance between planning plus reporting on the one hand and doing on the other. Otherwise we shall spend only some 40 per cent of our time on doing . . .

Thursday 26 April 2001

Olof Skoog told me this afternoon that the foreign office – Malin Karre – had called him and sounded him out as to whether he would accept becoming ambassador to Colombia. He was tempted, he said. Yes, I can understand it. Normally he would be second man in some bigger place. This would mean a jump. On the other hand, Colombia is not a dream place for a family with children. High criminality and risk of kidnappings. For my part I feel some resentment against the foreign ministry. They have really not cared a damn to make my job easier. And now they make an offer to my assistant, so attractive that he can hardly resist it . . . I really don't blame him. He is young and looks to his career.

Monday 30 April ('Valborgsmässoafton') 2001. New York

On the political front, not much is visible but a good deal happening. The 'Geneva Group' (*of main contributors to the UN system*) has been meeting in Geneva and on its margins the US, Russian, UK and French UN bureau heads are to discuss the 'smart sanctions' scheme. It seems the US and the UK are agreed and the French pretty close. Query whether the Russians are ready to come along and what prices they might ask. We are at the beginning of the bidding. Query whether the Russians are sufficiently tired of the Iraqis to leave them alone and to join the West. There are oil contracts and other goodies at stake, Russia is pretty friendly with Iran, too . . . .

Monday 7 May 2001

Sam (*Sanmuganathan*) was back today from his trip to Nepal, Bangladesh and Bangkok. He said Dacca was messy. They are nearly at war with India. Dacca was so insecure that he was not allowed to leave the hotel. Both the prime minister and the leader of the opposition are women. It seems it does not get any better for having women at the top. Same is true in Sri Lanka. Women's leadership as bad as men's. Not so surprising after all, if men and women are equal.

Friday 11 May 2001

The British briefed us about the planned proposals on 'smart sanctions' today: rather than having export of everything to Iraq prohibited and exceptions being made for foodstuffs, etc., every export will now be permitted except for items on the 'control list'. These will consist of all items on the 1051 list (dual use, now being revised by us) plus all items relating to conventional weapons and items on the Australia lists. UNMOVIC would examine all contracts

Dimitri expressed fear that UNMOVIC would become the paper shuffler. Well, well, we are not there yet. The oil money continues to go into the escrow account and Iraq must be longing to have it come directly to Baghdad. However, if they see little hope of that, they might prefer the status quo rather than accepting inspection. The US might accept with relative equanimity that inspectors don't get in. If their satellites were to spot something fishy or if their intelligence were to tell them something worrisome they can always send a cruise missile and destroy the site ... The whole thing may drag out. The escrow account remains, imports grow, smuggling continues, UNMOVIC is barred by the Iraqis. The Security Council does not modify Res. 1284 and the demand for inspection.

When Gerard Errera asked me to take the job (of Chairman of UNMOVIC) he suggested it would be for a year or a year and a half. His assumption was that Iraq would accept inspection relatively soon. I have accepted a prolongation of my contract for a second year and there could be pressure on me not to let UNMOVIC down. My resignation might be viewed by Iraq as a victory. I think my first ambition should be to produce a really fine-tuned report on what is known and proven about the Iraqi WMD programme and what are still question marks. We have very much work to do to get to this.

My second ambition should be to have groomed our staff and potential staff (on the roster) so well that we would have really good teams ready to go in at any time.

Wednesday 16 May 2001

Olof Skoog is definitely leaving at the end of August. Talked today to a Finn who has assisted President Holkeri as president of the General Assembly: Ambassador Jarmo

Sareva. Forty-two years old. Solid fellow with an excellent network of contacts among perm. reps and deputy perm. reps. Been a delegate in the Fifth Committee and dealt with disarmament, stationed in Moscow twice. Speaks both Russian and Swedish. Claims to write English very well. Wife is in UN secretariat in peacekeeping. This is a major reason why he wants to stay on in New York.

Saw the President of the Security Council, US Ambassador James Cunningham, yesterday. He is acting perm. rep. until Negroponte has been confirmed by the Senate. Jim is soft-spoken and very calm. He knows the Iraqi issue very well, especially as Dick Holbrooke did not deal much with it. He gave me a paper with the proposals for 'smart sanctions', hoping to use it for the June prolongation of the Oil for Food programme. The plan is combined with steps to get Turkey, Syria and Jordan to tighten border controls and to ensure that they place the money they pay Iraq for oil in escrow accounts.

Iraq has already voiced opposition and said they would consider it a hostile act (!) if neighbouring states went along. They have been hoping to make the whole sanctions system collapse. Now they might find that a more limited system would be there to stay. Query whether the Russians will protect them by a veto or only abstain. It seems the French might go along with the US/UK this time. The Russian foreign minister is to be in Washington this week (or next?). It would be nice for the Secretary of State, Colin Powell, to win this one. His standing vis-à-vis the Pentagon hawks would gain *standing*.

I can see an increasing risk that the Iraqi affair becomes dragged out. The Iraqi government can wait. So can the US. They will – so they hope – lose the stigma of starving the Iraqi people. They can watch Iraq by satellite, U2 planes and intelligence. If they fear there is some significant build-up of weapons production they can always bomb it to pieces. Saddam will not pose a danger to the region . . . Having UN inspectors in Iraq, the US knows, may give information about the inside of buildings, which is valuable (at least they would learn what not to bomb). The US is saying that they support Res. 1284, which is left intact, but maybe they are not so hot on it, except as a ground for keeping the escrow account . . . ? However, the UK and France want it applied. The Russians, too, but they seem ready to compromise about the firmness of inspections. That is enough for the time being. Get on with the profit making . . . If Saddam were to misbehave the world will cope with that when it happens . . .

Where is UNMOVIC in a dragged-out affair? 'Wir brauchen Geduld, Sitzfleisch and Fingerspitzgefuhl . . . ' (*We need patience, stamina and fingertip sensitivity*). For the next half-year, we shall have plenty of things to do. It will take time for our staff to eat their way through the archives and the reports and form intelligent opinions about the issues. It will take time merely to make the archives and the database user-friendly. But come the year 2002 . . . If we are not in by that time, I think we would need to appear (and be) expert also on the current situation in Iraq. We should have much satellite imagery to base ourselves on. And open-source information. Maybe we could be enabled to have more direct contacts with defectors. Our reports about the situation in Iraq might have greater credibility than partisan reports by member states. But our analytical capacity would be far behind ...

I was invited by the Argentine Ambassador, Listre, today for lunch at the Metropolitan Club. I thanked them for allowing us to go to Cordoba for the specialized missile training course. The ambassador told me he had met the new Iraqi ambassador, who had said that they had nothing against me. On the contrary, the greatest respect. However, it was the resolution ... He had no objection to Listre telling me. Well, I have not had occasion to be a nuisance to them yet ...

Friday 18 May 2001

Today I had the impression that the US may not be indifferent to future inspections in Iraq as required under Res. 1284, but may, indeed, really prefer that none come about! If they can get the 'smart sanctions' through they may really have attained what they want at the present time.

If no inspections are allowed in, there will be no occasion either to suspend or to lift sanctions! They will last for an indefinite time without any troublesome discussions in the Security Council as to whether Iraq has complied with 687 or 1284. Fine ... If Iraq were to let the inspectors in, the US could have problems on two fronts. The inspectors might land themselves in some dramatic situation, which would force the US to take action it would rather not be dragged into. As bad, from the US viewpoint, would be if the inspectors report that the Iraqis cooperate and that key issues are being solved, calling for a suspension and later a lifting of sanctions! If inspectors are not there, the US and the world will learn less surely about what is going on inside Iraqi installations, but satellites, U2 and intelligence may see larger things. Should they suspect that ABC is being built somewhere or there is a military build-up somewhere the US will simply send off a cruise missile or bomb ... 'take appropriate action ... '.

There is a good question as to whether anyone wants inspection at the present time!

The US secretly does not want them. Iraq is adamantly opposed. Russia speaks about cosmetic sanctions. The French (foreign office, not the military) also want mild routine monitoring for an indefinite period. UNMOVIC and not least the handbook we have compiled stands in the way of cosmetic routine monitoring! Paradoxically perhaps the Iraqis will be the ones who may wish inspection in order to have a chance to get UNMOVIC's testimony that they have 'cooperated in all respects'. We are not there yet ...

Sunday 20 May 2001

The US is reported to contemplate walking away from the draft verification protocol that is being drafted for the biological weapons convention. After some six years they were close to agreement. It may now collapse – unless they go ahead without the US ... Coming on top of the rejection of the comprehensive test ban agreement, the proposed scuttling of the ABM (*Anti-Ballistic Missile*) treaty and the refusal to go on with the implementation of the Kyoto protocol it is not making the US more loved – nor more respected ...

Friday 25 May 2001

A tiresome but not difficult week. We had the quarterly meeting of our College of Commissioners Monday and Tuesday. It went very smoothly. Our revised versions of fifteen unresolved disarmament issues were seen as real improvements on the first version. This is a comprehensive survey, not the list of key remaining disarmament tasks ...

The focus of attention this week has been the draft proposal in the Security Council to change *the Oil for Food* programme for the next period of 180 days to make all exports to Iraq permitted except such that collide with a Control List, consisting of three elements: the 1051 list, the Wassenaar list of conventional weapons items and a list of additional items. I think this is a smart approach. The US/UK want to change the image that they are responsible for the misery in Iraq by their blocking imports of a host of items. Hopefully they will succeed in this. They also try to persuade the neighbouring countries to pay for their oil purchases in Iraq only by paying into local escrow accounts. It is more doubtful that this will succeed. The Iraqis are adamantly opposed to the proposal. After accepting the Oil for Food programme the situation has steadily and gradually improved. Today, after an excellent harvest, the country is full of food and one of the greater problems is that the heavy import of food presses prices downward and is a disincentive for indigenous production.

The major reason for the Iraqi position is that they fear that once these weapons-limited restrictions are accepted they will last indefinitely. Suspending them can only be achieved by cooperation with inspectors and this Iraq wants to avoid.

Was invited to lunch by Iqbal Riza, the SG's chef de cabinet, today, together with Benon Sevan and U Tun, SG's representative in Baghdad. They inclined to think that there would be a postponement of perhaps two months of the British proposal ...

Wednesday 30 May 2001

Today it became clear that the UK will not try to push the resolution to reform the sanctions system in time for the rollover of the oil for food programme. *One* question is whether in the new system UNMOVIC will be asked to check contracts against the whole Control List or just the Res. 1051 list, which we already do. For us more check work means more operative activities at a time when we have no other and I can see that Rachel Davies would be glad to get the extra job.

Talked today to *our* new operation section head for missiles, Mr Jolly (Australia). He said that many staff seem to be pessimistic about UNMOVIC ever being allowed to go into Iraq. Well, it is not only our staff ... However, it is hard to make any educated guess. If there were to be unanimity in the Security Council about the new focused economic restrictions and continued escrow accounts, it would mean that these restrictions will stay until lifted by the Council because Iraq has complied with Res. 1284 and cooperated with UNMOVIC. It is this perspective that makes Iraq scream today about a 'perpetuation of sanctions' and a trusteeship being established ...

The Iraqis will be in a new ball game if and when the resolution is adopted. When the new situation has sunk in they might more seriously consider accepting inspection again. And will try to bargain.

Thursday 7 June 2001

Introduced UNMOVIC's fifth quarterly report in the Security Council this morning. The Russian ambassador, Lavrov, asked how I thought the new draft resolution would impact on UNMOVIC's chances of getting into Iraq. So, I had the opportunity to develop my analysis of the current situation. I noted that nothing remained of the leverage that was created *in* 1990 by the prohibition on buying Iraqi oil. As of 1999 Iraq could sell any amount. What was now discussed was a strong export control for militarily useful items, including weapons of mass destruction items, to Iraq. The controls were to be limited to such items and effective. This marked a new phase for all. Iraq had expected a total collapse of sanctions. If it were to dawn on Iraq that this would not happen, but rather that payment for all exported oil would continue to flow into escrow accounts, it might begin to realize that the only way offered out was implementation of the resolutions. Unanimity in the Security Council would likely impress Iraq. The greater ease of importing dual-use items, if inspectors were in the country to check end use, was another leverage. However, Iraq was bound to ask what 'administrative and operational' measures the Council would link to a suspension. This was the 'carrot' and Iraq would wonder how big and how juicy it was. The Council had not started to consider this question. I said UNMOVIC was ready to take on tasks of examining contracts under a new resolution. I think my comments made some impression. Lavrov looked quite happy and the American Ambassador – still Jim Cunningham – phoned me in the afternoon to tell me how well he thought I had handled Lavrov. Actually, I had worried a little that the US and the UK would be a bit unhappy about my clear language. My intention was to give an impartial and realistic analysis of the situation. I suspect the members of the Council were interested because they recognized that I was talking reality. A good morning and a good feeling that the political representatives of the Council seemed to like hearing a detached, dispassionate analysis from a Secretariat side.

Saturday 9 June 2001

Yesterday we had 'seminars' in the 'bunker' on three biological and three missiles issues in the category of 'unresolved disarmament issues'. Compared to the drafts we received early this year what we now get is far better. But it is still not good enough. We must have a second reading of what is now produced. Eventually we should have a compendium of cases described correctly and with the right nuances.

Friday 15 June 2001

The European Union summit has taken place in Gothenburg. Terrible riots. They don't want to be given the floor in the democratic room. They want to be denied it in order to scream, to strip, to throw rocks or whatever. Why should we tolerate their conduct more than one minute? With the Schengen agreement citizens from all over Europe can come and speak up at European summits. That's OK. This is the politics of Europe. But it is not OK to speak up with stones and fire. Curious that our tolerant welfare societies breed these extremes. The summit was about something as historical as the expansion of Europe from West to East. A new phase in the world. And all the discussion is about some hooligans throwing stones or baring their behinds!

I was angered by a column by Thomas Friedman today in the *New York Times*. He was lamenting what he saw as an ugly new anti-Americanism in Europe, citing the criticism of Bush, the missile shield, etc. Are Europeans 'anti-American' because they are as opposed to some US government policies as many Americans are? There are things I appreciate much here. Freedom of speech is very solidly defended although here as in Europe there is greater tolerance for showing violence than sex on the screen ... The policies concerning minorities have had long time to be developed in the US and while far from flawless they are probably more advanced than in Europe. We are at the beginning of our troubles with immigrant minorities.

Friday 6 July 2001. New York

Work-wise the week has been dominated by thoughts about the consequences of the collapse of the UK–US effort to get the Security Council to adopt a resolution on smart sanctions. The Russians signalled that they would veto, and the UK and US decided to refrain from pushing their text to the vote. Instead, a resolution was adopted which simply prolonged the old oil for food programme and the much maligned 'sanction' system.

It is interesting to speculate why the UK effort collapsed. The Russians said bluntly that the draft resolution was not in their 'economic interest'. Holds in the sanction committee on Chinese–Iraqi contracts were lifted by US–UK for many millions. Moreover, possibly the Chinese got friendly noises about no objection to

Olympics in Beijing or to entry into the WTO (*World Trade Organization*). In any case the Chinese declared that they were satisfied with the revised Goods Review Lists. Returning to the Russians one might also see the development in a more principled light. The Russian position might have been that either we – US and Russia – cooperate in world affairs and it is a two-way street or each pursues rigidly its own interest in each case. The US needs Russian support in the Security Council. OK, the US should then pay some attention to the Russian objections to the missile shield or NATO expansion ... The US might counter by saying that it should be in Russia's interest, too, to contain Saddam. Yes, but Russia does not find him as dangerous.

The Russians are right in commenting that the US seems interested only in cementing the sanctions by revising them to make them more reasonable. The US hardly mentions that it would wish Iraq to accept inspection, cooperate with UNMOVIC and have sanctions suspended and lifted. Of course, the US does not believe that Saddam would do this (and they are likely to be right). Yet, when no mention is made of this, it looks as if they just wish to 'keep Saddam in his box'.

Saturday 7 July 2001

Consequences to draw for UNMOVIC?

First, we cannot expect any change to occur in Iraqi positions. They can live with the current trade restrictions and the oil for food as it is. It will be a nuisance for them, but they have enough free money to improve their military potential. They are not going to accept inspection for an uncertain path to suspension of economic restrictions that are not felt very severely and that can be used as a scapegoat for the economic misery of the country. Thus, barring any upheavals in the political structure (*involving sons of Saddam – Uday, Qusay*) inspection will be firmly rejected.

The Security Council needs to have UNMOVIC ready to go in. If UNMOVIC were to disintegrate the Council could no longer demand the fulfilment of resolutions 1284 and 687. We declare that we are ready. Yet there is still a lot that can be done to improve that readiness: in training, analysis, logistics, consolidation of database and archives. We have come a good deal of the way, but there is no difficulty in filling the next five months with work that is genuinely needed.

There is an important distinct further mission we could embark upon. We have a good deal of knowledge of Iraq's military industrial capacity up to the end of 1998. We could now make extensive use of the satellite imagery – from the US, from France and from commercial source – to analyse expansions and changes which have occurred. We could use open sources to supplement imagery and we could get clues from intelligence. We might also report our conclusions to the Security Council. In all likelihood, the US administration has large resources devoted to such analysis. However, it does not report to the Council, and we would have much more credibility. In a way it would be a way of being useful and to adapt to a situation in which we cannot perform our main task of sending inspections. Kofi Annan sounded very positive when I related my idea to him.

Another idea I have come up with that meets French (and perhaps Iraqi) comments is to try to define criteria for 'key remaining disarmament tasks'. Iraq (and France) have complained that it is hard for Iraq to accept 1284 without knowing which items the country must clarify and we have said that we cannot tell before we have been in and done some re-baselining. (Lavrov said that we all know which these issues are ... a view I rejected.) OK, we shall stick to that position, but we can examine the criteria on the basis of which we shall assess the issues.

Sunday 8 July 2001

I have been reading the discussions of the Security Council from 28 and 29 June. It is conspicuous how difficult it is to explain in accurate yet simple terms the economic restrictions which Iraq has been subjected to. I shall try my own list:

> In 1990 (Res. 661) Exports to Iraq were banned – with the exception of medicines and foodstuffs in humanitarian circumstances. At the same time states were prohibited from buying Iraqi oil, thus depriving Iraq of income to import. In 1991 (Res. 687) the ban on exports to Iraq was confirmed but calibrated, lifting the ban on foodstuffs and establishing a no-objection procedure for essential civilian needs. The ban on the import of oil from Iraq remained. At the same time bans were to lapse when the Security Council determined that Iraq's weapons of mass destruction had been neutralized.

Clearly the two combined measures hit Iraq's economy hard. One would have thought sufficiently hard to make the regime cooperative on WMD. But no.

The resulting suffering raised humanitarian concerns at the UN.

- 1995: the UN adopted the oil for food programme (OIP), which allowed Iraq to sell a determined quantity of oil and use the proceeds – from escrow accounts – to buy what was called humanitarian items: medicines, food, but also other products. The sanctions committee was to consider all contracts.
- 1996: Iraq eventually accepted the OIP with a memorandum of understanding.
- 1999: Res. 1284 removed all restrictions on the volume of oil that could be sold. At the same time, it liberalized the objects for which the resources could be used: education, agriculture, etc. But the escrow account and sanctions committee remained in place.
- 2001: UK proposal: escrow account remains for all proceeds from oil sales, but all import contracts which OIP (*the Oil for Food Programme*) and the UNMOVIC do not find to contain items on a Goods Review List are automatically approved. Only those which are found to contain items from this list go to

the Sanctions Committee. A much faster procedure is to emerge. It is hard to avoid the impression that the misery is in large part the result of a mismanagement of the economy. The government controls everything and all is subjected to the political aims of the government: 1 billion dollars is promised to the Palestinians, oil production is stopped for political reasons for a period resulting in loss of income. Resources obtained through smuggling are devoted to paying the military and security apparatuses and weapons development.

Wednesday 11 July 2001

At UNMOVIC we are going through another batch of analyses and descriptions of 'unresolved disarmament issues'. It is heavy going. Even though the lawyers are now an accepted part of the teams they are not always consulted and horrible language results. We must provide coherent descriptions of the three programmes (biological, chemical and missiles).

Thursday 12 July 2001

Scott Ritter is going to present his film of UNSCOM 'such as it was'. He seems to have got a lot of footage from the Iraqis, some from the UN public information and maybe he has taken some with him from UNSCOM when he left. I think we shall try to avoid passing judgement on our predecessor. But clearly, if his view is that Iraq has 'qualitatively disarmed' – meaning there is nothing serious left – we have to report that the Security Council is of the view that there are things left and that new inspection is necessary.

Friday 13 July 2001

The news this evening was that China has been selected as host for the 2008 Olympic games. There was a lot of coverage of jubilant Chinese. Tiananmen Square full of people – mostly young. A reporter said there was a nationalist frenzy. China had been recognized as 'a great power'. However, a young man who was interviewed said China had been 'accepted by the world'. That is not the same thing. The reporter wanted to explain the popular enthusiasm in the power sphere. The young man, so I believe, saw the decision as a recognition of a great proud developing country coming of age – being accepted as a worthy member, not seen as an outcast. Maybe the difference is subtle, but it could be hopeful. And I would much rather sympathize with those who are elated that their 'dignity' has been honoured than those who are happy that their power has been noted.

Sunday 15 July 2001, Evening

I am reading Colin Powell's autobiography. Interesting and attractive. He is self-assured but not smug. Aware of his limitations. For instance, he realized that he was not fit for PhD work. More activist than research man. It also comes through that he is prudent – not to say cautious. Also ambitious, hard-working and not brilliant in everything: not physics, not computer science. He wins your sympathy. Only on one point have I found him erroneous. He reports that a visit to Russian Lake Baikal showed that there were industries all along the lake, implying that the Communist country squandered the environment. While this is true, I think it is completely untrue to claim that there is much industry on the lake. When I was there, I was told there was only one wood-pulp factory on the lake and it was controversial whether it should be allowed to continue. I did go by boat on two occasions and saw a good deal of the beaches but no industries.

Monday 17 July 2001

Went to a reception at Egypt's national day. Saw Ragida Dergham, the Druze journalist, and agreed to have lunch with her next week. I had a chat with the Saudi ambassador. He thought something was going on inside Iraq. There have been rumours to the effect that Saddam is about to hand over formal power to his son Qusay. It does not sound implausible. He might want to establish Qusay both in front of the wilder Uday and in front of the ruling elite. Reports today claim that Saddam is trying to make peace with the family of the killed Kamal (*son-in-law of Saddam*). Could also point to a wish to fix the succession. In reality, Saddam would, of course, retain power.

Thursday 19 July 2001

Iraq. The French Ambassador, Levitte, was in my office for a long talk yesterday. He thought a main reason for the Russian turnaround to go against the UK resolution (*on sanctions*) was that Bush had not said a word about it in his meeting with Putin in Ljubljana. He had left it all to Colin Powell. Putin had got the impression that it was not such high priority ... Levitte expects new attempts to bridge the gaps between the P5. It will not be easy.

Saturday 21 July 2001

Genoa G8 meeting. The enormous demonstrations – with one demonstrator killed – absorb most media coverage. Another matter is that the G8 group is somewhat questionable as an institution. Why is Italy a member but not Spain? Is it not awkward that a few rich industrialized countries discuss how to manage the world? This time Nigeria, Mali, El Salvador and Bangladesh were invited to some meeting with the G8 as a kind of token gesture to the developing world. They steered clear of Egypt, South Africa, India, Brazil, who might have staked claims to be permanent guests. Not to speak of China ... The problem is similar to the question of the permanent seats in the Security Council. How do you get a proper composition of groups to handle various questions? So long as you do not need a 'group' you can have something like the General Assembly. We know the weaknesses of that. Small states and mini-states have a majority. They could force decisions over the votes of states representing the majority of people in the world. An assembly with weighted voting based upon a variety of criteria, mainly population and economy, could be a possibility. But the industrialized states are hardly going along with giving so much more power to China, India, Pakistan, Indonesia, Egypt, Brazil. One would have to give much weight to economic power. This would hardly be acceptable to the poor developing countries. So we muddle along.

It is easy to say that if we form a shipping organization we should go by the states' registered tonnage – but then Panama and Liberia become great powers. It is a bit more complicated if we want a group for maintaining peace. Do we go by military power? No, that is only one factor. Economic power? Again, just one factor. Geography and strategic location? It is intractable and what we get are whims of history. The P5 were the victors in the Second World War and gave themselves the front seats. The G7 was formed by some industrialized states to confer on economic issues.

If the G8 cannot meet anymore because of the demonstrations, perhaps we should not weep. It is worse, in a way, when the WTO cannot meet (as in Seattle) or the EU (as in Gothenburg).

The US strategy – if there is one single line – is to say that we must ensure that Iraq does not again constitute a threat to oil supplies, Israel and neighbours. We do not seem able to topple Saddam. Hence, containment until he disappears from the stage. Prevent Iraq from building up its military power, especially weapons of mass destruction. Export controls in the rest of the world are not enough. We must keep control of Iraqi oil proceeds. Hence, stop the floods of free money for oil to Jordan, Turkey, Syria and smuggling. Control the borders (if feasible ...). Inspectors in, OK, but no concessions on the economic controls. In any case control through satellites, no-fly zones planes, intelligence and elimination of suspect new WMD sites through precision bombing.

The Russian strategy. Get Iraq to accept inspectors back by making concessions on what they can do – allowing them mainly the old type of routine ongoing monitoring and verification. Suspend sanctions and the escrow account. If there appear to be some dangerous developments, look to the US to act. Meanwhile, reap the benefits in the shape of oil contracts, drilling concessions or the import of Russian goods

The UNMOVIC line. We have to move on to be really ready to go in at any time. This means that all logistics – air transport, communications, equipment, lab network and other support contacts – must be there, planned and deliverable at short notice. The analytical basis must be fully laid: detailed knowledge of the Iraqi programmes and the moot points, awareness of what needs to be looked at first and most intensely, declarations forms to be filled by the Iraqis, the overhead arrangements (US and commercial satellite images, etc.) must be flowing in and analysed by us. The open sources must be continually tapped. The personnel must be in place or be available at short notice. We must have our report on 'unresolved disarmament issues' but also rather soon an idea of what we might zero in upon as 'key remaining disarmament tasks'. The handbook *on inspection* is *already* on the table. We should ensure support for it, because Iraq will seek to reduce it all to monitoring. This is why Fedotov does not want to allow the handbook to be public.

Sunday 22 July 2001

As one slowly moves with Powell's text and life one warms to his personality – and it seems he does so himself ... With consistent success and career progress he becomes more self-confident, perhaps sometimes even a bit self-righteous, though he tries to belittle himself. I became a bit sceptical when he tells his staff and collaborators to watch the mood of the boss, I would have thought the boss should control his or her moods as a private matter and that anything else would be self-centred extravaganza ... Nevertheless, he comes across as a solidly balanced, prudent and decent person which much experience of life and public life. With a sense of humour and, mostly, without any exaggerated view of himself. I cannot avoid thinking that he must be very uncomfortable with the hawks in the Pentagon.

Tuesday 24 July 2001

We watched Scott Ritter's film today. I doubt he will be able to sell it to many. It is one and a half hours and really interesting only for the experts. There were some points clearly interesting for us. The emergence of the 'modalities' is described and it is reported that Washington was very displeased. Ekéus appears and talks about it and says it was a declaration as to how he would conduct himself, but two seconds thereafter he calls it a 'contract'. The Iraqis call it an agreement between them and the UN. There is also a sequence about the last inspection, the attempt to inspect the Baath party headquarters. The core of the film is really the contention that Iraq is 'fundamentally' disarmed, by which Scott means that so much was destroyed that Iraq was no longer a danger to its environment. As to bio, no one knows very much what there is today. Another matter is the potential.

Tuesday 31 July 2001

Iraq. The situation looks more locked than ever. The Russians stick firmly to their line that Iraq's cooperation must be attained (not forced upon them as before). The Russians would be willing to settle for very thin inspection (and the French might perhaps also go along with that). However, I see no way in which the US/UK would go with that. For the US the 'smart sanctions' were difficult enough. Colin Power is getting flak for it ... Many of their hawks are sceptical about any inspection and for them to expressly go along with something weaker than we have is, I am sure, unthinkable. The net result is that the present system will continue – with more erosion. The US seems now to be planning some further military strikes. Condoleezza Rice said as much the other day. There is, of course, the possibility that the leadership in Iraq will implode.

Thursday 2 August 2001

Iraq. Yesterday, I tackled the draft which Olof Skoog had prepared of the report to the Security Council about the last three months. Olof and I wanted to paint the picture of UNMOVIC's life *as* vivid – that there is plenty of activity, above all analysis and training. The training serves both to refine potential staff's skills and to keep their interest alive. It is not difficult to get them coming. They are taken free of charge to Rio or Buenos Aires or Vienna for two weeks to meet people of similar interest. Not too bad even though we drive them rather hard.

Tuesday 14 August 2001. After Vacation in Sweden, Back in New York

The day after I had a farewell dinner with Olof Skoog at the rather elegant Swedish restaurant Aquavit. We have had a very good and nice working relation. He is the youngest ambassador in the Swedish service. He will do very well. Is both sharp intellectually, diplomatic, writes rather well and works hard.

25 August 2001. New York

Identification of 'unresolved disarmament issues.' For the last nine months quite a number of the UNMOVIC staff have been engaged in trying to identify disarmament issues in which there are open questions, in effect in most cases questions which open the possibility that there remain weapons of mass destruction or parts of such weapons. It has been a very tough process. The staff has had difficulty in finding their ways in the fragmented archives of UNSCOM.

Institut de Droit International at Vancouver, biannual session 19–26 August. I flew up on Saturday 18th. I stayed only for Monday and Tuesday *and* I got what I wanted, namely contacts with a number of colleagues. We had just read that the son of Tariq Aziz had been sentenced to over twenty years in prison for corruption. There was no evidence that the regime was shaky but the sentence must imply a censuring of the Vice Premier, Tariq Aziz. He has never been known to have a power base of his own and has, therefore, been seen as accepted and no potential threat to Saddam. Perhaps the imprisonment is a signal to others in the top echelon that unless they wholeheartedly accept steps taken to make Qusay, Saddam's younger son, successor, they are in danger.

It is Labour Day on Monday (3 Sept.), so this is a long weekend. I shall take the day plane to London on Tuesday morning and meet the British Foreign Secretary on Wednesday (5 Sept.). Jarmo Sareva, who is succeeding Olof Skoog as my personal assistant, should be coming in from Johannesburg on the Wednesday morning. Hope he is not delayed. He has been at the Durban conference on racial discrimination together with the Finnish President of the GA, whom he serves.

On Thursday I shall take part in the World Nuclear Assembly (formerly Uranium Institute) and deliver a twelve-minute statement, which I must craft this weekend. From London I go to Vienna on Thursday evening – to see Mohamed ElBaradei on Friday (7 Sept.). It is time we compare notes about Iraq. As Egyptian he may understand better. As stationed in New York and focusing exclusively on Iraq I may have more information through my antenna.

Monday 3 September 2001. Labour Day. (UN Free)

Beautiful and around 25° (*Celsius*). Today I must complete my speech for the World Nuclear Assembly, print it at the UN office and perhaps email it to London – if I can.

The New York moon. Last night around seven thirty, as I sat down to eat, the full moon was rising in the East, above La Guardia airport. It was so beautiful. Stark yellow. While one certainly does not see the stars here the moon is forceful. Somehow it also cut New York down to size. The city is not a miracle. The moon shines on it in the same way as it shines on other cities. All equal under the moon ... Later in the evening it sat higher up, making New York feel less big.

Göran and Bo came back from Turks and Caicos Tuesday night (28 Aug.). Göran came over and picked up the cat, who had been with me for nearly a week. She was well adapted to my apartment and me this time. They had tried to call me and the line was busy a whole hour. So they figured something was wrong. Göran used my internet (*mobile*) to check the website of Verizon ... and we got a promise that they would fix it Saturday morning. Actually, it was done already when I was back around 10.30 after dinner. *Nevertheless*, a repair man came this morning. I could only tell him that his enterprise had already fixed the problem. Apparently, no one else in this building had been hit by the problem. Perhaps they were installing a listening device somewhere ...

9/11: TERRORISM

19 September 2001. New York, Wednesday

(*After visits to London (meetings at FCO and Ministry of Defence on 5 September, speaking at the World Nuclear Association on 6 September) and to see ElBaradei in Vienna on 7 Sept. and to Stockholm 8–10 Sept. I embarked for New York in the morning of Tuesday 11 September – but arrived there five days later, on Sunday 16 September.*)

I left Stockholm, as foreseen, on Tuesday morning 11 September. After four hours' flying the captain said that he had turned the plane around and it was because there was an announcement that the whole US airspace had been closed. It sounded weird but my guess, like others, was that it had to do with some hijacking. It took almost an hour before we learnt that planes had slammed into the World Trade Center in New York. I could at first not believe it. As for terrorist acts it occurred to me that the General Assembly was to start on the third Tuesday of September. Maybe Bush was slated to speak?

We were lucky to be ordered to turn around – with enough gasoline to fly to Stockholm. Many planes were beyond points of return and went to Halifax or Gander or to Shannon. We returned to Stockholm around 7.30 in the evening. You, Mårten, had learnt about the events and found our landing time on the SAS web site. It was very sweet of you to drive out to Arlanda and pick me up! It warmed my heart. No other passenger, I am sure, came home faster than I. My suitcase came the day after. In fact, I got four full extra days at home. I phoned the SAS each day to enquire when they could fly and give me a seat. I was to have presented the UNMOVIC quarterly report to the Security Council on Friday 14 September. This had to be cancelled. The first SAS flight was on the Saturday (15 *Sept.*) and they did not put me on that one. However, on that Saturday afternoon they phoned me and said I had a seat on Sunday.

On Sunday morning I was off for Arlanda. Rather early because expected stiff security procedures. They were! A queue stretched across half of the departure hall of passengers waiting to have their baggage opened and checked. There were only three tables and searchers. It took nearly two hours before I was through.

Business class was only half-filled. I was amazed. I thought the backlog would have been enormous. However, we now learn that people are so scared of flying that some US airlines may go bankrupt. Returning to New York the taxi driver took me first toward the Holland Tunnel. I thought he wanted to get to Lower Manhattan to take the East Side highway up-town. I had a direct view of the cloud of smoke that rose above Lower Manhattan where I used to see the two towers of the World Trade Center. I was amazed that five days after the catastrophe smoke was still coming up. The other thing that struck me was that there were American flags everywhere – on cars, houses, shops. As I got to 200 East 61, I could see pictures of a young woman outside our building, with name and pleas for help to find her ... Candles and flowers too. Some 5,500 people have lost their lives.

At the UN, First Ave. is blocked between 45 and 42 Street. The UN building was evacuated both on the Tuesday and – for a bomb scare – on Wednesday. Olivia, my secretary, had to walk down thirty floors and could hardly move her legs thereafter. By and large a week has been lost for work.

Media carry little apart from the terror affair. In the field of travel security there is talk about a better partition between cockpit and passenger space, technical means of preventing a plane from leaving its path, etc. I suspect that one of the least expensive measures will be to have 'air marshals' on board. I have seen them sometimes – on Iran Air and on planes to Tel Aviv.

Who did it? There is much pointing to bin Laden's movement. He was linked to the bomb explosion in the World Trade Center in 1993 and might well have wanted to do the full thing. He was also linked to the bombings of the US embassies in Nairobi and Dar es Salaam and lately to the bombing of the US destroyer in the harbour of Aden. Bush said he wanted bin Laden 'dead or alive'. Some doubt that an enormously complicated organization and preparation could have been accomplished without a state helping. Naturally, eyes are focused on Iraq. They would certainly have the motivation. Yet Vice President Cheney and others say they have seen no indication of Iraq being implicated. Perhaps true, perhaps a ruse to lull the Iraqis into a false confidence of no risk. But which other state could have assisted? Syria? Hardly. Libya? Not now. North Korea? Not now.

Iraq is said to be the only country which has not sent condolences. Saddam has written two open letters to the US urging the US to be wise, etc. They are odd documents. You suspect the man is a bit jolted and scared that the US will come for him now. Maybe they have some money in the affair without taking part in organization?

What will be the response? There seem to be two schools *of thought* in Washington. Those who feel that the mighty and proud US must smash something somewhere to show its anger. The question is where? Alexei Arbatov (*Russian expert on strategic thinking*) said in Moscow that it would not be wise to avenge the killing of 5,000 civilians in America by killing 5,000 civilians in Afghanistan. If Iraq were shown to be implicated, I have little doubt they would bomb a lot of industries – for missiles, chemistry, pharmacy, etc. But in Afghanistan? As someone said you cannot bomb them to the Stone Age. They are practically there already. The other school proposes the building of an international alliance to combat terrorism – US and Europe, Russia, China, even Arab states and the PLO (*Palestine Liberation Organization*). Indeed, the US would have a chance in the present atmosphere to bring together practically all except Iraq! But the US would have to impose some restraints on itself. No attacks without good evidence.

Is it war? Bush went out and declared that 'this is war!'. Well, such exclamations should be taken for the rhetoric they are rather than a legal label. Was it an attack on the open societies? This has been said by many. However, I would be inclined to see it more as an attack on those who are seen as not respecting the holy Arab Muslim lands. Bin Laden, in particular, seems enraged that US troops are stationed in Saudi Arabia.

Impact on UNMOVIC? For the moment Iraq is not in focus and there is a lull in the Palestine–Israel struggle. Suicide bombings are not hailed as glorious anywhere at present. Saddam, who has been rewarding the families of the suicide *bombers*, seems lonely today. He still wants an escalation of violence, but the world has had enough of it for some time. For that reason, American strikes that would not be strictly pinpointing bin Laden or his training camps for terrorists will probably turn the rage against the United States. On the other hand, if evidence were obtained that Iraq was in it, both bombing and demand for the acceptance of inspection might be accepted by many. We have to be ready ...

Now that a large US armada is assembling in and near the Gulf Saddam might also become scared. Though I don't think it is likely, he might try to stave off attacks by accepting inspection ... Again, we have to be ready ...

Iraq's reaction. The first comments from Iraq were that the US has brought the attacks upon themselves by its behaviour – bombing Iraq, etc. Subsequently there came two open letters from Saddam in which he urges the US to be wise and prudent! One had the feeling that the dictator was a bit jolted. Iraq also denied having had anything to do with the acts in the US. It refrained from condolences, except for Tariq Aziz. An almost-macabre report came of comments by Saddam to the effect that Iraq would be ready to help the US clear up the rubble and ruins in New York. Iraq had acquired considerable experience in such work through the US bombings. Such comments must come from a weird mind set! It is in line with Saddam's earlier offer of $100 million (or some such sum) to the poor of the United States. Mockery about ruins, victims and graves seems, to put it mildly, a vulgarity.

Saturday 22 September 2001

I watched President Bush delivering a speech to a joint session of Congress on Wednesday evening. It was a good performance. Pronounced with much conviction and body language. Congress was packed. Lots of invited guests: judges from the Supreme Court, generals from the Joint Chiefs of Staff, Tony Blair, Mayor Giuliani, Governor Patakos, the widow of one of the victims, etc.

While it sounded very belligerent it did not single out military strikes as the most important. He avoided the term war. He went out of his way to say this had nothing to do with Islam. What I reacted against most was the assertion that those who are not with us are against us. The world joins in blanket condemnation and a wish to eradicate terrorism, but it is hardly ready to give a blanket approval of any measures decided by Washington.

An article in the *New York Times* today asserts that Bush has now found his mission, he is a changed man, one with a clear goal and purpose. This sounds a little worrisome. While the horrible events certainly require determination and action and tenacity, they are not the only problems that call for governments' attention.

Thursday 27 September 2001 (Yom Kippur)

Perhaps the city was a little calmer today – with so many Jews celebrating. But I did not notice much difference. All news is still about the terrorist attack and its aftermath. Today President Bush was at the O'Hara airport in Chicago to urge Americans to start using the airlines again. But no military action yet.

Kofi Annan and the UN management did a lot of meeting and talking. Actually yesterday our thirtieth floor was asked to assemble outside Dhanapala's office to meet the Secretary-General and Nane. He gave a short, warm talk and walked around and shook the hand or hugged everybody!

For our part, we had already long ago scheduled a meeting of all staff on 25 Sept. and I went through with that. Talked nearly one hour about the political background of our job and how the terrorist act and the responses to it might affect us. What I wanted to point out to them, above all, was that the political situation in which we find ourselves has changed a good deal. In 1991, the US mobilized the world against Iraqi aggression and banned the purchase of Iraqi oil as a pressure on Iraq to declare and destroy its weapons of mass destruction. In 1999, this pressure was dropped and thereafter we have seen how Iraq has increasingly tried to mobilize the world against the US. They have had good help from the situation in Israel and applauded suicide attackers and awarded 10,000 US dollars to each family with such a martyr. After the attack on the World Trade Center people all over have had enough of suicide attacks. The Iraqi line is not applauded and Iraq, alone in not condoling with the US, is again alone. I wanted all to feel that while we have not seen and do not see any sign of an opening for us to be asked to undertake our main job, inspection, the situation is increasingly volatile. Hence the need for increased preparedness. Everyone, wherever placed in the organization, should feel that he or she is engaged in a meaningful mission. The Security Council needs us. So, we must be ready.

How long the Iraqi neo-isolation will last and in what way the US can make use of it is not easy to see. If evidence were to turn up that Iraq helped finance or otherwise support the terrorist action, there would hardly be criticism of renewed bombing of Iraqi industry that could be related to arms production. So far, no such evidence.

Saturday 29 September 2001

Evacuation of the UN exercise. Yesterday at the end of the working day the whole UN was made to walk down and out of the building. It worked very well. We trooped down when the fire warden of our floor (thirty) gave the signal. It took about twelve minutes to walk the thirty flights of stairs! Not bad. In fact, much faster than I had thought. As we got out on the flat ground I felt a bit awkward at the hips and limped a bit, but nothing serious.

UNMOVIC preparedness. It is now nineteen months that I have been responsible for building up a capacity for effective inspections in Iraq. And I realize how much remains to be done. Of course, a lot has been done, too. Above all we have trained a lot of potential inspectors and we have a group of people here who know a fair amount about the issues. We also are clear about procedures available to us. However, what lately has struck me is how unsmooth our administrative routines are. With new staff all around and only a minority of old hands procedures are not automatic. People come from all corners of the world with different administrative orders. They are surely willing to adapt to the order here. But they do not know it. We do need to train our staff and give them an administrative manual and explain it to them. How letters, email, faxes are logged, shared and answered. How and when budgetary requests are to be made. How staff are to be interviewed and hired. All these things should be routine and not cost any thought at a time when we need all our brains for inspection. I would like to achieve this before I leave the organization. UNSCOM had a rather different working basis. Staff came from member states and were not UN-remunerated. And as it was the military who were the suppliers, it was prompt. They were used to be prepared. We shall be less reliant on member governments, more relying on the regular UN machinery. But this is notoriously slow. We cannot change that. However, then, we must have delegation to do more by ourselves. We must be an island of efficiency in a sea of slow motion.

Sunday 30 September 2001. *The Campaign against Terrorism*

I read today excerpts (in the *New York Times*) of what the supreme religious leader of Iran had to say. They opposed terrorism, he said, but not under US leadership. It would have to be a genuine UN action. Not one simply led by the US under a UN cloak. The Iranians may be the only one to say it, but I am sure that others would step in with much more ease, if there were a real UN lead: Saudis, Pakistan, Indonesia, Egypt, Jordan. The difficulty, as usual, is to give it real teeth if it is the UN. The Americans will not submit anything vital to international leadership, even with themselves dominating. They have not even asked for NATO support! What they want from the UN, for the moment at least, is rather a stamp of legitimacy. However, they might try to distribute tasks. Keep everything military in their own hands, perhaps with a few others, like the British. Have a small group for intelligence compilation with a larger group supporting. And maybe a UN group for the financial controls and getting better border controls. It must give them some pause for thought that the Saudis appear to have declined their request to use Saudi air bases for military operations. It is evidently too sensitive for the Saudis. They have enough trouble perhaps hosting the planes that bomb Iraq ...

The Taliban seem to be solidarizing themselves more closely with bin Laden now and threaten to join terrorist acts against the US, if attacks occur in Afghanistan. They probably never had any intention of extraditing bin Laden but only played for time when they asked for evidence. Their new position and threat might make it easier for the US to attack Taliban military installations.

I have just watched a film on CNN about the current inside of Afghanistan. It is totally shocking. Ruins everywhere and complete misery and oppression. Perhaps there is order – totalitarian order and terrorizing of the population, especially the women. While they have not systematically exterminated people, like the Khmer Rouge, they have established their regime by massacre. They seem almost as mad as the Khmer Rouge.

Saturday 6 October 2001

Göran was in Philadelphia yesterday and received his prize for his essay on a book by Zola. I am happy for him to receive public recognition. It is also a good professional merit. His essay will be published.

Mårten turned thirty-three yesterday and I sent an email and phoned. I recalled what I was doing in October 1961, when I was thirty-three. It was really a turning point in my career. I was attending my first UN General Assembly session in the Sixth (Legal) Committee. I was still docent (associate professor) and aiming at an academic career. However, as it turned out the foreign minister, Undén, thought I was competent and when I returned to Stockholm in early January (1962) he had made me International Law Adviser of the ministry. So that autumn was my first thorough brush with the UN.

Eva will be invited to Wilton Park (UK) for a conference discussing Arctic issues. It is the same week that I go to London for the Chernobyl Fund, so we should be able to get a weekend together.

UNMOVIC. I am pushing and pushing to have several long-lasting projects finalized: the handbook, the list of Unresolved Disarmament Issued (UDI), the checklists, the administrative manual and a few others. The method I use is to call meetings in my office where they report where they are and we discuss and give directives. It is slow but by the end of this year many of the projects should be ready. I like that.

Sunday 7 October 2001

It is almost four weeks since the attack on the World Trade Center and still no strikes by the US. The talk is no longer of punishment and the ending of states but of finding bin Laden's network *and* training camps and of dislodging the Taliban by creating a new, broad Afghan coalition. Wisdom and prudence have prevailed over hawkish eagerness of doing something muscular fast with the risk of rather spectacular failure.

Rumsfeld, the Secretary of Defense, has come back from his trip to Egypt, Saudi Arabia, Oman and Uzbekistan. He is not talking about an alliance but about many bilateral ones, each suited to the particular conditions set. There seems also to be a policy line in this. In an alliance there would have to be joint consultations, and this might be an impediment. This line is consistent with the new Pentagon philosophy. The US is strong enough to go it alone. The role of others is, first of all, to applaud. It was even reported that the first Pentagon reaction was negative to the NATO allies' proposal to declare the NATO *Article* 5 applicable, making the attack on the US an attack on all allies.

According to the *New York Times* Kofi Annan had suggested that the US should obtain the Security Council's approval for any armed action, and this had been declined. Washington may feel that it already has what it needs from the UN in the form of the Security Council resolution. My guess is that so long as such action is limited to presumed bin Laden camps and Taliban military installations, the reaction is not going to be so strong.

A decades-long campaign against 'terrorism' led from Washington with assistant roles for all other countries is no easy scheme.

A new security order. There has been a good deal of talk of the 'tectonic shift' that has occurred. States and regimes are now assessed on the basis of where they stand in the campaign against terrorism. Iraq will be an interesting test case. Clearly it is not in focus now. It is a little further down the agenda. If no indications are found implicating the Iraqi regime in the recent deeds the US will have a hard time to get any support for dislodging the regime and would have a hard time doing it through subversion. Where would Russia stand in this case? If the Russians plead for a new security order, they should be anxious for guarantees that Iraq has no weapons of mass destruction. They cannot achieve this by negotiations with Saddam.

Sunday evening, 7 October 2001

Attacks in Afghanistan. I sat glued to CNN. It was a relief that at this serious moment they did not have any advertising. The opening seems as good as it could be. Attacks on military installations or strategic points in Kandahar, Kabul, Jalalabad and in the North as well. The US mainly but with British participation as well. We shall soon learn how accurate the cruise missiles and the bombs were and how many civilians were hit. The Pakistani government expressed understanding and hoped the process would be quick. The West supports. The Iranians condemn the action as not being under international lead. Bin Laden and his Egyptian ally speak on Al Jazeera TV. Apparently taped speeches in anticipation of the attacks. Fascinating that this TV station by being even-handed and trying to be objective has attained a tremendous audience and is evidently – for that very reason – favoured by the bin Laden people as a forum for their speeches! The reward of virtue. People want a channel that is not allied to anybody, but just reports.

Tuesday 9 October 2001

Anthrax. There is a lot of scare in the US that a case of anthrax in Florida is the result of terrorist action. If so the scare of biological weapons will increase. Would there be a link to Iraq? It is doubtful that the bin Laden group would have produced anthrax by itself.

UNMOVIC checklists. It has proved to be a good initiative to ask all divisions to prepare lists of what they feel is needed to be undertaken before any inspection begins in Iraq. The lists turn out to contain a great deal of necessary action and measures. The divisions will feel that they have work for a long time.

ANTHRAX IN THE US – AND AT THE UN?

Tuesday 16 October 2001

All the talk here is now about the anthrax attacks by letter. I find it hard to believe that the source should be some nut in the US. The targets have been media and the Senate minority leader. There is currently no link to Iraq, but I would not be surprised if there was one.

Thursday 18 October 2001

So now I have lived it first hand! From ten this morning we had a meeting in the UNMOVIC 'bunker' on the thirtieth floor. At some time around noon, Jarmo Sareva, my assistant, complained that white particles were falling from above on his jacket. He brushed them off. Igor Mitrokhin, who sat behind him, is our expert on health and safety and Jaremo joked with him and asked: 'what is this?' In no time Igor phoned for UN Security. By the time they came with masks and gloves and protective clothes we had adjourned to move from chemical to biological issues in our discussion. The two UN guards opened a small suitcase with instruments and proceeded to apply it to the table and to pick a few particles from the floor. They ordered all to wait in the room outside. Ake Bovallius came back and asked what kind of examination they were undertaking. It turned out to be for chemicals (toxic, I suppose). Ake asked if they did not make any bacteriological check. To this he got no proper answer and the chief guard tried to exercise some authority – which was lost on his microbiological audience authority. *Our experts* were rather indignant that a biological threat was met with a chemical check and they thought the sample taking very amateurish. Was OK. The guards took off their masks and soon left. All returned to the discussion. But at the end of it apparently Bovallius and Diamantidis went down to the medical division and asked to be checked for anthrax. Medical alerted security again and the machinery slowly moved on. I was happily having my lunch at my desk and working away. By five o'clock, I was asked to come to the UN

Office of Security (Mr McCann). It had contacted New York City with experts and a doctor. Mr McCann, poor soul, was nervous. He is responsible for security and a white substance is not to be neglected. I said I thought the office of Iraq inspection was not the most likely target (at least not by Iraqis who do not wish to draw attention to themselves...). More likely was that some white paint was falling down. Yet once the machinery was set in motion it could not easily be stopped. However implausible, if we had stopped it and were wrong, we would carry an awful responsibility. So, the solution was that further samples would be taken and analysed as soon as possible (twenty-four hours...) If something was found, all those who had been at the meeting would be tested and antibiotics would be given...

Sunday 21 October 2001

Was called by Alice Hecht in the afternoon and asked to come down to the UN. It turned out that the American labs had analysed the samples from our 'bunker' and the cultivation had shown no anthrax bacteria, but two additional biochemical tests that were expected to be negative had been positive! So, they wanted to take more samples and needed another seventy-two hours for tests. Meanwhile they felt staff who had been in the 'bunker' should begin to take Cipro. The incubation time for anthrax is around six days and as we were in the 'bunker' on Friday, we should not wait for tests any longer but take the medicine prophylactically. OK. Alice and I set out phoning all we had on our lists. Some were not reachable, but I did reach a sleepy Dimitri in Vienna. I got hold of Jarmo and of Surya Sinha and Bovallius. As I have been on doxycycline for several months (*for Lyme disease*) I don't need anything more. McCann, the Security Chief, had emailed all UN staff that an investigation was underway re: the thirtieth floor. I bet this will get into the media tomorrow. However, we shall refer every inquiry to the UN press spokesman, Fred Eckhard.

Saturday 27 October 2001

The news is dominated by the war in Afghanistan, the anthrax letters and the continued investigation of the roots of the attacks on 11 September. Yesterday the big news was that one of the terrorist pilots, the Egyptian Ata, had met an Iraqi intelligence agent on a quick trip to Prague last April. It is hard to avoid the guess that there was some Iraqi involvement, money, passports or other.

I have been reading the New Yorker this afternoon. There is an article about terrorism, containing a good deal of interesting observations. Adelman is interviewed. It is chilling reading. He says it is hopeless to hit the terrorist. Just go for countries. Though without *advancing* specific evidence, he feels that Iraq is in it and should be 'wiped out' together with Afghanistan. I wonder how. He says he does not care what comes after an ousting of the Taliban. Probably some incompetent group.

UNMOVIC. The long work to identify unresolved disarmament issues through analysis of UNSCOM documents, Iraqi declarations and inspection reports is coming to its conclusion, almost a year later than we had thought ... And yet the quality is far from acceptable. Now begins a phase of clustering the cases and reducing them from some eighty to about half of that and to begin to see what is of greater and of smaller importance. Fedotov, our Russian commissioner, tends to see it all as *rather meaningless*. I must say I rather resent his saying this. If he thinks so he should say nothing. We are asked by a valid Security Council resolution to 'address' unresolved disarmament issues. It is then logical that we define which these issues are. He may be convinced that the inspectors will never be let in, but he should not tell us that it is meaningless for us to do what the Council has instructed us to do. Perhaps it is remarkable that morale is so good. Despite the fact that most of the staff would love to go into the field, travel, do something thrilling, they are also taking to the forensic detective work and our discussions are lively and engaging. Another question is what the atmosphere will be when we are finished with the current analysis which absorbs a lot of people. We certainly can go for renewed and refined analysis, using the better tools we shall have to access the archive and database.

UN Day 24 October 2001. Went to the Celebration in the General Assembly Hall

Brought Rachel Davies as I had the right to two seats. It was pretty full.

The new American commissioner, John Wolf, visited me last Monday with quite a group, including Ambassador Jim Cunningham. We talked about one hour. It did not shed much light on future US intentions. He probably does not know. If anyone does. The US supports the demand for inspection. He did not know whether Bush had brought up Iraq in his talks with Putin in Shanghai. He was quite complimentary about my stewardship. There was a difference having a diplomat in control and having an experienced manager of a large organization. Yes, I think the organizational work has been fine, but more important would be how I direct inspections.

3 November 2001. Saturday. The Anthrax Situation

I have spent much time on the subject this week. The American investigators seem inclined to think that the spread of anthrax by letter is the work of indigenous American nuts and not linked to Bin Laden or Iraq. Four people have died from anthrax by now and a number have been cured by antibiotics. The hawks have wanted to direct suspicions to Iraq and pointed out that apart from the US and Russia Iraq did have a large-scale programme for anthrax. American media interview former UNSCOM inspectors, like Richard Spertzel and Scott Ritter. Not to mention Richard Butler, who seems to be on CNN every morning. For a while I was thinking that perhaps we should stick out our neck and appear at the UN spokesman's press briefing and say what we knew about the Iraqi programme. However, Eckhard was hesitating and perhaps this was wise. He reminded us that the Security Council had resented that Butler went to the media before he came to the Council. So, we put together a paper with succinct points describing the essentials that UNSCOM had learnt about the Iraqi programme. We passed a copy to the Irish who had the presidency of the Security Council in October and one to the Jamaicans who have it for November.

So, what do we know? In the 1980s, Iraq developed a large-scale programme for the production of anthrax. They managed to buy seven vials of various strains on a commercial basis from the US (and we know which they were). They tried – unsuccessfully – to buy strains in the UK and succeeded buying two strains in France (we don't know which). They claim to have used one of the American strains for production but UNSCOM never analysed any sample, so we have no verification of this declaration by Iraq. (However, it is hard to see why they should have lied on this point in 1995.) They declared that they had produced about 8,500 litres of anthrax in liquid (slurry) form and to have filled a rather large number of warheads and bombs with it. The declared volume of production is unverified. So is the declared volume of destruction (in 1991). A warhead was found to have degradation products from anthrax so the weaponization is not in doubt. While UNSCOM did not see evidence of the Iraqis having dried anthrax and to have treated it to suppress the electrostatic force which makes the spores clump, UNSCOM did find that Iraq had mastered the technique of drying bacilli both by freeze-drying and by spray-drying and that they had used the technique of avoiding clumping by mixing slurry bacilli with wet bentonite clay particles before spray-drying. We do not pretend to know anything about the current US inquiries, but it seems that the only strain found is one called Ames (from Iowa) and that the fine white powder which has been inhaled is not the result of any bentonite coating but rather of silica. However, if asked, we could not rule out that Iraq had had access to the Ames strain and to silica.

There are several intriguing twists to this story. It was revealed that France had prepared a resolution for Security Council adoption, condemning the recent use of anthrax. They found to their surprise and chagrin that the US opposed any such resolution being tabled. The dissemination could be an internal American affair... If so, the Security Council had nothing to do with it... Well, I might have thought that each party to the BWC had the duty to make sure there was no anthrax production on its territory and that the recent cases placed this in doubt – whether the powder came from the US or elsewhere.

Sunday 4 November 2001

Nuclear installations have been in focus during the past week. The US has banned flights (of small planes) in the vicinity of nuclear power plants in the US. The IAEA has had a symposium in Vienna and Mohamed ElBaradei came out with rather agitated statements that nothing could be excluded but perhaps putting together dirty bombs was the more likely path for terrorists. Of course, the Agency is in a bit of a dilemma. It needs to speak up as the most knowledgeable and directly responsible (*authority*). It will be most heard and cited if it says something agitated. If it says something calming it may be accused of playing down.

Friday 9 November 2001. Stockholm. At Home

Arrived from New York by seven this morning. Fast flight: six hours and forty-five minutes. Half-empty. No wonder the airlines are going bankrupt (Sabena, Swissair). New York had around 8° (*Celsius*). Here it is just below freezing and some snow on the ground. Sunny and nice. The autumn has been mild and lovely in New York.

Wednesday 21 November 2001. Back in New York

Came back to NY Sunday night (*having been in Stockholm 9–14 and London 15–18 Nov.*). I parted from Eva at Heathrow and left London around 6 pm. Plenty of work in the office Monday, Tuesday and today. We have a meeting of the College of Commissioners next Monday and Tuesday, so there is much to prepare. No documents to submit. In fact, there is little to consult the College about. No policy questions we want to submit. We have chosen to let each director of a division report on the preparatory work they have made or plan to make to achieve readiness for inspections.

Let me go back in time and note things chronologically.

Wednesday last week –14 Nov., I spoke to a Nordic security police meeting about what UNMOVIC is doing.

(*On Saturday 17 Nov.*) Dinner at high table in Trinity College (*Cambridge*). Amartya Sen, Nobel Laureate in Economics and Master of Trinity presided. His wife, Emma Rothschild, sat next to me. I have heard that she was a close friend of Olof Palme (*Swedish Prime Minister, assassinated in 1988*). She told me that at one time she had a flat in Stockholm. I have also heard that she was rather leftist. In any case, she had been a member of the SIPRI board for a number of years. Knew Swedish politics extremely well. Mr Sen, whom I sat next to at coffee, talked a good deal about Boutros Ghali and Kofi Annan (to whom he is an adviser . . .). He asked me what the Americans had had against Boutros. I think he was too articulate. Perhaps not sufficiently deferential to Madeleine Albright. But he was also caught by the general anti-UN attitude of the Republicans and the unwillingness of the Clinton regime to defend the UN.

(*Return to N.Y. on Sunday 18 Nov. and meeting of College of Commissioners on 27 and 28 Nov.*)

Tuesday 27 November 2001

Iraq inspections in focus. Yesterday President Bush said that Iraq would have to accept international inspection. Or else . . . Journalists asked 'or else what?'. And he replied: 'They'll find out . . . '. We have lived without any media attention for a very long while. Hardly anyone asked us about what we knew about Iraq's anthrax programme and 'terrorist training camp', although newspapers speculated and several UNSCOM inspectors – especially Richard Spertzel – gave interviews revealing facts that they were obliged under UN rules to keep quiet about. We would be foolish to demur and there was really no harm in the revelations. After the interview with Bush, we must have been rediscovered. Today I had a long talk with the *Wall Street Journal* and a shorter one with AP. Tomorrow is the Los Angeles Times . . . It is always risky but inevitable. While our inspections still seem *distant* and Bush's remarks may be just the first salvo in an escalating war on Iraqi nerves, the 'smart sanctions' have moved decisively in the last few days, envisaging a much greater role for our contract checking without media having yet noticed it.

Smart sanctions. It seems that the Russians are meeting the Americans more than halfway on this scheme. We have not seen the resolution yet, but it seems to be a rollover of Oil for Food for another six months but with a proviso that next time the Council will adopt the GRL, i.e. the goods review list, covering those items' contracts which must be submitted to the sanctions committee. We are to examine whether contracts contain such items. If, in our judgement, they do not, they are automatically approved. Iraq is adamantly opposed because although they will be able to import a number of items which may now be stopped, the procedure will make sanctions look more reasonable and this is seen as a great propaganda disadvantage. An important aspect of the resolution will be precisely that Iraq's objections will be overridden by Russia and China. The Council will again be unanimous. It would appear that this is a result of the new wish of the great powers to cooperate in efforts against the further spread of weapons of mass destruction. For the Russians this may cost valuable orders in Iraq. They must have concluded that the gains in Western goodwill (or alternative loss of goodwill) was important. Of course, it is still highly uncertain that Iraq would go along with inspections.

Yet, for Iraq (as for most others), the world is a bazaar. Only a few weeks ago they said they would never again contemplate inspections. The chapter was over. Finito. Now they are saying that inspections could only be contemplated if sanctions were lifted at the same time. In some statements they may add that US/UK no-fly zones must be lifted and in yet others they say that other countries in the region must also then accept the same inspections. There are many bargaining chips to play with. The greater the risk of unilateral American action, the less they will demand and the same is probably true about the Russians. They are surely willing to make quite a few concessions to the Americans in order to maintain the operation as a common one. More American 'alleingang' (*solo walking*) is not a habit they want to see developed . . .

UNMOVIC College of Commissioners. We have had a meeting yesterday and today (27 Nov.). With new Commissioners from China (Li) and the US (John Wolf). As there were really no significant policy issues on which we could ask advice we had envisaged all directors to give crisp pictures of where their preparations for inspection stood. Brian Mulladay started fast and fun on logistics. Rachel was also good. Alice was well prepared on personnel. Diamantidis knows a great deal and works hard but is hopeless as a presenter. We were able to hold a discussion about the political issue of the prospects of UNMOVIC going in. I must note that the members from the lesser players appear pretty naïve or off-tune in such discussion. Some think the College could push the Security Council to reach consensus, etc. The College is much better when it concretely discusses inspections. Several of the members have direct personal experiences as former UNSCOM inspectors. On these matters they can speak with authority, while the political heavyweights of the P5 do not. This might prove helpful to us in the future. It is clear that the Russian, Fedotov, will often be the odd man out. He will sometimes be supported by the Chinese *commissioner*, sometimes by the Ukrainian. But the others will almost invariably support Secretariat positions.

Friday 30 November 2001

End of the week. Jamaican reception at the Helmsley Hotel to celebrate the last day of their Presidency of the Security Council. *All minds were* filled with the adoption of the new resolution on sanctions on Iraq. A compromise between the US and Russia with many uncertain elements that should be sorted out before 1 June. The resolution speaks about the comprehensive settlement on the basis of past resolution. Whatever that means. It squares with the Russian talk about a package. It also calls for the 'clarification' necessary to ensure implementation. The Americans will ride on the word 'clarification', which is not the same as 'modification'. The Russians will ride on the word 'necessary'. Whatever the Iraqis demand as a condition for implementation will be 'necessary'! I don't think any of these clarifications are of great importance to the Iraqis except as a means of blocking Res. 1284. The only point of real importance would be the clarification of what administrative and financial arrangements would be connected to a suspension of the sanctions.

Sam, Muttusamy Sanmuganathan, my old friend from *Sri Lanka*, who is now the secretary of the College of Commissioners, has succeeded in making himself as indispensable and accessible to all these commissioners as he was to the members of the Board of Governors (*of the IAEA*) which he served.

Saturday 1 December 2001

The *New York Times* cites Richard Armitage, deputy secretary of state, today as saying that the US will increase the pressure on Iraq to accept UN inspectors. It may look like a tougher action, but when you look closer it appears rather as a scaling down from the expectations of military action, which were raised when Bush said that the Iraqis will 'find out' what will happen if they don't accept inspection. They are disclaiming any intention to use force at the present time. Sending a signal to their camp to keep cool. And a signal to Saddam to keep quiet and not stop selling oil, not provoke the US by armed measures against the Kurds. It will be interesting to see how the Iraqis will react to the new resolution. My guess is that they will swallow. They cannot change it. But they can tell the Russians that if they help getting lenient conditions for Iraq end of May when the new sanctions system is to be launched, they will continue to get most favoured nations treatment. The amendments of the Memorandum of Understanding will give them a chance to try to put their foot down. The US and Russia will have a tough time to agree. All will depend upon the general climate prevailing between them. If Russia gets goodies in other fields, it may yield on Iraq.

I don't see Iraq accepting inspections in the spring. Why should it before they have seen what the new comprehensive implementation of resolutions will be? They know that the US will not start anything military until they are finished with Afghanistan and will be held back by allies, Arabs and Russia. Saddam will try to get a better control on the Kurds and the Shias to prevent them from collaborating with the US. He will trim his air defences, perhaps accelerate production of chemical weapons. Intensify support of Palestinian uprising and reward 'martyrs'.

For UNMOVIC the work is laid out. Get on with the 'clustering' of issues. And prepare for inspections. We need interpreters, some technical people and more training of chief inspectors. We need space for new staff to handle the examination of contracts.

Thursday 6 December 2001. 22.15

Tired. Introduced seventh report of UNMOVIC at an informal meeting of the Security Council this morning. Everybody kind and appreciating. No pull and push. Yet it was not difficult to see how the French and the Russians were trying to get an early list of what Iraq would have to do – under key remaining disarmament issues. No one else contradicted them, although it is evident that if an early list is provided the Iraqis will challenge it and claim it is old UNSCOM hat and declare that unless the list be reduced by two-thirds, they will not accept inspection ... The US and UK wait to intervene. They feel we can take care of the current comments. OK, I did. Despite the friendly atmosphere of the Council, the charged atmosphere is taxing. Lunch with the Chinese. The talk was very good. We managed to hover over most of the crucial matters. While they apparently hated Butler, they are very helpful to UNMOVIC. It seems likely that they will offer for us to have a training course in China and offer for us to use Chinese labs for analysis of samples. They want more Chinese in our staff. China is clearly taking its place in the Iraqi affair.

And fairly pragmatically so. They have much less of an axe to grind than Russia. Hence, they are more balanced. They invite me to come to China in the spring (no doubt instigated by my staff member, Pang, who must have claimed I wish to make a tour of the P5 ...

Sunday 9 December 2001

Kofi Annan urges US not to bomb more countries according to Eva, who had heard him speak in Oslo in connection with the Nobel Peace Prize. I wonder what scenario Kofi sees for Iraq. An increased pressure – through P5 consensus – on Iraq to accept inspection? And what if Iraq refuses to accept the inspectors? Are we to resign? Or what if Iraq accepts inspections but resumes the cat-and-mouse play and we do not find anything and solve rather little? What if they extend the two years they have had without inspectors by another year with stalled inspectors and use the three years to develop more weapons? The risk (not big but not negligible) is that they might succeed making a nuclear weapon while we are talking and trying. Once they have a weapon, they will be even more difficult to handle. Not surprisingly some Americans think they must strike before this happens.

Monday 17 December 2001

Inspections in Iraq. There pops up various comments to the effect that inspections will not help. Saddam will just hide things (which is probable). Or, today, Mr Hamza, defector, former nuclear scientist and well known here, wrote that the new inspectorate had protocols not allowing them to insist on immediate access! I can hardly imagine that he had put the piece together himself. It was ignorant of Res. 1284. However, the tendency was to say that the new inspectors would be useless. But then he added that the old were also denied access ... I have no regret that they point out the limitations of what inspectors can do. We are not an occupying army. But it should preferably be correct. Tonight on CNN there was a similar statement that the inspectors would be fooled by Saddam. Well, well, the job of inspection would surely be easier if the US first removed the Saddam government ... Then we might go in and have a cooperative regime to help us establish what there was ...

Thursday 20 December 2001

Inspections in Iraq. We wrote a press release in my name to counter Hamza's claim that UNMOVIC inspectors had said our protocol did not demand immediate access. We underlined that the Security Council resolutions consistently demand immediate, unconditional and unrestricted access and that we have said repeatedly that we do not give any discount on these resolutions. Moreover, that giving immediate access will be an essential part of cooperating in all respects, which is required as a condition for the suspension of sanctions. We let the UN spokesman read this at his press conference and we are also getting it into the *New York Times* as a letter to the editor. I saw at our senior staff meeting today that our Russian Nikita Zhukov was not very happy. Of course, the Russians are trying to persuade Baghdad to accept inspections and want to display them as more benign under UNMOVIC than under UNSCOM. However, this is not the consensus view that emerges from the Security Council resolutions. True, our rubbing in 'immediate access' will not make the Iraqis more inclined to invite us. But it is good that they have no expectations of any leniency. I feel on good ground to say what we did because we have repeatedly taken the line that we don't give any discount and in all discussions of what is meant by 'cooperation' I have given the two examples 'immediate etc.' access and security of the inspectors.

I shall see Kofi Annan tomorrow. He sent me a contract to prolong my service by one year. I have not answered, but I feel I must tell him that I would like to return home as soon as it is reasonably possible. I cannot responsibly rock the boat and I would surely do that if I left when my current contract expires, i.e. on 28 February 2002. I must ask his advice for the exit strategy.

Year 2002

TUESDAY 8 JANUARY 2002

Iraq. Met with Kofi Annan today. We agreed that the interview with Pentagon hawk Wolfowitz today in the NY Times signalled that the idea of an armed attack on Iraq was shelved for the time being. We also agreed that this signal from Wolfowitz meant that there would be no inspections in the spring. Why should Iraq accept inspections if it were not to be a way of avoiding invasion?

For the US, the course apparently decided on meant that they would be good multilateralist boys for a while, insisting on the implementation of Res. 1284 including, notably, inspections. The Arab states will support that, feeling that the US had met their concerns and refrained from early military action against Iraq. In reality, the US is surely choosing to avoid such action anyway at the present time, because it might be costly in military terms (no allies sending troops) and politically (would offend friends they need in the Israel–Palestine conflict). The Arabs will say, however, that Iraqi acceptance of inspections, which they support, should be coupled with a lifting of sanctions. For this they will get applause – and commercial contracts – in Baghdad, but the US will evidently not buy it – and there will be no inspections... When the insistence on the implementation has failed, as one would expect, it might be easier for the US to build an alliance supporting or at least acquiescing in military action. In any case, the US would have tried the multilateral path before it went unilateral...

Amr Moussa, the Secretary General of the Arab League, had phoned Kofi during the weekend. He was going to Baghdad and was thinking of asking Saddam Hussein to invite Blix to discuss inspections. Kofi had discouraged this step, knowing that I would be sceptical. He had said that if the Iraqis wanted to send a delegation to him (Kofi) in New York, they could do so. I agreed. If Iraq talked to me, it would only be to ask me for concessions of some kind and I have none to give. I have talked often about not being able to give any discounts on SC resolutions. Of course, Kofi is likewise unable to give any discounts, but he could relay Iraqi proposals to the SC.

My UN contract. I told Kofi that I was ready to continue to the end of June. This would allow me to ensure that analysis and identification of unresolved issues would be finished. The inspection train would be ready and loaded at the station. It was uncertain when it could depart and not reasonable for me to sit and wait. After the report to the Security Council on 1 June would be a suitable time for exit. Kofi agreed and we concluded that I would sign the one-year extension which they had sent me, but it was understood that I would leave by the end of June. I said Eva was taking retirement end of February and we wanted to reunite.

MEETING IN WASHINGTON WITH COLIN POWELL, JOHN BOLTON AND OTHERS

Saturday 12 January 2002

Thursday 10 January was the day of official visits and talks in Washington. A very full day! Beginning with discussions about the resolution on smart sanctions and the future role of UNMOVIC in that context. It was good we brought Rachel Davies with us, as she knows the subject much better than I or Dimitri. We agreed that we would need bilateral detailed talks about procedures later in New York.

Next was full-scale meeting with the Secretary of State, Colin Powell. He was well briefed and it was a pleasant talk. With me were Dimitri Perricos, Rachel Davies and Jarmo Sareva, my personal assistant. Powell confirmed that the US demanded implementation of UNSC Res. 1284 and the acceptance of inspectors. Apart from that, the US had an interest in the removal of Saddam Hussein. But these two interests were separate. Jarmo will write a summary. At the end and as we were walking out Powell took my arm and said he really hoped I would stay on and I replied that de Gaulle was reported to have said that 'the cemeteries are full of indispensable men ... '. I described the state of readiness and how we still could use time for the analysis of what questions remain.

After Powell I went to see John Bolton, now undersecretary in charge of disarmament. He had not changed a bit during the last ten years. We also talked about the value of inspections (which he has *rejected in the context of* the biological convention ...). I discovered that John Wolf was extremely negative to any mentioning of the Middle East zone free of weapons of mass destruction. He had taken part in the negotiation of SC Res. 687, and the reference in Art. 14 to the zone was, in his view, just a mishap ... I noted that the zone was supported by a consensus – including Israel – in the General Assembly.

Then a working luncheon with John Wolf (my direct opposite number and assistant secretary for non-proliferation) and a number of the people dealing with smart sanctions plus the assistant secretary in charge of international organizations and the deputy assistant for the Middle East. The former expressed his admiration for what we had achieved at UNMOVIC. I thanked him but pointed out that the proof of the pudding is in the eating. He agreed but said that also the baking of the pudding is difficult and important. *Touché* ...

MEETING AT THE PENTAGON

After lunch, trip to the Pentagon and a little guided sight-seeing tour. When you come from the State Department you are struck by the patriotic atmosphere and decoration in the Pentagon. The corridors and walls are full of portraits of generals and of people who have defended the country: heroes, women in uniform, etc. Secretaries of War (until 1947 when they became Secretaries of Defense), joint chiefs-of-staff, etc. My host was undersecretary for defence policy, Douglas Feith. He hid his scepticism against inspection fairly well and was courteous enough not to contradict my sermon on the benefits of inspections (which were effective and the results of which were not exaggerated). He did ask, however, if there was not a risk that inspectors of some nationalities would learn the inspection techniques and report on this to the inspected parties. Well, the techniques are not very secret. It is a bit like war. The enemy will soon learn about the weapons and techniques you use.

MEETING WITH CONDOLEEZZA RICE

Then on to the White House and the Presidential Security Adviser, Condoleezza Rice. I could only bring one adviser into her small office, so Dimitri and Rachel left us. We had a less hurried talk this time than on the first occasion – in April last year. She is very alert and articulate. She expressed great satisfaction about our work.

MEETING WITH JIM SCHLESINGER

On Friday morning I saw James Schlesinger, former Secretary of Defense and Energy and former head of the CIA (*Central Intelligence Agency*). He was as always exuding self-confidence and a fair amount of irony. We had a full hour of interesting talk about Iraq and nuclear power and global warming. When I left, he said he was pleased that I had seen him and that he had feared that his support for the rejection of the complete test ban agreement had put me off from seeing him. I replied that I did not admire the rejection of the test ban but that I always valued and enjoyed meeting him – which is true. He was somewhat critical of the global warming argument. He agreed that it was there, but not as strongly as claimed ... Even an increase of ten degrees could be absorbed by the rich countries over a period of time without disasters. I wonder if he is not belittling it ...

The programme I had worried most about came at lunch on the Friday. Speaking at the Washington Institute of Near East Policy (WINEP). This is the Jewish lobby and Hebrew was spoken right and left in the audience of over 100 people including the ambassador of Israel. I think it went very well vis-à-vis this group. Whether what I said would be also acceptable to more pro-Iraq people I do not know. Naturally I try to tailor my comments so that they will not lead to offence anywhere (if this is possible). We shall see. At any rate I am confident they all found me knowledgeable on the resolutions and the substance. After it was over the executive director said to me that he wished that all UN officials were as clear in what they say as I was.

Wednesday 16 January 2002

Dinner with the Secretary-General. The dinner was the annual one for the Security Council. Ambassadors and their wives. Plus, Undersecretary for Political Affairs (Prendergast whom I have always found a bit pompous), Humanitarian Affairs (Oshima, nice, unassuming, perhaps not very forceful), Chef de Cabinet (Iqbal Riza, experienced Pakistani player), Secretary of the Security Council (Stephanides, friendly but somewhat Byzantine-minded Cypriot eager to manipulate for the good cause of solutions). The SG welcomed us but said it was not a toast so there was no need for a reply. It is noticeable how hungry people are in these situations to laugh at something. Almost any feeble joke or turn is good enough to bring enthusiastic laughter and applause.

I managed to have a few words with Kofi about Iraq and my job. On his question, I confirmed that the end date we had agreed on was 1 July. He does not seem to question that. I said further that Danilo Turk, assistant secretary general in political affairs, in my view, would be a very good successor and an alternative name to the Hungarian Erdos. Kofi wondered whether Turk had enough disarmament experience. I said he had played a crucial role in the drafting Res. 1284. (The Iraqis would not like it, but I think he was the one who advanced the idea of 'suspension' as an alternative to 'lifting'.) I also said that in my view Turk was balanced and seemed to be a good manager.

Kofi is not likely to take any initiative in the Iraq issue. I think he will leave it to the Iraqis to come with new approaches – if they have any. The French ambassador, Jean-David Levitte, seems to hope that if he and a few others can stitch together a package with various 'clarifications', notably on the 'timeline', on the administrative and financial arrangements linked to suspension (the escrow account) the Secretary-General could be the one who would put it on the table. In Levitte's view a package with the Security Council's unanimous support should be in the US interest – I wonder. The US may worry about a package which others accept and they reject. I think they will warn Kofi not to put on the table something they would object to.

The Russian ambassador, Lavrov, said he hoped for an additional resolution, which would 'explain' a variety of things in Res. 1284. He has no problem accepting as 'clarifications' what really are modifications. However, he will run into a wall with the US. They will even have a hard time thinking of any 'needed clarification' and appearing to have been in good faith when they accepted the reference to clarifications. It would not surprise me if they argued that it is up to the Russians to make a case for something being a 'needed verification'. Lavrov is rumoured to become UN Undersecretary for Disarmament in a year's time – to succeed Dhanapala, who has just received a one-year prolongation. Well, the Russians are, indeed, in favour of disarmament, in distinction to the Americans headed by John Bolton... Lavrov is seen as a (very forceful and competent) hardliner, and they will be glad to get rid of him in the Council. He sometimes seems to be more rigid than Moscow.

Sunday 3 February 2002

Washington's sabre rattling has clearly rattled the Iraqis. But also the Europeans. Lots of political lights in various corners remind the world that it has not been proven that Iraq is behind al Qaeda or any of its deeds. Well, the US government has not asserted that at this point. While it has tried seamlessly to move from al Qaeda to Saddam to shore up broad support for possible actions against the latter, it has consistently held that Saddam qualifies for action in his own right, regardless of al Qaeda. The strongest argument that the hawks have is, I think, that waiting a year to tackle Saddam is not likely to make it easier. Maybe so. Maybe he has more BC weapons, he will hardly be ready with any nuclear. Yet who knows what weapons there may be in a year's time...

The Germans, French, Swedes, even the Brits are against any military operation to take out Saddam. However, there are even more serious obstacles. First, my guess is that the US military (not the civilian leaders) in the Pentagon are against it. They make cautious, not optimistic scenarios and they see that a campaign might cost many lives. Iraq is not Afghanistan and there is no Northern Alliance. Second, the US is aware that their friends in the Middle East are hard pressed because the US has been so soft on Sharon and his panzer policy against the Palestinians. To keep any support in the region the US needs to avoid another unpopular action. People in the street in the Arab world know that Saddam is brutal, but they admire him for full support for the Palestinians and for standing up against the US, which they increasingly – and wrongly – identify as anti-Islam.

THE 'AXIS OF EVIL'

Bush's State of the Union appointment of DPRK, Iran and Iraq as the axis of evil has shocked many. It certainly sounds as if it came out of the Christian right wing rather than the Brookings Institution. It is rightly objected that there is not all that much of an axis between the three – except that perhaps both Iran and Iraq have imported missile technology from North Korea. They have in common that they move toward weapons of mass destruction, but an axis they are not. Never mind, the speech and the expression achieved what politicians want: attention.

To return to the rattled Saddam. He is busy offering conciliation with Iran, Saudis and even Kuwait. However, they are hardly misled by this wolf dressing up as a grandma. He generously offered Kuwait that they could come in and visit any prison or camp or his own palaces to see that he was not keeping any Kuwaiti prisoners. Ergo the matter of the missing Kuwaitis is closed ... It is interesting that Iraq has the same approach vis-à-vis UNSCOM and UNMOVIC: You can see for yourself! If you cannot prove that there is something, it must be taken there is nothing. They cannot prove the negative ... The most likely is that the Iraqis killed the 600 Kuwaitis at the beginning of the war. They know what they have done, and they might even have records or witnesses. But they find it a better tactic to say they know nothing than to confess ...

Amr Moussa, now Secretary General of the League of Arab states, has recently been to Baghdad and talked to Saddam. It was he who came back with the 'offer' to Kuwait about visiting Saddam's prisons. The Kuwaitis angrily rejected the offer and even said that Amr had exceeded his functions. However, Amr has more to report and I am going to meet him tomorrow. One line is that the Iraqis want the SG to invite them to a continuation of the comprehensive dialogue. Apparently, Amr has also talked to Saddam about renewed inspections. It will be interesting to hear firsthand what Saddam answered. My guess is that he said he did not mind if Amr explored the issue, in particular what quid pro quo Iraq could get for accepting inspections. I don't think they will invite me to Baghdad although they know that a trip by me to Baghdad would get great publicity as a possible sign – loved by media and a peace-longing world – that they are on the verge of accepting inspections.

Monday 4 February 2002

The Secretary-General asked me to join him at noon to meet the Secretary General of the League of Arab States, Amr Moussa. Saddam wanted the SG to resume the 'comprehensive dialogue', which had begun early last year but had not been continued. They set no preconditions. Moussa had told them that they must consider implementing resolutions, including inspections. Saddam had referred to three grievances: there had been spies among the inspectors; the inspectors had misbehaved (not observed decorum in presidential sites, there ought to be some code of conduct); and little credit had been given to eight years of information from the Iraqi side. What use had been made of it? Moussa had assured Saddam that Blix was very different from Butler. Moussa had known Blix for a very long time. Kofi said that he would be ready for a continuation of the dialogue, but it would have to be more 'focused'. If it was not, it would be playing games. After conferring with me he said that Blix would be available to join if they wanted to discuss inspections. Moussa tried to get Kofi to say that there would soon be a meeting, but Kofi said he would have to consult his calendar.

I said I would talk about how we would go about inspections. Iraq knew it from the IAEA: demanding but correct. I also said that the main question was whether Iraq was ready to rid itself of weapons of mass destruction. Otherwise, there could be the same cat-and-mouse dance as earlier. Moussa cautioned we should take one step at the time. Kofi said that if he were to resume contacts Arab states had to work on Iraq to comply.

Kofi handles himself very well in this kind of talks.

Friday 8 February 2002

I have now been suffering a great deal to write the lecture for our next training course – in Geneva. It does give me an opportunity to say a lot of things that Iraq and others can jolly well read. But it must be instructive to the trainees as well.

Iraq. The latest rumour was that the Iraqis may be invited to come rather soon to see the SG. I would hope for the week 4–8 March when I am scheduled to be here. The second part of the rumour was that the Iraqis soon will want to see me alone. Well, that would really start the speculation about coming inspections. This presumably is what they would want in order, if possible, to fend off US action. However, I doubt the Iraqis are ready for me yet. They will want to play for time and space out their gestures. Surely, they would try to get some discounts on inspection before they go for it again. The US does not like the dialogue with the SG, but they have no problem if there are discussions with me. These, of course, should be about practical arrangements about inspections. So, how could the US object? I think it will be some time before the Iraqis go that far. Unless the US moves the thermostat even higher . . . Psychological warfare – and possibly real preparations for armed action – are pursued by the US.

Vice President Cheney is going to the Middle East – to practically all countries there! Is this to sell an American armed action against Iraq? German troops – not so many – are to go for some months to Kuwait for joint exercises on the detection of biological, chemical and nuclear weapons use . . . Part of a war on nerves or real – or both . . . ?

Saturday 9 February 2002

Hard work. I finished a draft today of my lecture to our fifth training course. It also contains a good deal of messages to the Iraqis, about the burden of proof, etc. Tomorrow I must start writing the paper for Tokyo on 'Efforts (including international inspection) to prevent the proliferation of WMD to states and terrorists'.

Sunday Night, 10 February 2002

I have had a rather good day. Managed to write four pages of my presentation for the Tokyo workshop on proliferation in March.

Had a superb dinner. Bought three rather small pieces of tenderloin yesterday. At reduced price. Last day of sale. I have noticed that this gives a good chance that they are mature and tender. They were excellent. I added purée of parsnip. Wow! Shame I had no red wine. But it is Sunday and a heavy day ahead. So, tea had to do.

Wednesday 20 February 2002, Stockholm

The College of Commissioners in Geneva 18–19 Feb. went well. We had quite a lively discussion about the prospects of going into Iraq. It was clear that the Russian, Yuri Fedotov, was not in the mood for restraining us. The College discussed in fair detail our role of verifying contracts under the new regime of Oil for Food. It seems likely that the new resolution on oil for food will be taken in May, at the latest. The 'clarifications necessary for implementation of Res. 1284' are not discussed and I doubt they will be . . . This was always a device under which the Russians intended to modify 1284 to try to make it more palatable to the Iraqis. However, the US is not going to take one step to make 1284 more palatable to Iraq. If Iraq does not accept the mandatory resolution, well then force is needed . . . This is in good conformity with the legal situation. The US is on more shaky ground if it holds that regardless of Iraqi cooperation the US will intervene to topple the Iraqi government. Hints to this effect are frequent and they have the good effect that the Iraqis may be more inclined to call for inspection to pre-empt the US. If armed action seems really credible and certain, on the other hand, there will be no incentive for Iraq to accept inspection. Why suffer inspectors if you are going to be invaded anyway?

TOP JOBS IN THE UN

I learned in Geneva that the Russian UN perm. rep., Lavrov, had been offered to succeed my old friend Vladimir Petrovsky as head of the UN office in Geneva (with a wonderful residence on the UN grounds), but he had declined. Lavrov had also been offered the disarmament department which Dhanapala now has, but he had felt that was too unimportant. Well, I think Geneva is even less significant.

Friday 22 February 2002 in Stockholm

I went from Geneva to Stockholm and yesterday (21 Feb.) we had a reception for Eva's colleagues at the Foreign Office, saying farewell, as she is retiring at the end of this month. Some thirty to forty persons. Speeches and handover of big flower bouquets and presents. Eva had made quiche lorraine and bought all kind of pâtés and cheeses. I made guacamole and acted as chief butler.

Monday 25 February 2002. Back in New York

While in Stockholm, I saw Pål Wrange about the Stockholm *Declaration* (*on the UN Environment Conference 1972*). Pål is a good lawyer. He had brought in a young staff to dig into the dossiers. With very good results. I got the whole stack of papers in copy and having gone through it I have a somewhat better idea what I might dwell on in my presentation in Stockholm on the thirtieth anniversary of the Stockholm Declaration, 23 May.

On Saturday 23 – *still in Stockholm* – took a walk with Eva in Lill-Jansskogen *and on Monday 25 February before embarking for* NY *I had a meeting with State Secretary* Dahlgren. I thought I owed it to him and the government to tell them that I want to return home as early as possible on condition that I do not jeopardize the work of UNMOVIC and that it does not look as if I fled from the job. After all, when I was persuaded to take the job, I was told it might be for a year or a year and a half. We were also agreed that the Europeans were a bit too negative to the American position on Iraq. They urged a multilateral approach and one based on diplomacy, claiming the need for a 'political' solution. OK, but does anyone think that Saddam would do away with his weapons of mass destruction unless he is under strong military pressure??

In NY *this afternoon (25 Feb.)* Vladimir Gratchev in SG's office told me on the phone that the Iraqis are coming for talks with the SG (and me) on Thursday 7 March, i.e. next week. Excellent. Then there is no collision with my trip to Japan and to Italy. It now only remains to find that the European Bank is not scheduling a Chernobyl meeting inconveniently to complicate our wedding anniversary trip to Italy ... We have asked Giorgio (*Giacomelli*) to go ahead with the booking of the hotel (Santa Lucia in Naples).

Wednesday 27 February 2002

Began with a visit to the February President of the Security Council – a Mexican. Then came our American Commissioner, Assistant Secretary John Wolf, with a number of associates, Jim Cunningham, Tom Duffy and two or three more. At my side, I had only Rachel Davies. John warned us against any polemics against the statements by Secretary of Defense, Rumsfeld, that inspections in Iraq would have to be much more intrusive than they had been and that UNSCOM had only done some 'snooping around' and relied on defectors. You cannot win an argument against a saint ... The frustration of the State Department was obvious.

After lunch came CNN with Mr David Ensor. It was not easy. I have since seen the passages that he let go to the screen today. It was a long interview. What they showed on CNN this time was only a short passage. What did they select? Was I soft? Interesting that this claim – which no government has ever advanced – comes back so often. It really emanates from David Kay, Milhollin and perhaps a few other UNSCOM fans. My answer to Ensor was not particularly good. I said I do not like to shout. Soft speaking and strong leverage should be enough. I also said – and it was fortunately included – that cosmetic inspections are worse than none.

Saturday 2 March 2002

Everything now seems to be working out for the trip to Japan and Italy. Leaving New York on Sunday 10 March and back Tuesday 26. First Tokyo and one day for the Foreign Ministry (I am now more interesting to them as the Iraqi issue is getting to the centre), then two days of public and closed discussions. Then to Rome and Tuscany for the weekend. Sunday 17 March is our fortieth wedding anniversary. On Monday 18 March we go by train to Rome and to Naples, where we stay until the Friday 22 to see Pompeii, Capri, Vesuvius, Sorrento. Then fly to Stockholm and on Sunday 24 to London. Meeting with the Chernobyl Shelter Fund on Monday. Dinner with John Ritch (*World Nuclear Association*) Monday evening. On Tuesday morning perhaps UK intelligence, then Foreign Office talk and round-table lunch. Then off to New York. Hope nothing will intervene (from Iraq) in this beautiful schedule ...

Lectures to write. First comes my introduction to our latest quarterly report to the Security Council. It does not have to be long but should be well targeted. The report is public, but the introduction is not. Then I have to write a thirty-minute presentation for Tokyo on non-proliferation. I have struggled with it and must finalize it this weekend. Then I have to prepare a twenty-minute presentation for Columbia University which will give me the Wolfgang Friedmann award 11 April. Lastly a thirty-minute piece about the Stockholm Environment Declaration for 23 May.

THE UNRESOLVED DISARMAMENT ISSUES (UDI)

I am concerned about the process of analysing and formulating these issues. There may be about eighty of them. The raw texts that came out of the hands of the experts and the seminars are not neat and disciplined pieces ending with precise questions. I have Jarmo Sareva, Ewen Buchanan, John Scott and Surya Sinha working on them. If we were not to get into Iraq it would be nevertheless important that we have defined the questions we think are open. There should not be only the report by UNSCOM (UN Doc. 1999/94). That report was written in the spirit that 'if we get the answers to these few questions, then it is all over'. I think if anything it was too mild in tone. Rather consistently it seemed to assume that all that was needed was more documentation supporting Iraqi contentions. What it should have said – more starkly – was that if documentation could not be produced, we could not exclude that such and such a weapon still existed in such and such quantity. If we all suspect that Iraq may retain weapons, why not say so?

Congressional hearings on Iraq. Senate Committee on Governmental Affairs. 1 March. Bob Einhorn, the former Assistant Secretary for Non-Proliferation, now in the Centre for Strategic International Studies (CSIS) had a superb analysis which largely supported the idea of US armed action against Iraq. He noted that inspection would be of value for making it more difficult for Iraq to run its weapons programmes but pointed rightly to the fact that after a year or so Iraq might again throw out the inspectors. Another testimony came from Richard Spertzel, the former bio inspector. Very expert and very alarming. Charles Duelfer, Andrew Cordesman (both from CSIS) and, yes, David Kay. Congress gets pretty expert views!

Wednesday 6 March

Talks with the Iraqi foreign minister tomorrow. It will be Kofi, Ralph Zacklin (from Legal in the absence of Hans Corell), Kofi's two lieutenants i.e. Gratchev and Moller, the spokesman, Fred Eckhard, my assistant Jarmo, and a note taker. On the Iraqi side, the foreign minister, Naji Sabri, Amb. Saed Hasan (former UN perm. rep.), Mohamed al-Douri, present UN perm. rep., General Hosama Amin, head of the National Monitoring Directorate, plus two younger fellows from the foreign ministry.

Iraq can be expected to first say they have fulfilled Res. 687. Hence sanctions should be lifted. More interesting might be to hear what kind of 'package' they want to go for. They may say they are not averse to inspection, but their experiences were very bad. Can they have a guarantee that it is only for a year? A guarantee that there are no spies?

It is entirely possible that they simply want to look a little more ready for inspection in order to encourage Europeans and others to protest to the US that it must not launch an attack just when the Iraqis are getting better behaved ... However, it is clear that the Iraqis would not have moved one inch in this direction if the US had not threatened to be 'ill behaved' ... Thus, perhaps simply a dilatory action.

Media which have hardly observed us in the past year have woken up with a vengeance. I have had three or four TV interviews and lots of newspapers coming. Barbara Crosette reported in the *NY Times* today. Quite good. Ragida Dergsham wrote a whole page (!) in the London issued Al Hayat. Also positive, it appears. On the whole, I have come out rather hard-line. What I do is to stick to strict interpretations of the resolutions.

Saturday 9 March 2002

The Iraqis were here on Thursday (7 March). A lot of media attention. Kofi Annan tried to keep the meeting small, but there were fifteen of us anyway: Gratchev, Moller, Ralph Zacklin, me, Jarmo, Fred Eckhard (spokesman) plus a note taker. The Iraqi foreign minister, Sabri (former newspaper man), brought Amb. Hasan (former perm.

rep. NY), General Amin (head of the National Monitoring Directorate), al-Douri (present perm. rep. NY) plus three. It is too many. Kofi did have several meetings with the minister only. I hope he was less diplomatic and more blunt in those.

My main impression was that if Sabri genuinely believed in what he said, they live in a different world. In his eyes Iraq is wronged by sanctions, by no-fly zones and by threats of invasion and subversion. The main problem – as they see it – is how Iraq can get confidence in the Security Council! As Iraq has fulfilled its obligation and done away with all its weapons of mass destruction, the Security Council only has to lift the sanctions. Not a word of recognition that the Council does not have confidence in Iraq. In their world, only two states – the US and the UK – doubt Iraq. I can well understand that they harp on the no-fly zones because the legal basis is feeble. However, they should recognize that the Council does not give them credence on the weapons.

Other participants who had been present a year ago thought the atmosphere was dramatically better and noted that they did not say they ruled out inspection. Well, what can they do? They are not ready to say that they will accept inspection. If they were to say that, this would indicate that they are beginning to negotiate and they are not ready for that. If they have decided they must accept inspection, I have no doubt that they will say 'provided that . . . '. So, to say something now about inspections they must do it in the form of a lament . . .

Reading their nineteen points in the quiet of my room it strikes me much more than when I listened to them that although they press for being treated not as a culprit but a state on equal footing with all others, they nevertheless are raising the question of inspection and asking specific questions. I translate them into frank language.

> How many disarmament questions remain? How much has been cleared up? Answer: We do not know until we have received new declarations and done essential re-baselining and formulated our work programme. If a list of items were given to them now they would start negotiating about it.
> Alleging that US and UK alone believe questions are open, what needs to be inspected? How long will it take? How are inspections to be done? Iraq is not against the idea of inspection ('We are not against certainty as a principle'). However, which sites, what activities? Iraq seeks to limit the scope . . .
> 10. New inspectors could be used again to spy again on Iraqi leadership. Is this a way of objecting to inspection of palaces?
> 11. Can the UN guarantee that new inspectors are not spies? Answer: Is there really any information that would be useful for US? Perhaps it would be to know which industries do not contain anything weapons-related; they would be spared attack in case of conflict . . .
> 12. Here they talk even of 'the coming inspection formula'.
> 13. How long will inspection have to go on? And: what methods will the inspectors employ. Are they compatible with 'relevant international conventions'?

14. How can there be US and UK members on the inspection teams?
15. How can UNMOVIC re-employ persons from UNSCOM (Smidovich and Mitrokhin)?
16. What are the limits of the powers of the chairman? How will the SG supervise the work of UNMOVIC?

Thursday 28 March 2002. New York

The Korean laundry-shop man said I looked tired as I picked up my laundry this evening. Maybe. I came back here Tuesday night and have been two days in the office. Two days in the office were well calculated, however, to fix the essentials. Last night I was invited by my Vienna friends Horst and Rita Jeschek for dinner at a posh Viennese restaurant in the Tribeca area: the Danube. The dinner reminded me of Chinese banquets where you never know what you have eaten and how much remains.

Good Friday 29 March 2002

Arab summit in Beirut. It ended yesterday with the main news being a strong endorsement of the peace vision of the Saudi Crown Prince: peace and normalized relations offered to Israel in return for a complete evacuation of occupied land. The new move is regrettably shaken by a Palestine suicide bomber succeeding in killing a large number of Israelis at a Passover supper.

On Iraq there was also remarkable news. Iraq has promised to respect the independence and borders of Kuwait. How credible such a statement is one might query, but it might well silence the Kuwaitis in the public discussion. There seems also to have been some kind of mutual non-aggression agreement between the two. Perhaps this will mean that no American attack on Iraq could be launched from Kuwait. The Summit also declared that any attack on Iraq would be seen as an attack on all Arab countries. The disenchantment with the US's Israel bias is costly . . . I did not see any request to Iraq to implement UN resolutions. Maybe it is somewhere. The CNN website had nothing at all about the summit! The NYT reported that the Iraqi minister of information, Sahaf (former foreign minister?), had said that Iraq was ready to implement UN resolutions if anything did, indeed, remain to be implemented. My hunch is that the position of the summit in combination with the removed imminence of any US armed attack will lead the Iraqis – in effect – to reject inspection as we explain them. They may say that there are no guarantees against espionage, etc. They will drag it out. So long as they do not see the armed threat as real, they will not let inspectors in, only appear to be positive. The US, of course, will not take one step back from Res. 1284 and the stalemate will continue. Meanwhile, the US and the UK will seek to show that Iraq is again producing weapons of mass destruction. In three weeks time I shall be in the SG's meeting with the Iraqi foreign minister and explain how we plan to run our inspections . . .

Easter Saturday 30 March 2002

Full moon. New York is never so attractive as when the moon hangs over the East River. It does tonight. Actually, more in the direction of La Guardia. A full yellow moon. Everything else within sight is man-made.

Dialogue with Iraq. I have spent today working on a presentation at the next meeting with the Iraqi foreign minister. The New Yorker today has an article in which they predict US military action in the fall. The planning is so advanced. They assume that either the Iraqis won't accept inspections as required or that once inspections start, they Iraqis will thwart action. Not such bad hypotheses . . .

Easter Sunday 31 March 2002

Yesterday I celebrated alone. Spent the day working on a presentation for the meeting with the Iraqi foreign minister 18 April. A little shopping at my favourite Korean grocery store. For supper I had – necessarily at Easter – a hard-boiled egg topped by anchovy (a whole tin!). Then puréed parsnip and pastrami. As dessert fresh raspberries. And after, a piece of marzipan (incredibly from the Korean store . . .).

America – the Empire. There is a good deal of writings about this subject. After the collapse of the Soviet Union and Communism it was the US – the only superpower. Now it is the empire. Incomparably stronger and more powerful than anybody else in every respect. Richard Perle can say that they don't need any agreements (on disarmament at any rate); they can take care of anything and should not feel constrained by obligations. Richard Haas seems to say that, yes, they need agreements and multilateral cooperation, but two things cannot be tolerated: spread of weapons of mass destruction and governments waging 'genocide' on their own populations. I have no difficulty in understanding the view on WMD. A further spread of ABC weapons and long-range missiles is certainly scary. But it would be becoming if the old sinners who started down this road also articulated the aim of ridding themselves of the stuff in the end.

As to 'genocide', real genocide is not common: Rwanda, Cambodia. However, governments which terrorize their own populations are more common: Iraq, Afghanistan with the Taliban, Uganda under Idi Amin. I think it would be justified to move the goalposts in the UN Charter and accept intervention in these cases even if international peace and security were not threatened by national terrorism. However, it would still be preferable to have a Security Council decision. I am not sure that the US would bother with that. However, would the US really care to take the lead in military operations that might be costly in lives and material merely to prevent people from being terrorized by their own governments? If there was no threat to oil supplies or the terrorism spreading to other countries? I doubt it. In Iraq, it is the oil and the stability of the Gulf that underpins the demand for intervention. In Afghanistan it was the risk of the country serving as a base for terrorist acts against the US. Thus, again self-interest – not the idea of liberating a people from its own oppressors. The liberation should really come from the organized international community – the UN. But, again, who will pay in lives and money for such interventions? It will only happen when the feeling of global solidarity is sufficiently strong. Perhaps that will come through media exposure. Governments are likely by themselves to calculate more coldly why they should use resources to stop oppression that does not threaten their countries. People in general may be more inclined to act on the moral feeling that certain things cannot be tolerated even in remote places.

I wonder whether the US 'empire' discussions are not a bit premature. After Afghanistan some of their theoretical strategists seem a little dizzy. They can do anything ... All the more now that the recession appears to be over, and the US might be sailing into good growth again. There is nothing that holds them down to the earth. This may pass. Japan was a bit dizzy, too, with confidence fed by their booming economy. They are more restrained now. East Asia in general was heady when the economies boomed. Asian values were superior to Western. With the bust, modesty returned. It would be becoming if all showed modesty and awareness that neither success nor failure is in only one place. The Europeans will need to get their act together. They are certainly handicapped compared with the US by their different languages and cultures. However, it is moving. The (European) Union is in many respects awful but is it surprising that integration of countries which have fought each other through the centuries will take many decades to unite?

Sunday 7 April 2002

Speech at Columbia. On Thursday (11 April) I shall receive the Friedmann award at Columbia and I am asked to speak about international law topics for some twenty minutes. That means about ten pages. I have now about ten, mostly about various treaty law problems that I have encountered in practice. Will now switch to implementation – compliance – peer review and inspection.

Iraq dialogue. Saw Kofi Annan Friday afternoon. He will try to limit the meeting with the Iraqis so that we can finish before lunch on Friday 19 and have time to go before the Security Council and see the media. I am sure there will be a lot of interest.

The Iraqi delegation has a lot of weapons specialists, headed by the General Amir al-Sa'adi, senior adviser to Saddam Hussein and knowledgeable about the whole Iraqi weapons programme. This might suggest that they would attempt to get into a discussion of substance – which would be inappropriate at this stage. We must think through how we respond to various proposals and requests from them.

Michael Gordon came out with his interview with me in the *New York Times* today. No damage. We do not appear naïve, just 'stoic' ... Got the interview in the

Figaro. It was excellent! Tonight, Swedish TV should have the interview that Lisa Karlsson did with me last Friday. She was kind but knew very little, so the questions were repeatedly 'Do you think they will let you in?' 'How soon will you get in?' 'What have you been doing all this time?' Colin Lynch of the Washington Post is the other extreme. He knows too much and asked as his first question: 'Do you plan to go by the "modalities agreement"?' This is to get into really sensitive stuff ... I tried to avoid being pinned down too much.

THE BUSH–BLAIR MEETING

Bush went out directly and said it was his government's policy to remove Saddam. Blair said they were agreed that Iraq would be better off without Saddam. They were also agreed that Iraq had used weapons of mass destruction and must be rid of them. All options were open. Bush said maybe he should be more nuanced ...

Friday 12 April 2002

The Iraqis are not coming next week. A likely reason for them to postpone is that they don't want to appear conciliatory (especially to the US) at the current moment of fighting in the Middle East. Another reason is likely to be that they do not feel that armed US action is imminent yet and need not look positively toward inspection yet give arguments against such action.

A small group of Jarmo, Ewen and Salwa (*Barberi*) are looking into what questions the Iraqis might put to me after my presentation. The composition of their delegation, as reported to us, shows a group very strong in experts in the various disciplines. One gets the impression that they may wish to get into discussions of substance! We will have to counter that we welcome any supplementary information they may have. It may help in our analysis. However, the Security Council has not envisaged our replacing inspections and verification in Iraq by discussions in New York ...

Given the Friedmann award at Columbia (Thursday 11 April). Friedmann was a German-born, Jewish professor at Columbia. He was killed by some thug in Morningside Heights in the 70s. In his memory an award is given every year to some prominent international lawyer. The first two to get it were Jessup and Lissitzyn. Others were Steve Schwebel, Jack Stevenson, Rosalyn Higgins, Boutros Ghali ... So, I felt honoured.

It was a much bigger affair than I had thought. Oscar Schachter who was to have introduced me had heart surgery the day before, so Dick Gardner did it in his place. I have a liking and admiration for him. He is hard-headed and constructive. This is the combination that I like. The American Conservative hawks are just hard-headed – not constructive. And most of the 'idealists' are just constructive.

I had not realized how many young students there would be – perhaps a hundred. Had I realized this composition of the audience I might have stressed more the things that lie ahead for international law and spoken less about things that I have experienced. Well, I missed that chance. Even so I received a very gracious letter of thanks from the editor of the Journal who said that many participants had told her that this was one of the best banquets in many years (I hope they meant my speech, not the chicken ...).

20 April

IRAQ. The meeting that should have taken place in the past week was postponed and is now likely to take place 1–3 May.

I have spent a great deal of time and effort in the past weeks on preparing a statement answering the Iraqi questions in the sphere of UNMOVIC and on writing a paper with possible questions and answers. I have sat up until midnight every evening in the past week.

I learnt some time ago that the Pentagon had asked the CIA about me and got an answer that was much more positive than they would have liked. This burst into public view last Monday, when the Washington Post (Colum Lynch and my old pal Walter Pincus) had the inquiry on its first page ... Chance had it that I had agreed with the Post to come to them that very morning (15 *April*) to speak with the editorial board. Well, the editors at the Post were fairly sceptical about inspection but I don't think they found me *naive*. It is not that inspection is a panacea. To be sure it has weaknesses. It is rather that the alternative of invasion also has many drawbacks ...

As Jarmo Sareva, my assistant, and I got to Reagan airport (15 *April*) Kofi Annan reached me on my mobile phone and wanted to tell me how angry they were about the Wolfowitz (Pentagon) inquiry at the CIA. They termed it an attempt to 'intimidate' an international official. I did not feel it that way. I thought it was a bit silly, but I had no difficulty in seeing that they want to discredit the idea of inspection in all possible ways: the method is hopeless and the people who will do it are softies ...

What is more remarkable is that the US can allow itself to have a President, a National Security Adviser and a Secretary of State who all say that they insist upon UN inspections while at the same time the Secretary of Defense (Rumsfeld) publicly expresses serious doubts that inspections are meaningful. He even casts doubt on UNSCOM, saying that they only found a few things and then only when defectors had given them tips where to look ... As if inspectors should go around at random or – even worse – try to examine every square inch of a large country ...

Most likely is that now that *since* the US is heavily engaged in the Israeli mess and the – less visible – Afghani troubles, Iraq will drag its feet. However, the US planning of invasion and gradual deployment of staff and weapons to the area continues. I think they will first see if Iraq accepts inspection. If they do not then the US can say: OK, that is it. Now we go for it. And if inspections are accepted, they expect that soon enough there will be denial of access or other trouble and they can say: OK, we have had enough. Now we go for it ... The worst scenario for Pentagon hawks would be if the Iraqis really were cooperative with tough and effective inspections. Well, the risks are not that great. The indications are that the spots have not disappeared from the leopard ...

Going to China and Russia. Tomorrow, direct to Tokyo (21 April), then two hours on the ground, then four hours more to Beijing. However, we have two easy days in China before the politically interesting things start with a meeting with Mr Qian, the Deputy Prime Minister in charge of Foreign Affairs. It is an interesting structure they have had for a long time, with a senior cabinet minister in charge and a foreign minister under him. Since I have known Qian for many years, I get to see him.

On Saturday next week (27 April) we fly on to Moscow. Have a free Sunday and then to see Foreign Minister Ivanov on the Monday. Then back to NY on the Tuesday and on Wednesday (1 May) we shall meet the Iraqis. A tight schedule that includes a meeting with the 'quartet' – Ivanov, Powell, European Union and Annan.

Saturday 4 May 2002. New York

The above schedule was followed. The trip was not quite as tiring as I had feared.

Both in New York and at Narita in Tokyo I had to take off my shoes for inspection in the security control and they examined my hand luggage including the toilet kit. I had neither nail clipper nor razor so there were no problems.

Stayed in Beijing's Hilton International (22 April), which was fine. But the air in Beijing was terrible. They get a lot of dust from the Gobi apparently and much smog from all the cars. On our last day we were taken for sight-seeing to the 'lanes'. This is something new. So much of old and squalid Beijing has been torn down and given way to high-rise buildings (storing people vertically ...) that they now are determined to keep some old parts as they were – one-storey square, grey cement blocks with an atrium in the middle. We were told that these blocks were laid out by the Manchus around a well. Now tourists are taken around to look at these somewhat slummy – but centrally located and valuable – old residential areas. It is not the elegance of the modern city they show but the nostalgic picturesque primitive quarters of the past!

Talks in Beijing were fine. I had an hour with Qian (25 April) who had aged a bit since my last visit two years ago. He and I are the same age – which he, too, had noticed. I told him that Kofi Annan recently had opened the conference on the aged (in Madrid) on his own sixty-fourth birthday and cited a Beatles song saying 'who will need me, who will feed me when I am sixty-four ...'. I told Qian that I had consoled Kofi by telling him that there was hope even at seventy-four. It may well be that this quip was lost on my vintage friend, but a journalist who interviewed me a few days later and who had been present at the beginning of my meeting with Qian had heard and was amused. Both in the talk with Qian and the round table led by Vice Foreign Minister Wang, which I had in the Foreign Ministry, there was great scepticism about the Iraqis and good support for UNMOVIC. But in their public accounts of our meetings, they cite themselves as stressing that they want a peaceful solution and use of diplomacy ... As they have little trade with Iraq (not like Russia) and are eager that the US shall use the Security Council, they are ready to take steps toward the US position to have joint action rather than US unilateralism.

On the second day (23 *April*) we were flown (forty minutes) to Dalian (old Port Arthur). It is now a model city – with over 5 million people. Already from the plane you could see that they had advanced town planning. Houses in any given area were of the same height. There is lots of colour and broad streets. No bicycles. Question is how economic it is. Just a showcase? They have a huge locomotive industry and lots of petrochemical plus the old harbour. Was or is China's third largest (*port*) (after Shanghai and Hong Kong)? Their dynamic mayor gave a 'banquet' in our honour and we realized that many prominent foreigners are taken there: Boutros Ghali, Kissinger, Schroeder, Klaus Topfer et al. I was given a beautiful suite in the Shangri La Hotel. Dalian was Russian until 1906 when the city was lost to the Japanese. One can still see the influences on the architecture from both periods, though most is new. The other day someone slipped me a paper notice that a North China aeroplane had crashed into the sea just outside Dalian when approaching Dalian! All were killed ...

The Talks in Moscow. 29 April 2002

We had Sunday for rest in Moscow; stayed at the Arbat which belongs to the Presidency's industrial (?) enterprises ... Old hotel of the Central Committee. Had been refurbished. Still not up to modern standards, but not too big and sufficiently comfortable. On the Sunday we were taken to the Hermitage and saw centuries of gifts to the Russian tsars from the royal houses all over. The collection is well displayed. We also saw the collection of jewels and gold and platinum of the Russian Treasure. Also well displayed. Then we had lunch at an Italian place outside Kreml, Sbarro. Food OK, but a pickpocket stole Jarmo's fine digital camera worth 700 dollars. Bitter. We went to the Pushkin Museum and admired the marvellous collection of Gauguins and French nineteenth-century painters: a couple of splendid van Goghs (the prison march).

On my way from the airport to the hotel I went to the Swedish Embassy and saw Sven and Marianne Hirdman and had a nice chat on their terrace. Sven has been given another year but intends thereafter to leave the service. He is now a doyen in Moscow. He was very negative to an American invasion of Iraq.

The talks in the Russian foreign ministry (*on Monday 29 April*) were led by Vice Foreign Minister Saltanov, a highly sophisticated diplomat with the Middle East as his specialty. I had the feeling of a good deal of support for the UNMOVIC mission. And a good deal of frustration with their Iraqi relations. The later talks with (*Foreign Minister*) Ivanov were a little less easy. I said I thought the only thing the US cared about in Iraq were the weapons of mass destruction. If they were taken out the US would not bother about human rights. Ivanov evidently thought that the US wanted to establish its control in the region.

Saturday 11 May 2002

It is one week later (*since the entry of 4 May above*). The notes recorded below about the meeting with the Iraqis (1–3 May) and about follow-up were sent up to the thirty-eighth floor yesterday.

It seems fairly settled that the next meeting in the 'dialogue' will be in Vienna 31 May and 1 June, a Friday and a Saturday. So we have moved our College of Commissioners from New York to Vienna to take place Weds 29 and Thu 30 May. I shall come from Stockholm, where I am giving a talk about the Stockholm 1972 Environment declaration on 23 May.

It is really thrilling to see where the Iraqis are going. Foreign Minister Sabri has given the New York meeting a positive spin on his return to Baghdad, while Tariq Aziz has said that they cannot accept inspection so long as the US threatens with invasion. However, the US will certainly not withdraw that threat, so Iraq might be painting itself into the corner if it were to make acceptance dependent upon a withdrawal of the US threat. The US would want nothing better than an Iraqi refusal. Iraq's best chance lies, in my view, in accepting inspection and appearing to make them a success. It would then be difficult for the US to attack. Iraq might realize this but prefer to wait as long as possible. The US invasion would require quite a lot and while the planning is going forward here, the actual mounting (*of an invasion*) is a graver step.

While the spin in Baghdad – possibly to prepare Iraqi public opinion for new inspections – was positive, the Iraqis seem to have spread the word in New York that Blix had been as bad as UNSCOM. Either they are hoping that missions here will try to press me to be softer or they are beginning to prepare the ground for rejecting new inspections on the grounds that UNMOVIC under Blix is as bad as UNSCOM. *We'll see at* the talks in Vienna.

Monday 6 May 2002. Iraq

Below is my analysis of the meeting last week (1–3 May) with Iraq's foreign minister and high (weapons) officials and the Secretary-General, me and others:

At the meetings 1–3 May, Iraq continued to claim:

- that it is the innocent victim of a US/UK-led UN Security Council, which does not lift sanctions, although Iraq has fulfilled all the harsh obligations laid upon it,
- that it abandoned its weapons of mass destruction programmes long ago and has presented all the documents and evidence there were,

- that it was scandalously harassed and mistreated by UNSCOM, which acted for a few member state and ...
- that it is subjected to the threat of aggression and illegally imposed no-fly zones.

The Iraqi delegation further stated:

- that it cannot be expected to persuade its country to accept resumed inspection, if it is under the threat of aggression,
- that Security Council Resolution 1284 is vague, ambiguous and unimplementable,
- that the resolution requires clarification and a comprehensive approach,
- that it sees some points on which UNMOVIC differs favourably from UNSCOM but feels some concerns (which were not specified) as well,
- that it would like to learn that UNMOVIC differs from UNSCOM not only in organization and plans but also in its assessment of disarmament issues and remaining tasks.

While the Iraqi delegation said that UNMOVIC should not expect any new evidence forthcoming on weapons issues, it became known during the meeting that Iraq will soon return as much as 90 per cent of the Kuwaiti state archives to Kuwait.

The Iraqi side said it had expected that the very experienced and high-level weapons experts whom they had brought along would have an opportunity during the days of talk to learn from UNMOVIC how it assessed the 'unresolved disarmament issues'.

It is hard to understand how the Iraqi side could have expected that any meaningful discussion of substantive and complicated disarmament issues could have been undertaken in the course of two days.

While welcoming any new Iraqi comments or data on unresolved disarmament issues that were listed in 1999 by UNSCOM (doc. S/1999/94) and by the Amorim Report (S/1999/396), I (UNMOVIC Executive Chairman) declined to enter into a discussion of the substance of issues. *I (Blix)* said that UNMOVIC would have to follow the procedure laid down in Resolution 1284 and present a draft list of 'key remaining disarmament tasks' in a work programme to be submitted to the Council. This, however, would only be after UNMOVIC had started to work in Iraq, received requisite declarations by Iraq and had performed essential re-baselining inspections.

Next Steps

At the conclusion of the meeting the Iraqi foreign minister said that it was necessary to 'develop confidence'. Perhaps we can be a little more precise as to what is needed: the inspection authorities cannot base their work on confidence in unilateral Iraqi declarations. If they had such confidence, why should they inspect? Rather they are to seek evidence that proscribed programmes are ended, that proscribed items have been eradicated and that nothing has been revived. When they find convincing evidence to that effect, supporting Iraqi declarations, they will report accordingly, which should lead to confidence.

It may, of course, further be justified to talk about the need for a measure of confidence between the inspecting and the inspected parties, namely, as a basis for both the dispatch and the acceptance of inspections. Iraq may need to feel confidence that UNMOVIC will act independently as a UN body and in accordance with its declared procedures and plans for effective inspection. UNMOVIC, on its part, needs to feel confidence that Iraq will respect its obligations to facilitate inspection, e.g. at all times guarantee the security and safety of UNMOVIC staff, at no time reject inspectors of certain nationalities and give access as required.

Iraq's future attitude to inspections may well be chiefly influenced by its assessment of the risk of armed action against it . . . If it deems (*armed*) action possible but not certain it might invite the resumption of inspections in the hope that a period of trouble-free inspections will make it politically harder to start armed action and might eventually lead to a suspension of sanctions.

Inspections having that result would require 'cooperation in all respects' by Iraq. Would the Government of Iraq be ready to provide such cooperation? In practical matters, like providing access to sites and accepting air operations by UNMOVIC, cooperation would only be a question of goodwill and should not cause much of a difficulty. Iraq might find it harder, having repeatedly claimed there existed no new evidence, to turn around and present sufficient new evidence to solve some remaining unresolved disarmament tasks. Even the 'discovery' of another chicken farm might be felt as an embarrassment. Yet the claim that no more evidence exists may be a negotiating position and some way might be found to present proscribed items that had been 'forgotten' somewhere or bring more evidence. If Iraq could not – or would not – provide 'forgotten items' or new evidence resulting in 'progress' in the resolution of key remaining disarmament tasks, these would regrettably remain unresolved.

It would seem that a third meeting could be constructive for both sides, if it were to address and seek clarifications and understandings on a number of matters that are practically important for a future launching and operation of inspections.

Indeed, if the full benefits were to be attained from an acceptance of inspections under Resolution 1284, there would have to be 'cooperation in all respects'. Only a prior understanding of practical arrangements in line with existing agreements and Security Council resolutions would give some assurance that controversies and crises would not arise when inspections were launched and operated.

A list of items could be drawn up in advance to allow the sides to prepare themselves for discussions. Below are examples of what could be included in such a list on the subject of inspection:

Clarification of a number of practical arrangements connected with the starting up and operation of inspections, e.g.:

- regarding BOMVIC (*Bagdad Office of UNMOVIC*), including upgrading of bio-lab,
- entry and exit of inspectors,

- accommodation of inspectors,
- international air links and landing place in Iraq,
- air operations inside Iraq,
- regional offices,
- cooperation between NMD (*National Monitoring Directorate*) and UNMOVIC,
- communications, etc.

NOTE

Between 11 May (the last diary entry before the summer) and 30 July 2002, computer diary accounts are missing – whether because they were not written or have been lost. My pocket calendar shows the following Iraq-relevant events during that period:

29–30 May: College of Commissioners in Vienna
6 June: Security Council briefing
18 June: Washington meeting with Rice – Powell – Biden (Chair of Senate Foreign Relations Committee)
4–5 July: Third round of Iraq talks – in Vienna
16–17 July: Paris meetings with Villepin, Errera and MoD

Some non-computer recorded notes from this period were found. One concerned my thoughts on remaining in the job; another that covered the three sessions of the Secretary-General's so-called dialogue with Iraq during the first half of 2000; a third about the Paris visit 16–17 July.

First Note: On My Contract

Before Xmas last year I talked to Kofi Annan and said I would want to be released. It had been expected that the job would be for a year or a year and a half. It was soon two years that I had been here. Kofi was understanding. We discussed the matter again in early 2002. I maintained my wish but indicated also a readiness to stay until around 1 July. The reason was that I wanted to see finalized the two analytical documents, which had taken so much time: the one about the unresolved disarmament issues and the other about the clustering of these issues. They should be ready by the end of the spring. I would like to have them ready to serve the Security Council as a kind of UNMOVIC testament, if we were not to get in.

I am 'lucky' that we have not been called upon to report on our analytical efforts. If we had been invited to inspections, we would have had to make up our minds about the list of 'key remaining disarmament tasks' without sufficient analytical basis …

If I tried to leave now it would be interpreted the wrong way by all: as an escape before a possible and difficult period of inspection or as a protest against US plans for invasion which make inspection pointless.

Second Note: On the Three Sessions of the Secretary-General's 'Dialogue' with Iraq during the First Half of 2000: The First, in March in New York, the Second, in Early May in New York and the Third in Early July in Vienna

The meetings were initiated by the Iraqis after Amr Moussa, the Secretary General of the Arab League had met with Saddam Hussein and – *inter alia* – praised me as very different from Butler ... Iraq asked for talks without any preconditions. Kofi Annan responded positively but noted that he had to act on the basis of existing resolutions. The Iraqis raised no objection to UNMOVIC chairman taking part. This was seen as a step forward, as Iraq had earlier been consistent in ignoring UNMOVIC. I made a presentation of UNMOVIC at the first meeting (7 *March. Comment on the meeting in entry above*). Little they did not know before, as my four lectures to future inspectors are on our website and they probably get all our documents for the College of Commissioners.

The first meeting ended by Minister Naji Sabri presenting nineteen questions to Kofi Annan. About half of them concerned inspection. The rest were about no-fly zones, US threats, the lifting of sanctions and other things that the SG could not very well answer and on which the Security Council would not have a common view.

At the second meeting (*1–2 May. Also commented on above*) Iraq had asserted that the principal problem was how Iraq could regain confidence in the United Nations. I pointed out that it was not just the US and the UK that were concerned about the possible retention by Iraq of weapons of mass destruction. The whole Council referred to 'unresolved disarmament issues' and 'key remaining disarmament tasks'.

The May meeting with the Iraqis comprised also discussions at the 'technical level'. They had brought General al-Sa'adi, reportedly with Cabinet rank and, in any case, totally knowledgeable about the Iraqi weapons of mass destruction programme. They also brought General Amin, who had headed the National Monitoring Directorate (the minders). Lastly, they brought the famous Dr Jaaffar, the father of the planned Iraqi nuclear bomb. These were the 'technical' experts who were to discuss with us. I was a bit perplexed by the initiative. What 'technical' discussions could we have? It became soon clear that what they had in mind was to try to learn what UNMOVIC considered were 'unresolved issues', to discuss them and hopefully to clear them up or else perhaps tell us that if we insisted upon one awkward issue or another, they would consider us biased and would not accept inspection ...

They feigned surprise that I did not want to go into this discussion – apart from giving as an example of an issue we found 'unresolved', the case of anthrax. My main line was that we would go by the order prescribed by the Security Council in Res. 1284: first, unconditional Iraqi acceptance of inspection and a relatively short period of inspections, which would comprise 're-baselining', i.e. inspecting what might have changed since 1998; thereafter, and in light of the results of the re-baselining and submission by Iraq of the backlog of biannual reports, submission to the Security Council of a work programme, listing *inter alia* what we considered to be 'key remaining disarmament tasks'. We would not replace this order, which left the decision to the Council after proposals from us, with negotiation and agreement with Iraq. More directly I said in discussions with the Secretary General that we are not replacing inspection in Iraq by discussions in New York.

At the third meeting – in Vienna during the first days of July (4–5 July) – the Iraqis repeated their line. Already in discussions about the agenda they had tried to make Iraqi and UNMOVIC assessments of what had been achieved and what remained the topic of the technical discussions. We repeated our position that we would welcome if they discussed issues and gave any new material they might have, but we would be mainly in a listening mode. From our side we suggested that we should discuss 'practical arrangements' for inspections. It would be highly undesirable to resume inspection work and quickly get into frictions, clashes and crises. A compromise on the agenda was reached to the effect that both items would be listed, but the first item, 'the assessment', would be Iraq's assessment.

In Vienna al-Sa'adi spent more than an hour going through and criticizing the Amorim Report's list of unresolved priority issues. He said that UNSCOM had sold these issues to the Panel and little notice had been taken of Iraq's comments. In reality the issues were bogus and were meant to serve as excuses to visit military installations and to report to the US. Iraq had eliminated all its WMD, there were no more documents. They wished to hear our assessments, discuss them and agree how to proceed. Thus, again: look at the items, agree on a finite list and an approach to them. Thereafter perhaps an Iraqi agreement to inspection. We made a few comments on their assessments but presented in detail (through Perricos and Mullady) our ideas on practical arrangements for inspection. We said we were not in doubt what UNMOVIC's rights were, but we thought it would be wise to go through the long list. We mentioned the possibility of regional offices in Basra and Mosul (which the Amorim Panel had recommended) and the possible use of U_2 and Mirage planes in the same manner as UNSCOM had done. Al-Sa'adi limited his response to saying that practical matters could probably be solved, if we were agreed on what needed to be analysed . . .

However, the order of proceeding was not the only obstacle to inspection. The Foreign Minister, Sabri, stressed again that the main subjects of the talks were the no-fly zones, the threats to the Iraqi regime, the lifting of sanctions and a zone free of weapons of mass destruction. In the context of the solution of these major items it could be possible to undertake the verification needed to refute the US allegations about weapons of mass destruction. Sabri does not even take the word 'inspection' in his mouth. He talks about 'transparency' or 'certainty' or similar concepts. I have the feeling that he is on tight leash from Saddam and his Revolutionary Council. Perhaps they are caught in their own propaganda: Iraq is innocent (apart from hiding a few things . . .) and subject to completely unjustified encroachments on its sovereignty (no-fly zones) and threats to its integrity (US-threatened invasion). Seven years of inspection is enough. Whatever they have squirrelled away is nobody's business if it cannot be found.

Sabri rejected ElBaradei's suggestion that one might begin with inspection and it might facilitate a solution of the other problems. There is no link, Sabri said (except that they would not go for inspection unless the other issues were included). I retorted that 'I am optimistic. I think there is a link.' Of course, it is conceivable that the US is so hung up on the person of Saddam that it might attack Iraq whether they believe there are WMD or not in the country. However, I doubt this. If they were really convinced that there are hardly any WMD, I suspect they would leave the Iraqis to their dictator. Thus, I think that if the current regime really made an all-out effort at opening up and declaring and destroying what might be left, it would make a strong impression and make it much more difficult for the US to decide on invasion.

I said as much in our 'technical' talks. I said they used to complain about UNSCOM moving the goalposts (when one issue was solved UNSCOM found three new ones), but they, the Iraqis, too, could be said to have moved goalposts: the 'modalities' were meant to 'rectify' the total authority which UNSCOM had had. And what had Iraq gained by this? The Ba'ath Party HQ inspection in 1998 (of a building that had been emptied) which had led to a famous standoff, had simply led to the feeling that Iraq denied access and wanted to hide something. Would it not be wiser to drop all restrictions? To say that inspections are awful and resented but nevertheless open up without any restrictions ... Go for it! I think they were a bit shocked. I did not throw out the so-called 'modalities', but I questioned whether they had been useful to Iraq.

Kofi Annan was quite clear that he would not set a date for a fourth meeting, if there was no significant progress in Vienna. Sabri knew that and he knew that he had delivered the same song in Vienna as in NY. He did not have authority to do more. Yet it is clear that they have an interest in looking eager and open for a dialogue. All the world except the US want to avoid armed action and have some hope that if inspection starts armed action will be more difficult to launch. Iraq may or may not believe this. If they have concluded that US invasion is inevitable, whether or not there is inspection, there would be little reason to invite inspection. However, they must appear as if they are ready to take inspection to satisfy all those who are against US armed action. All the conditions they pile up are relatively sure ways of blocking inspection. So far, they have not met any understanding for their conditions.

Their aversion to inspection could have several other grounds than the fear that invasion is coming anyway. First and foremost, they probably understand that although UNMOVIC will try to be respectful and is different from UNSCOM, we are not soft but will be quite demanding. This could lead to standoffs, denials of access. That would be handing the US precisely the kind of *casus belli* that they now are a bit short of. Another possible explanation could be that they fear that UNMOVIC would find proscribed items. A third could be a genuine fear that UNMOVIC despite efforts would be closely knit with the US and provide the US with information about Iraqi defence arrangements just before the US attack.

After the Vienna meeting Sabri made a couple of statements in which he tries to put the blame on Blix for the stalemate. However, in the main he has repeated their stand, which is not received with much understanding anywhere: a comprehensive solution as mentioned in SC Res. 1382 is what is requested. Perhaps they are under the illusion that Russia and China stand by them. I think they are wrong. Russia and China will talk about the need for a peaceful solution, but they will hardly lift a finger against an American invasion. Their greatest concern about such US action is its unilateral character. They will be left out. The veto loses its value.

The most important obstacle to US intervention is probably inside the US. How costly would the invasion be in terms of life? Is the threat against the US from Iraq sufficient to justify the cost? It seems that the US military are sceptical on this point. They do not think that Saddam is such a threat. He has been kept rather neatly in his box. In the longer run he might be risky, but then at some point he will die ... This has to be weighed against the cost – military and political – of intervention.

Iraq still talks about the need for a dialogue, but Kofi Annan sees no signs of any diplomatic move on their part and feels that the next opportunity for a talk is the autumn session of the General Assembly, i.e. late in September. Perhaps the Iraqis feel that the US invasion is in doubt or is not so imminent and that they can wait *to play* the card of inviting inspectors?

At UNMOVIC we are benefiting from the delays inasmuch as we can refine our analyses of unresolved issues, give former trainees further advanced training and prepare the logistics. Each division has had to present a checklist of items that have to be ready before inspections resume. It is updated from time to time.

The Third Note

Reports that after the Vienna talks (4 and 5 July) and a marvellous week with Eva at Rosten (6–14 July), I went to Paris (16–17 July) with Jarmo Sareva and met the new foreign minister, Dominique de Villepin and the new minister of defence, Mme Alliot. Extremely solid support. No questioning of the firm positions we had taken in Vienna. Unconditional acceptance of inspection was their bid. It struck me that the French now automatically speak English at the highest levels! Villepin did so throughout. Mrs Alliot spoke French but did not need translation of my English. A young French official said that this is the 'globalization'. Thérèse Delpech was with us a good deal. She is forceful, solid and most helpful.

EKÉUS ON RELATIONS BETWEEN UNSCOM AND NATIONAL INTELLIGENCE

Tuesday 30 July 2002

Yesterday news came from Stockholm that in an interview Ekéus had said that UNSCOM had been subjected to pressures from all the P5 except China. He had succeeded in withstanding it, but with difficulty. He had learnt after he left that there were two infiltrators from US security services in his staff. This had 'irritated' him. The US had tried to get information about Iraqi conventional weapons locations and about Saddam's movements. They had used electronic eavesdropping. He did not think the US had got so much out of it. Sometimes UNSCOM had been pushed to provoke e.g. the inspection of the Ministry of Defence. The US wanted an excuse for bombing. On other occasions UNSCOM had been asked to hold back ... There were several interviews. Query *what reverberations there will be* ... ? The response that I have concluded should be ours is that we are not asked to look into the archives of UNSCOM to look at the past, but in order to prepare for future inspections. The substance dealt with by Ekéus was not entirely new. Scott Ritter has frequently talked in similar terms. However, it was certainly more credible coming from Ekéus. These were part of the circumstances why the Security Council did not prolong the mandate of UNSCOM at the end of 1999 but decided to create a new successor body – UNMOVIC – with a much stronger and clearer UN profile: it is wholly UN financed and all staff are UN employees rather than state employees with per diems from the UN. I did not have an American deputy chairman. When I am away the acting chairman is selected among the directors. We do not propose to utilize the US base in Bahrein as a place for briefing and debriefing but hope to have our own office. I have declared that we will not make use of electronic eavesdropping. I have also said that while we like to have information from national intelligence agencies it must be a one-way traffic. Moreover, these positions of UNMOVIC seem to have been accepted and supported by member states. They – including the US – have understood that the inspection authority must be independent.

Whatever the explanation in this bizarre case, I am sure that the Iraqis are going to utilize it: see, this confirms what we have said, namely, that UNSCOM was simply a US tool, the inspectors were spies. How can you expect us to receive them? Well, it is not UNSCOM they are to receive but UNMOVIC ...

HOPES AND DESPAIRS FOR INSPECTION

I went first to a Moroccan reception tonight (30 July). (*I met*) Abdulhasan, Ambassador of Kuwait, and he told me that the Iraqi foreign minister, Sabri, really had been nasty about me in his talk with the Belgian foreign minister. He had said that I was so hard-line. I did not even follow the line of the Secretary-General ... Later in the evening I was in for some more. One of the elderly lady UN correspondents (Reuters) said to me that the Iraqis were saying that I was homosexual! Well, that was something I had never encountered before. But would it be so damaging these days .....???

15 August 2002: Back in NY after Vacation at Home

My previous note was from Tue 30 July. Before I left for Stockholm on Friday 2 August a new turn of Iraq events occurred.

Iraq. On Thursday evening, as I walked home to pick up my laundry before 7 p.m. my mobile rang. It was Iqbal Riza, Kofi Annan's chef de cabinet, who told me that the Iraqi foreign minister, Sabri, had sent a letter to Kofi, in which he proposed that I should come to Baghdad for technical discussions, continuing the dialogue ... Jarmo, who was still in the office, got the text and took it to me. We read it carefully and concluded that Iraq had not changed their positions one bit, only suggested we come to Baghdad. They want a finite list of issues, an explicit list of means of solving them and perhaps also a timeline. Thereafter a decision on invitation.

I drafted a response for Kofi during the evening and began to doubt that I would be able to leave on the Friday afternoon for my home leave, as planned and booked. Kofi phoned me shortly after 10. Fred Eckhard (his spokesman) stood next to me. Kofi was away somewhere. He agreed to our approach and instructed Fred to respond to media that had already got the text from the Iraqis. He also agreed that I could go for my home leave. I had an advantage that it was Kofi and not I who responded. I might have been criticized. Kofi was not.

Jarmo and Ewen kept me informed about the Iraqi reactions to Kofi's letter. They explained that Blix was an American spy and that the US had exerted its influence to achieve the negative reply. One day Mr Sahaf (former foreign minister) said that the time for inspection was over. Another day Saddam himself said to the British pro-Iraqi Labour MP Galloway that Iraq accepted unfettered inspection. In any case, the ball is now in the Iraqi court, and I am back here to see where they next kick it.

Jarmo had been offered to become second man at the Finnish UN mission. Higher level and guaranteed five years. He cannot resist it, although he says he finds UNMOVIC much more interesting. I feel bitter that both Swedes and Finns have no hesitation to take a good fellow from an important UN position. Do they care how we operate or don't they? It was the same thing with Olof Skoog, whom the Swedes enticed to go to Colombia as ambassador. Now I have to search for a plausible successor.

Saturday 17 August 2002

Yesterday we learnt in the afternoon that Iraq had sent a new letter following up on Kofi Annan's negative response to the 1 August letter. Mrs Lederer, who interviewed me for AP, knew of it. Her Cairo office had it and were translating it. They had got it from the Iraqis in Baghdad. It was ten pages long. So, she concluded, it was not an invitation ... The SG's office confirmed that the letter had come and that it was sent for translation. Around 6.30 a summary translation of one and a half pages arrived (!). By that time Mrs Lederer had phoned me and read relevant parts of the AP translation. There does not seem to be any significant change from the latest letter. The request is still there to examine the issues as they appeared in the Amorim Report (1999). There is a contention that I should have rejected the earlier invitation before Kofi had it. Actually, the interview with Ragida in Al Hayat was done before the letter had arrived.

26 August 2002. Monday

Iraq. It has been the most active media week that I have been through. Fox TV spoiled the Sunday morning (*of the*) 18th. The interview (by Eric Shawn) was reduced to some two minutes because they had some technical problem. One almost feels cheated after all the adrenaline one has produced for the occasion.

On Monday 19 Egyptian TV (Good Morning Egypt).

On Tuesday 20 I had the Middle East editor of Der Spiegel. He claimed he had flown over just to interview me! Maybe? He did a good job of the article and sent it over to us. I corrected a couple of small errors.

I also had BBC World on Tuesday. I really dislike this sitting with an earplug and listen to London and staring into the camera. The BBC is especially my horror because their earplugs do not fit and I have a hard time hearing what the hell the fellow asks me in London. Concentrating so much on hearing you lose some of the power you need for thinking quickly of the answer.

On Thursday 22 I had Neue Zürcher Zeitung, Reuters and NBC. I must say the NZZ came out very well: concentrated and correct. About this time, we were informed about an Iraqi demarche made to the Secretary-General (received by Riza) complaining that I had declined the Iraqi invitations before there had been any Security Council consultations about them. It reminded them of Butler ... The Ambassador (al-Douri) had also claimed that I went to Washington every two weeks ... In the case of the two letters I had actually not seen them when the interviews were done. Ragida Dergham (the so-called Druze missile) had interviewed me for the Al Hayat Arabic London daily. She insisted on asking me if I would go to Baghdad, if invited. I suspect she knew that an invitation was coming and wanted to be the first to come out and proclaim 'Blix is ready for Baghdad!' As it turned out I was rather sceptical, saying such a visit could raise unfounded expectations ... She made the interview as a direct transcript. It looks just as awful as transcripts of normal persons look.

I had to spend a good deal of time writing a memo for the thirty-eighth floor countering the demarche the Iraqis had made. It is vexing. Query why they do it. Their enormous frustration must come out somewhere. Or do they wish to intimidate me to keep quiet while they themselves dominate the scene with their propaganda? Or are they preparing for the definite turning down of inspections? Their proposal – to discuss which issues were important at the end of 1998, and how we can agree to tackle them – may look deceptively attractive to the uninitiated. What they want is to share control of what is to be inspected and how . . . If their credibility had not been so low, they might have had an impact. As it was, I think we helped to shoot it down rather quickly in conversations with various members of the Security Council. They had a hard time seeing that there was any difference from the first letter which Kofi Annan had declined.

So, Saturday evening 24 August I took the Delta Shuttle to Washington and stayed at the Ritz Carlton and went to the NBC Meet the Press programme on Sunday morning and was interviewed by Tim Russert. Twenty minutes and it came out very well. Back in NY by Sunday lunch.

The thirty-eighth floor is not so happy about all my interviews, which irritate the Iraqis. The UN mostly tiptoes. Especially Iqbal Riza, the Pakistani chef de cabinet. He is cautious to point of self-effacement. I shall not *do more interviews*. I have sung my song for now. Today I visited the US ambassador, Negroponte. When I asked him why the Iraqis are jumping at me, he said that I am the only one in the UN Secretariat who speaks clearly . . . That draws flak. OK. They don't like to target Kofi.

Tuesday 27 August 2002. College of Commissioners, 29 and 30 August 2002

I had prepared a rather long and detailed introduction to explain why I was opposed to the Iraqi proposal of joint examination of the issues of 1998: a process not foreseen in Resolution 1284 and clearly prejudicing the Security Council's decision of which items are key remaining disarmament tasks and what Iraq is to do to help solve them.

There was a lively discussion in the College. Yuri Fedotov, the Russian member, said that Iraq had given up the demand for a package approach (no-fly zones, end to threat to the regime, lifting of sanctions and zone free of WMDs) and were really asking for discussion of inspection. Well, it does not emerge from the torrents of words they launch in the letters. If they get more rattled, their language might become more direct.

There is the other side: the US. After a week during which Brent Scowcroft and Baker (*former Secretary of State*) went public with doubts about a unilateral US attack, Vice President Cheney stormed onto the stage with a real broadside, the gist of which was that it was more dangerous to wait than to do something now. He also asserted that inspectors would not give any assurance whatsoever. (The very same day Ambassador Negroponte assured me that the US supported unfettered inspections in Iraq . . .) I had the feeling that the hawks thought they were losing the battle and had to open heavy artillery. I doubt it worked. The Europeans were appalled. German Chancellor Schroeder declared that Germany would not support the US in any armed action against Iraq and characterized the project as an 'adventure'. Chirac said that there must be Security Council authorization and Blair has difficulty with his own party in sustaining his support for the US hawk line. Even the US polls are showing declining support for armed action if it were to be costly in lives. And Congress is increasingly demanding to be heard before anything is started.

It is a bizarre spectacle. The top Pentagon team: Rumsfeld, Wolfowitz, Feith plus Cheney pushing hard, Colin Powell mute, congressional figures divided, the debate raging and the President simply saying that 'Saddam is an evil man' and 'I am a very patient man. No decision has been taken ... '. He cannot go on with that posture very long without looking ridiculous. If only all this were by design to rattle the Iraqis, but I fear it is all by lack of leadership. A strong-willed group of desk generals has been pushing for a line and gone public, probably felt somewhat encouraged by the President. He might have wanted to let them test the water. The opposition did turn up rather forcefully. If Bush now pushes on, he may be seen as adventurist and – certainly – unilateralist and God knows what they will get into. If he retreats and joins the Europeans in calling for a spell of inspection, he will look meek to the hawks and, indeed, be disavowing his own Vice President! The hawks have some good arguments: time may not be on the US side. The longer they wait the further the Iraqis can get on the nuclear. However, if they do not succeed in acquiring enriched uranium or plutonium in sufficient quantities on the black market – and that is difficult to do – they would be far away from a weapon. Another argument is that inspectors can be thrown out after a year and at such a time public opinion might not be prepared to support strong action.

The difference to the Europeans is partly due to the fact that Europe does not really feel threatened by an Iraqi nuclear weapon, while the US does see it as challenging them. But how are we to view Iran? No hawk suggests the US should attack Iran, which they suspect of building a nuclear weapon ... And North Korea?

What will Iraq do? I shall not be surprised if at the eleventh hour they ask for inspection, provided they think the US action is imminent. The US may not like to see inspection, but there may not be much it can do to prevent it. We deploy as soon as the Iraqis allow. They would be smart to be cooperative. If not, we could have clashes and the US would be given an opportunity to say that inspections do not work. This may well be what Iraq fears. Why should it call for inspection if invasion is inevitable? They also worry about leakages from inspectors to the US about military arrangements.

The College of Commissioners met 29 and 30 (*August*) and came out with a good summary of its discussion, supporting the approach I had taken both in the talks with the Iraqis and in my statements to media. It also endorsed the view that talks before Iraqi acceptance of inspection should concern practical arrangements for inspection, implicitly turning down the Iraqi request for joint examination of the issues of 1998. Very good! In fact, it could not have been better. I felt much sustained. Mr Sylla, the Senegalese, is superb. Always focusing on the central matters and sensible. Thérèse Delpech is also of great help.

Tomorrow, we go to the EU in Brussels. Jarmo and I travel to brief the permanent foreign affairs committee and to meet *EU external relations chief* Solana. It is timely and this is the group that seeks to get the European act together. After Brussels we fly to Nuremberg and get picked up by the German protocol to take us to Würzburg, from where we shall go to join German Foreign Minister, Joschka Fischer's, election caravan and have an hour with him on the road. From Fischer I go to Munich and a plane for London, to attend the World Nuclear Association. Eva arrives the same evening.

Thursday 12 September 2002. Late Evening

Bush in General Assembly. This morning the US President spoke to a full house. I came down half an hour early and was lucky to get a seat in the last row for UN higher dignitaries. The speech was very well delivered. It was mainly Iraq. Noting that Iraq had defied UN resolutions for over ten years. It was time to take up this challenge. The Security Council must be engaged, and the US will participate. If Iraq wants peace, it must disarm, destroy, etc. ... But not a word about inspection. I suppose the hawks in Washington did not want to mention the reprehensible word. Nevertheless, the speech was about enforcing resolutions and logically inspection should be part of that. There was also no deadline set. It was more implicit that if the UN does not act soon the US will do something alone. This puts good pressure upon the Russians and Chinese. If they want to avoid unilateral US action, they had better go along with a tough text in the Council.

How tough will the SC resolution be? The Brits and the French are dealing with it. Sir Jeremy Greenstock, the UK ambassador, sent his new Iraq man, Adam Bye, to me yesterday to discuss ideas for the resolution. It will certainly demand that Iraq accept inspections unconditionally. That word is important and a rejection of Iraq's current positions.

Jessica Matthews, President of the Carnegie Endowment, today sent me the report of their seminar on 'inspections backed by force'. We heard about this seminar quite some time ago. *Tom* Kono (*of the UN disarmament department*) and Thérèse Delpech were there and were astounded at the suggestions that inspectors could be accompanied by (US) helicopter gunships. Reading part of it today I found the plausible suggestion that forces should be close to Iraq and be ready to intervene if Iraq did not cooperate with the inspectors. OK. But a little further on you find that there should be a large, mostly US force and that it might accompany inspectors. Intelligence is to be provided by this force. The executive chairman is to select sites for inspection. (But if the intelligence is all from the US side the influence of the chairman might be limited ...)

I had an email from Gary Dillon, former head of the IAEA action team. He had been at the Carnegie seminar and claimed that all who were there and who had had some inspection experience thought the ideas were nuts. I had certainly heard the same from Thérèse. Dillon claimed that the ideas were the brainchild of Jessica Matthews and Ekéus! The ideas have been discussed recently in Stockholm. John Wolf told me he had been there and Thérèse, too. I learnt today that Ekéus and Jessica Matthews are going to see Kofi Annan tomorrow! I am surprised that he will receive them. Jeremy Greenstock told me tonight, however, that these ideas were going nowhere. Condoleezza Rice had told him so. I hope not. If they were to be realized (though I don't for a moment see how the Russians and Chinese could be brought to support them), I would go (*resign*).

UNSCOM lost legitimacy by its close liaison with the US. UNMOVIC was told to have a UN identity. The Carnegie proposal would do away with it.

Tomorrow is a horrendous day, ending with dinner given by the British foreign minister, Jack Straw. I have sipped water the whole week. But I need some sleep.

Friday 13 September 2002

Just back from Jack Straw's dinner at the British residence at 1 Beekman Place. Had not been there before. I wonder how many perm. reps. live there. For sure the Dutch are there, the Australians and the Kuwaitis. Close to the UN and with a view of the East River. Much better than Sutton Place which is better known. Jeremy Greenstock, the British perm. rep. introduced his two children, teenagers, and later the chef. A nice touch.

Iraq. Tonight, I really don't know where we are going. After Bush's speech everybody said 'fine, the US is going the multilateral path to the Security Council'. No unilateral attack. If they first try inspections and the Iraqis stall, OK, then maybe we have to move to the use of force. Then I talked to the Dutch ambassador last night and he said the Russians and Chinese were on board for the use of force and this morning I had the Norwegian Sommer (?) who told me that it was clear that they were going to load so much into the resolution that there was no way the Iraqis would swallow it. The Russians and Chinese were on board. The *NY Times* talked about including paragraphs on the protection of minorities. Others said that they might demand reports about the 600 missing Kuwaitis, etc. The impression was for a while that there would be no chance that Iraq would accept. And that this was precisely Washington's intention. My reaction was that this smacked of insincerity: appearing to go the multilateral path while in reality preparing for armed attack.

Then I had Amr Moussa, the Secretary General of the Arab League, in my office. He thought that Sabri, the Iraqi foreign minister, would announce in the General Assembly that Iraq accepts inspections under the relevant SC resolutions. And he felt they should hurry to do it – before the Security Council adopts something stronger than the current resolutions. I said it would have been smart if they had done this earlier, e.g. during the summer. If they did it while a new SC resolution is being worked out, it will be too late. We will say that we have to await the outcome of the new resolutions. And a lot of new demands will be placed on them. Moussa, who I think still sees me as an old pal, did say that it might be wise to have a low media profile. I replied that if the Iraqis kept quiet and refrained from attacking me and UNMOVIC I could also say less.

The evening at Sir Jeremy's place tonight began with the impression that the US had given up on regime change and that the central part was again elimination of weapons of mass destruction. Jeremy did not think that they would put anything about minorities or Kuwaitis in the disarmament resolution. Only defiance of that resolution would be a *casus belli*. Someone said that Colin Powell wanted to keep the ball in New York. Ivanov had said at the Secretary-General's luncheon for the P5 foreign ministers that with some difficulty the Russians would be able to vote for the use of force against Iraq ... (Incidentally, I was puzzled about the luncheon. I had not been invited. Perhaps it was oversight? Or only Secretariat people from the P5? Or did Kofi keep me at a distance? Hans Corell told me that the Secretariat people tonight had been *named* by Kofi. Whatever, the luncheon had been illuminating on the Iraq issue. So, I missed something. Curiously, when Bush was to speak in the GA, there was again a privilege for the P5 group from the Secretariat: Connor, Prendergast and the French were invited to the office behind the podium to meet the President. Hans Corell reserved seats for them in the front row and I found a seat in the last row ... I am not keen to regurgitate protocol matters, but I do notice. Why make distinctions in an international secretariat? Is it not bad enough that the P5 have practically guaranteed undersecretary positions in the Secretariat ... ?)

Tonight, I am back where I was this morning. I don't know whether the intention is to give inspection a chance and give the Iraqis a chance to be open and cooperative – admittedly an unlikely conduct on their part. Perhaps the reality is that the US factions are still fighting their fights? Those who think that inspection has worked sufficiently well as containment and wish to avoid the use of force and bloodshed and those who feel he is too dangerous to be kept contained in a box and, perhaps, also feel that Saddam is so evil to his own people and the world that he must be taken out. It is true that not to take out the regime does have the serious drawback that the worst possible bloody dictator is left in place to continue terrorizing his own people. That is not appealing. On the other hand, it is true that UN and international law (until now) do not endorse taking out odious dictators, unless they really constitute threats to or breaches of world peace. I have really been astonished that much of the US political world seems to be prepared to spend a lot of lives and resources to do away with Saddam, when the much less costly containment might work for another period, during which Saddam might fade.

I must write a para about the Carnegie study on 'coercive inspection' or militarily enforced inspection. A report is now circulating. I have read part of it. UNMOVIC would be left intact, but there would be an American–international armed force outside Iraq ready to intervene if Iraq did not cooperate as it should with the inspectors. So far, maybe OK. However, it emerged that UNMOVIC could also call on this force to accompany it on sensitive inspections. Sort of half-invasion? If civilians protested, inspectors should be able to call in riot control force ... I felt this was going one step further than the UN–US–UK blend that led UNSCOM to lose international legitimacy.

It is hard to avoid the conclusion that the outside US force would, in practice, be the one which took decisions about where to inspect, etc. It would be responsible for intelligence and it was suggested that inspection decisions should be taken by UNMOVIC in Baghdad – not New York. In the end it looks like a thinly disguised US counter-proliferation squad. Jeremy Greenstock told me that Condoleezza Rica had put her thumb down. Nonetheless, Ekéus had met Kofi Annan today. Jeremy said that he had, himself, seen Ekéus and told him that this project is out of the question. (Nevertheless, an op-ed article pleading for the idea appeared in the NY *Times*.)

In the Carnegie study that Jessica Matthews sent me, Ekéus is pleading for greater liaison between the inspectors and national intelligence. This is somewhat curious considering that Ekéus has recently publicly described how UNSCOM was pushed by their national parties (presumably first of all the US). If the collaboration which UNSCOM had was too much for the UN, how could a new organization have more without losing legitimacy?

Saturday 14 September 2002: An Eventful Week

Mårten phoned from Ft Lauderdale. Tonight was his last evening. He was enthusiastic about the course. He had been diving down to sixty-two metres with helium, which avoids the nitrogen (*narcosis*). He is leaving Florida tomorrow and starts working Monday morning. Eva should be back on Tuesday and is then off for an art excursion to St Petersburg until the end of the week. Adventurous mother and son . . .

Iraq. If I was at a loss yesterday to read where things are going, I am a little clearer today. Meeting various individuals at the German Foreign Minister's buffet luncheon and at the Bulgarian President's reception tonight has helped.

Reading reports in the NY *Times* this morning about what Bush and Bush aides were saying, I was left wondering whether the agreement to go to the Security Council was just a short gesture of courtesy to the UN majority: the US is kindly willing to listen to the outside world for a little while, including some sessions of the Council. After that US planning proceeds as before. The fighting season for Iraq is January when it may be bearable to put on protective garb against chemical weapons. The US might expect that either they would succeed in getting such a tough resolution (or several) accepted in the Security Council that Iraq would reject it (them) or the Iraqis would balk in the field. In either case there would be a *casus belli*.

However, at the German buffet I talked to Jim Cunningham, second man at the UN mission, and asked him whether what we now see is just a perfunctory bow to the UN. No, no. It is a real chance. Maybe Iraq will not seize it, but there is an avenue opening. He said the MOU about presidential sites would be thrown out. I would be asked what conditions I needed (eliminate modalities . . .). I told Jim I did not want a dual command with the SG though I would seek his advice. The Iraqis are constantly trying to play down UNMOVIC as 'technical' to play up the SG. OK, but once we are into inspection UNMOVIC must not be on a leash from the thirty-eighth floor. That floor contains not only the wise and nice Kofi but also a number of actors who may claim to speak for and on behalf of Kofi. Jim Cunningham assured me that there would be no double command. I raised the same point with Jeremy Greenstock tonight at the Bulgarian party. He did not see a problem. Res. 1284 rests on UNMOVIC and there will be no change. We'll see.

At the German buffet – where I said a short hello to the foreign minister, Joschka Fischer – I also talked to the Irish Ambassador (member of the SC). He thought the Iraqis would be smart to rush to accept 1284 before the SC began to write a new text. I told him I did not think a quick Iraqi acceptance would stop work on the new SC resolution. [Events have proven me right.] If the Iraqis had accepted 1284 last summer, it would have been different. But now new conditions are in the air and Iraq will have to say yes or no to what is offered them.

A short talk with the bearded Ambassador from Mauritius was amusing. He said that his greatest wish was for this year to end so that he would no longer be on the Security Council! I can well imagine that having little analytical back-up from home and being obliged to react to momentous global issues with the spotlight on a country between East and West and North and South, they are in difficulties?

Saturday 21 September 2002

IRAQ. This week has been dramatic. I was called last Sunday (15 Sept.) to come down to the UN and see the Secretary-General at 11 a.m. Between the meetings with two foreign ministers Kofi told me that Iraq was going to announce the acceptance of resumed inspections. He left it open whether I should now approach the Iraqis or I should leave any initiative to them. In the evening he called me again on my mobile when I was having dinner with Göran and Bo. The Iraqi letter actually came only late on Monday. (I had left the office and Ewen Buchanan received the letter from the thirty-eighth floor and read it to me on the phone.) It was stated from the Iraqi side that it was due to the appeal by many Arab and non-aligned states and the work of Kofi Annan. OK, OK ... it is evident that it was above all due to the US threat of war ... The letter declared not only that Iraq would allow resumed inspections but also that they were ready for talks about practical arrangements (undoubtedly Kofi had advised them to put this in the letter).

On Tuesday morning there was a wreath-laying at the memorial plaque for (*UN Secretary-General*) Hammarskjöld near the meditation room. As Kofi was not there, I asked Iqbal Riza, his (Pakistani) chef de cabinet, if he thought that I should approach the Iraqis and invite them to discuss the practical arrangements necessary for inspections. Iqbal said yes, indeed! Maintain the momentum that had been created by their announcement!

Considering that UNMOVIC has tried ever since the dialogue meeting in May to get to talk about practical arrangements I concluded it would be logical for me to phone. So, I called Ambassador al-Douri, referred to the letter, the talks in Vienna and asked whether we could now have some talks, profiting from the presence an Iraqi delegation. Could meet the same afternoon? The ambassador agreed straight away to talks but asked that the meeting should be a preliminary discussion. OK.

The Iraqis (Ambassador Saed Hasan, former perm. rep. in NY) and hardliner General Amin and the new deputy perm. rep., Mohamed Ali, came at 4 p.m. We talked for nearly two hours. It turned out they were not ready to go into a discussion of substance. They had only taken some notes at our briefing on the item at Vienna in early July. We gave them Perricos' detailed talking points paper from Vienna. (Both the Russians and the Chinese have got it when they asked for it.) They tried to suggest substantive talks in Baghdad. I declined. They did not insist. I suspect they had heard through their friends that we thought Baghdad would raise false expectations. They tried mildly for Damascus and Amman but fell rather fast for Vienna. They were the ones who suggested that the meeting should be held to 'complete', 'finalize' the examination of the arrangements. I said that I needed to be in NY for some days in case the SC wanted advice from UNMOVIC. They needed some days for interagency contacts in Baghdad. So, we agreed on talks in Vienna in the week beginning 30 Sept. I thought this would be welcome for those who were working on a new SC resolution. We would be glad to see it before we focus on practical arrangements. These would very likely be affected by a new resolution.

Immediately after the meeting we issued a press release (with substance that was agreed with the Iraqis) about the results of our meeting. From that moment we were the hottest prey in the media world! I was asked to innumerable TV shows and for innumerable interviews. Buchanan had to put on a tape on his telephone advising that we were not taking any interviews and referring to our website (for the press release). The media were not very pleased, but with the situation being extremely sensitive and any misquote or misunderstanding from me potentially endangering progress, it was necessary to maintain what the military call 'radiotystnad' (*radio silence*). This had the advantage, also, that you get some time to work rather than concentrating on the right formulations for media.

During the day there was a slightly comic wrangling going on regarding my briefing the Council. I said to the President that I, a humble servant of the Council, would come whenever they summoned me. Vcegda gotov! (Be prepared!) In the end the quarrel (between the French and the US/UK) was ended by agreement on a briefing Thursday afternoon. So, I got some time for thinking during Wednesday and half of Thursday.

On Thursday (19 Sept.) at 4 p.m. I came down with the elevator to the second floor and walked to the SC briefing room. The place was packed with media and cameras and I had to stop and pose for pictures.

The briefing went very well. I talked freely from the notes. I stressed that I had taken the initiative in the talks with the Iraqis. (Some would have suspected an Iraqi ploy to move fast to inspection in order to avoid a new resolution.) I told them it was the Iraqis who were not ready to respond yet. We distributed a list of the spread of nationalities in our roster of potential inspectors. (Tariq Aziz had had the cheek to tell Nelson Mandela in South Africa that half the number of UNMOVIC's inspectors were American! Actually, we have as many Americans as Russians and French.)

Then I explained the 'timeline' that one can deduce from Res. 1284. Since few have the patience to read the complicated text and even fewer to understand it, my sketch (which we distributed) was probably helpful. It did indicate the talks in Vienna for 30 Sept.–2 October (should have been 1 October. Just one day). Then giving 15 October as a possible day for the arrival of an advance UNMOVIC team in Baghdad. I could foresee that this would be the news. It gave two months for preparing for inspections before these could be regarded as 'started'. I explained that we would need to have our instruments – inspectors, helicopters, planes, jeeps, labs, etc. – in place before we would 'start to work'. I agreed with speakers who asked about acceleration and admitted there would probably be impatience, but I pointed out that we had now been waiting for four years for renewed inspections and it did not seem all that wild to prepare for two months to get a solid basis. I added even within that period we would mount some early inspections and early re-baselining. Several speakers in the Council expressed support.

In the discussion and question period which followed it was interesting to note that quite a number of delegations had now come to a positive attitude to a new resolution. Most importantly that Lavrov, the Russian Ambassador, said that if such a resolution could help, well ... So, he kept Russia's options open. On Tuesday I think there had been a much less welcoming attitude to a new resolution. Iraq had now accepted inspection. This was what the Council would have asked for in a resolution, why then bother ... Of course, what these people wanted to avoid was an authorization in a resolution to use force in case Iraq were not to cooperate ... I think that by Thursday (when this briefing in the SC took place) the US and UK had got to work and lobby. They had a strong *argument* in saying that a resolution must condemn Iraq for violations and expressly counter future cat-and-mouse play by Iraq.

WORK ON A NEW SECURITY COUNCIL RESOLUTION WHICH BECAME RES. 1441

Work on a new SC resolution has, indeed, moved on this week and I have been consulted. I have said that, for instance, the 'modalities' on sensitive sites worked reasonably well in many cases but did not work in a number of high-profile cases. Clearly, it involved a certain erosion of the right to 'immediate' access. I have also said that if they want to reduce the room for cat-and-mouse play they may use the resolution – and I think they would have the Council with them. I also suspect that any scrapping of the Memorandum of Understanding (MOU) of 1998 between Kofi Annan and Iraq about inspection of eight presidential sites will be the hardest point to put in the resolution. On Friday they had a meeting with the E10 (non-permanent members of the Council). If they do not overload the text absurdly, they could get it through – provided they get the Russians to agree.

Today, Saturday (21 Sept.), media have *reported that Iraq declares that it will not accept a new resolution*. However, my guess is that *this* latest Iraqi move will not stop the work on a resolution which strengthens the inspections. I think it will scrap the MOU re the presidential sites. (Iraq could live with that although it would be humiliating.) However, the US and the UK had better avoid any absurdly far-reaching rights for us. They would lose support among the members of the Council on such a course. And I think the US might have to give up a clause about the automatic right to go to armed force if Iraq does not comply. Or to fuzz it. After all, the US is ready for unilateral force if need be and the Council would be aware of that if and when Iraq gives us a denial of access or other trouble . . .

Sunday 22 September 2002

Iraq. I have now seen the text of the latest Iraqi message and it says it will not accept any resolution differing from the 'agreement' it reached with the Secretary-General. That is the MOU on the presidential sites – nothing else. No surprise! I had thought that the pride on the Iraqi side and the contempt for Saddam on the US side would make this the most touchy issue. Query whether the implication is that anything else can be toughened up: sensitive sites, interviews, helicopter paths, what not?

The effects of the new Iraqi move on the various actors will be interesting to watch. I suspect that it will make the US doubly eager to have the resolution scrap the MOU and make presidential sites as accessible as any other site for UNMOVIC. Moreover, the US will hope that, once the resolution is accepted, Iraq will stand by its rejection and the US can launch an attack. Query, still, whether the Council will go along with a clause authorizing force in case Iraq rejects the resolution. I think the US will have a hard time getting that clause through . . .

My guess is that the US will now manage to persuade Russia, France and China to throw out the MOU and that Iraq will retreat again. Perhaps the US will now add that Iraq must accept inspections in accordance with the new resolution before 15 October . . . ? So long as the US would be prepared to drop an authorization to use force in case of Iraqi non-compliance, I think the other will go very far.

Thursday 3 October 2002. *Iraq*

What a time it has been since I wrote last! Last week – 23 to 27 Sept. – the new resolution on Iraq percolated. I was shown some versions and while the early ones were tough, they were not out of this world. Toward the end of the week, I got the text which the UK and US were said to be negotiating with others. They were to send an envoy to Paris on the Friday and to Moscow for the Saturday. The text stipulated that any P5 member could 'recommend' to UNMOVIC and the IAEA to inspect sites, call for documents, interview persons, etc. What was more, they should also have the right to have reports on the result. Clearly the idea was that P5 members (which one?) should be able to direct UNMOVIC. Further, the draft prescribed that any P5 members should be allowed to nominate a representative on any inspection team. Clearly such a person could take part in the inspection of Iraqi military sites and then go on to report to his government, which might launch an attack the next week.

UNSCOM was criticized for being too close to the US and UK and for being led by US intelligence. With UNMOVIC a more solid UN identity was sought, and we have tried to conform. Now comes a draft that almost openly says that the US would control the organization. It certainly is far from the concept of Res. 1284 and I think that if it were to be adopted, I would resign. Tonight, I am not inclined to think that it will be presented in its current extreme form. The British are not enthusiastic about it and the Russians, Chinese and French find it awful.

Back to the end of last week. On Saturday (*28 Sept.*) having had lunch with Hisashi Owada – who is campaigning for a seat he will get on the International Court of Justice – I flew to Vienna, arriving on Sunday. Met with Mohamed ElBaradei and his and my staff in the afternoon to discuss the next day's meeting with the Iraqis – General al-Sa'adi, General Amin and Ambassador Saed Hasan (former perm. rep. NY). On Monday and Tuesday, we walked our way through lots of practical arrangements necessary for or facilitating inspection. We began by giving them (in Mohamed's office) a paper in which we suggested they give up the sensitive site and interview modalities and the memorandum of understanding on presidential sites.

I have to admire these (Iraqi) negotiators. Their country is pretty close to being invaded and crushed by the US armed forces. This is why they are talking with us. They would have continued to consider us a 'nonentity' otherwise. Yet even now they have the cheek to propose that payment be given to the Iraqis who work overtime to escort our inspectors! Iraq is privatizing and each state organization is to make money ... The minders would be more enthusiastic if they were paid by us (in dollars) ... I answered that it would be their job to keep them enthusiastic. We would stick to the old order. I also said I did not think the SC would go along. In any case Iraq would be the ultimate payer. However, under their proposal Iraq would get more dollars at its disposal. Considering that they already make some 2–3 billion dollars in smuggling, the Council would not wish to add further money. They also had the nerve to suggest that UNMOVIC should supply its budget and audits to Iraq, since we lived on Iraqi oil money ... I said we were responsible to the Security Council and submitted our economic reporting to UN audit. Accordingly, I did not feel we owed Iraq any reports ...

The greatest success was that after drawn-out talks the Iraqis did away with the 'sensitive sites' modality. They could not touch the MOU about eight presidential sites, outside their authority. On interviews and air operations in the no-fly zones, they did not make many concessions.

I have never seen so many journalists than the hundreds who came for our press conference on the Tuesday (1 Oct.) evening. Lucky, we *and the Iraqis* had drafted *a joint* press release *about what we had agreed on*. I read it to the crowd in the Vienna International Center rotunda and then answered questions together with al-Sa'adi and Mohamed ElBaradei. I have been told that it went well.

Today I have briefed the Council about the outcome. I had been cautious not to brief media too much in Vienna, so there were a number of things which I could tell the Council, and which were fresh. Relations with the Council members improve much with this restraint on my part. Actually, I have good relations with all of them. In the afternoon of today the P5 came to my office to discuss with me and ElBaradei the new draft resolution. I think we helped them to move to a new resolution.

Tomorrow (4 Oct.), I go to Washington to see Colin Powell. Invited to the meeting – it will be interesting to see if they come – are also the National Security Advisor, Condoleezza Rice, the CIA boss, Mr Tenet, the Deputy Secretary of Defense, Mr Wolfowitz, and others. Quite a meeting. See if we can convince them that moving UNMOVIC to become a façade for CIA is not a good idea ...

Large Washington Meeting. Tuesday 8 October 2002

Past 10 o'clock NY time and past 4 in the morning my biological time. Just back from Vienna. Left NY for Washington last Friday (*4 October*) after lunch. First a meeting with our US commissioner, Assistant Secretary John Wolf, then with a lot of people from the joint chiefs of staff, the National Security Council and what not. Briefings by me and by Mohamed ElBaradei. Time for some questions. I thought it was a rather friendly audience. We explained what inspection can do and what limitations it has. We have had inspection in Iraq between 1991 and 1998. It did a great deal of things but did not give a high degree of assurance about the absence of BC and missiles. What it demonstrated was that if you have a non-cooperative party and a tightly controlled state there are limitations on what you can achieve. It does not mean that inspection in general is useless. Also, it does not say that monitoring in Iraq is not helpful in placing significant obstacles in the way of the production and stockpiling of weapons. It has shortcomings but they have to be compared with the drawbacks of an alternative approach, armed action with its effects of death and destruction.

After the meeting at the medium level, we moved to the Secretary of State, Colin Powell, where we also found Condoleezza Rice, the National Security Adviser and Mr Wolfowitz, Deputy Secretary of Defense and a lot of other high figures. Here the discussion was brisker, with Wolfowitz and Rice taking rather tough lines. Wolfowitz asked me if I did not believe that Saddam Hussein had WMD. Had I answered yes, it would have been all over the papers the day after. I usually reply that if I had solid evidence, I would tell the Security Council. I said I thought the British paper was balanced and good but simply referring to 'intelligence suggests' or 'intelligence tells us' is not evidence. This is what I need. The aluminium tubes that are talked about may or may not be for nuclear. Here some alleged evidence is on the table. But it does not seem to convince everybody.

During the discussion I made it very clear that some of the provisions in the US draft resolution for the Security Council were very helpful, others not. I said I thought that some sanction clause was helpful to the inspectors as leverage. Iraq needs to be under a constant pressure to be cooperative. The economic sanctions have their effect in making it more difficult for Iraq to import war material and important dual-use items, but they do not amount to leverage. I also supported the idea of a general declaration. This was the original concept in 1991: Iraq declares. We verify. Later it developed into Iraq is to hold sites open. Inspectors are to look. It became a *game of* hide and seek. However, I turned rather sharply against the idea that the P5 were to be able not only to recommend sites to be inspected, people to be interviewed, etc. but also to have reports on the results. I also said that for each P5 to be authorized to send a 'representative' on each inspection team was a bad construction. What will the Chief Inspector do if five P5 representatives suggest five different actions? The Council must give us broad responsibilities, not seek to micromanage. In 2000 the French and the Russians suggested I should have five political advisers in my office. I declined saying that it would be hopeless to be exposed daily to conflicting advice. Once it was proposed by the Soviet Union that the UN Secretariat should be headed by a troika, representing East, West and non-aligned. It was rightly rejected. It would have paralysed the Secretariat. A 'pentoika' in the UNMOVIC is no better.

After the meeting. Colin Powell, Condoleezza Rice, Mohamed and I withdrew to Powell's chamber and Powell expressed concern about the security of information in UNMOVIC. They could not provide intelligence without being sure that it would not be compromised. Well, I responded, we cannot allow ourselves to have US representatives handling US intelligence within UNMOVIC and become an extended arm of the CIA. It is a one-way traffic.

After that smaller meeting Powell came with us downstairs and stepped outside the front entrance with us. Thereafter I jumped into a stretched-out Volvo from the Swedish Embassy and went to Jan Eliasson's residence for a chat with him. His driver took me to Dulles Airport where I boarded a United Airlines plane for London.

Arrived in Stockholm on Saturday at 2 p.m. On the Sunday (*6 October*) Eva and I had time for an hour's walk in Lill-Jansskogen. Then I had to work on the lecture to be given in Vienna for our sixth training course for future inspectors. In the afternoon an hour's talk with Hans Dahlgren, Undersecretary, and Torkel Stiernlof who is going to join me here in NY. We were at the foreign office and before the talk Lars Adaktusson of Swedish TV did a short interview with me.

Sunday evening, I went to Vienna and on Monday morning I gave the lecture (to UNMOVIC's sixth training course). Then I worked on the draft letter about our understandings from the talks with Iraq one week back. Spent the afternoon with Mohamed, polishing letter to General al-Sa'adi. Mohamed and I work well together on such things. He is an excellent draftsman and sensitive politically. We spelled out a good deal and asked for confirmation and said we would report to the Security Council. I think they will be eager to show themselves cooperative – unless the avenue to Security Council consensus is closed and armed action appears inevitable. At such a point Iraq has no further reason to be conciliatory.

Dinner Monday evening at Aioli with a lovely view of St Stephan's Cathedral. Vienna is magnificent and the cathedral, bluish cold. Beautiful.

Today (8 Oct), off to the airport for flight via Paris to New York. Thérèse was on the same plane, so we had a long talk. She is knowledgeable and realistic and with very independent views.

Thursday 17 October 2002

Colin Powell. Shall meet him today at Waldorf Astoria. We shall no doubt talk about the resolution in the Security Council. Signals are conflicting. Some say, US is just feigning interest in the UN. The war plans are finalized. Others say the resolution is moving forward.

Much work. We have an extra meeting of the College of Commissioners tomorrow and I have not yet concluded writing my introductory statement. On Monday I plan to go to Moscow and give a paper on non-proliferation at a workshop organized by Los Alamos and the Russian Academy of Science. And to meet Mr Ivanov, the Russian foreign minister. I must write the paper over the weekend.

Saturday 19 October 2002

Eva called this morning from Arusha in Tanzania. She was now at a good hotel and had washed off all the dust of Kilimanjaro. Stomach troubles were not serious. The roads were as bad now as twenty years ago. But the main road was fine. She is now going on a safari, beginning at Lake Manyara, then Ngoro Ngoro crater (where she and I were some twenty years ago). She was also to visit some rock or cave, where they found the remains of some early man creature.

Colin Powell was in town on Thursday and I saw him at the Waldorf Astoria for a one-to-one talk over half an hour. He wanted to convey to me that the US is serious about wanting a solution in Iraq without armed force. It is clear that they see strong inspections as the only alternative today to armed force. The draft resolution which they have given to the French (but hardly to anyone else) and which we and media have and which envisaged the P5 taking over much of the control of inspection has been regarded as very extreme and it is doubtful whether it would even have had a majority. The US seems now to abandon the P5 privileges in the text and to have a sanction clause, which is blurred and would enable the US to take unilateral action if the Council did not get its act together and support armed sanctions. The impression is that France and Russia might be able to live with that. It would put even more responsibility on UNMOVIC and me. A breach of compliance obligations by Iraq would be reported by us to the Council, which then would take a stand. I am rejecting the view – advanced by drama-loving journalists – that we have in our power to decide on war and peace. We shall be accurate – and reasonable – as an accountant in our reporting. It is the Council and its members who decide on war and peace. That the US may retain the possibility to use force even without Council support strengthens our position in Iraq. They cannot count upon a veto to shield them if we were to report non-compliance.

The US would now like us to beef up our inspection plans and machinery. It is a little late to come to us after nearly three years to say how they think we might function. After all, we have submitted our plans regularly to the College of Commissioners and the Council and had their support. A sizeable and rapid upscaling now would risk involving many mistakes. I understand the American impatience, but query whether ingenuity would not be better than quantity. We must have competent chief inspectors and we do not want to rehire any old UNSCOM hands who were war-scarred from their many skirmishes with the Iraqis. We are a (rather) new creation and might get away from some of the past conflicts. Regrettably, the Iraqis are reported (by the Americans) now to be busy hiding a lot of things, moving things around. The chances that they would declare proscribed items for destruction are not great. This means our task would be to look for smoking guns and – more probable – smoke. Sad.

Iraq's ambassador, al-Douri, visited me yesterday. It was a first. He wanted to talk about the joint letter Mohamed ElBaradei and I had sent to General al-Sa'adi and the two letters he has sent in reply. They chose to accept our joint press statement and my briefing note to the Council as valid descriptions of our Vienna 'understandings' but avoided a straight answer to the letter, which covered more points than the two documents they endorsed. Of course, we wondered whether there were some points in the letter they wished to avoid: regional offices in Basra and Mosul? Arrangements for U2 flights? No unilateral destruction of proscribed items? I suggested to al-Douri that the best way to clear up the situation might be a third letter in which they refer to the confusion and say that they endorse all the points in the letter. If they don't, the resolution to be adopted by the Council may well ensure that all the points will become binding on them.

Saturday 19 October 2002

Moscow trip. The programme is shaping up. Meeting with the foreign minister, Ivanov, on Tuesday afternoon just after my arrival. On Wednesday at the opening of the workshop and then talks with Fedotov and his colleagues and lunch. Thursday morning my 'keynote' speech. Then lunch and off to Sheremetova and a plane for Stockholm. Today, Saturday, I have been working away on my paper on non-proliferation for Moscow. I have also done a few chores. Ordered my high-blood-pressure pills. Went to Bloomingdales and bought an air travel carry-on bag. Why is it that the credit card they have sent to me has such a low credit limit? 250 dollars was more than I could take on it! Ridiculous.

Kofi Annan phones me from time to time. Today I was in front of the laundry shop when he called from Uzbekistan to hear how work on the resolution proceeded. He had talked to Colin Powell, who felt that the resolution was doing well. I said the most obnoxious provisions – about P5 privileges – were gone but the US was now canvassing us about an upscaling of the whole inspection effort. This was a bit late in the day... Nevertheless, we are positive toward innovations and will be glad to talk to them.

Monday 28 October 2002

Moscow. Went to Moscow last Monday (*21 October*) after a hectic day. In the morning I phoned the former Bahrein ambassador Buallay in Bahrein to tell him that we were now making arrangements to have our field office in Cyprus. He sounded a bit disappointed but it might have been fake. Kofi Annan told me today that the Bahreinis probably would be relieved. The talks with Cyprus went well and fast and today Kofi and Mohamed ElBaradei signed the agreement.

Arrived Tuesday 22 in Moscow and stayed at the Marriott Royal Aurora, which was the nicest hotel I have lodged in so far in Moscow. Close to Red Square. Good service.

Talk with Foreign Minister Ivanov Tuesday 22. The talk was in his private bureau with only Fedotov and a fellow from their Middle East bureau. I felt Ivanov's reading of the revised US Iraq draft was unnecessarily negative. I doubt, however, that they would go so far as to veto it. (Later, Nikita Zhukov in my office told me that Putin had authorized a vetoing of the first draft.) I said that my reading was less negative but pointed to specific matters, which I thought were awkward.

Media showed up already at my arrival at the Sheremetova Airport. Took some footage and put some mild questions. They were ignorant. In the period of intense media interest, I have learnt that for many of them all that is needed to 'cover' is footage of Blix going into or out of an airport! They will illustrate that something is happening, not what is happening! Some of the ensuing media reporting was encouragingly correct and straightforward. Good accounts. Old-style journalism.

Sven Hirdman is still Swedish ambassador (I think nine years now. Just as long as Lavrov has been PR in New York) and doyen. He and Marianne picked me up at the hotel, took me home to their residence and provided a nice supper with morel soup and cheeses. We talked about Iraq, of course. He has been kind enough to insist within the Swedish foreign office that reports on Iraq of relevance to UNMOVIC and me should be transmitted to me. Sven might go into retirement next year.

Los Alamos–Russian Academy of Science workshop was not located near the hotel. A bus took us there on Wednesday morning. Lots of people I knew: Hoskins (formerly UK) recruited by me for IAEA intelligence. Tarek Rauf (Canadian of Pakistani extraction, earlier Monterey), now IAEA. David Albright, Roland Timerbaev, etc. Many interesting presentations. Mine was only in the morning of Thursday. I had been worried that New York would call me back to brief the SC on Friday morning, but it turned out that they saved me and Mohamed for Monday. So, I only had to move my trip from Stockholm to New York from the Monday to the Sunday.

Russian 'banquet' for the workshop. Wednesday evening in the restaurant on the top floor of the ugly Science Academy skyscraper. Fine view of Moscow. High Russian spirits! Many toasts. Great Fun! I, too, made a speech. *Inter alia* about scientists and inspectors, who both have a vocation to seek the truth . . .

Velikhov, I think President of the Academy and a central figure in the 'fusion mafia', was there and told me a hilarious story of questionable truth about why I and Rosen and Konstantinov had been taken by helicopter – and not by car – to Chernobyl in 1986. After the dramatic decision to invite us there (in an early application of 'glasnost') Petrosyants (Chairman of the Atomic Energy Commission) had laid down that we were to go by car from Kiev to Chernobyl. However, Velikhov thought it unwise to go through the closed zone with many spots of high radiation. To change such a decision was difficult. He phoned Gorbachev and said that they could not possibly take us on a several hours' excursion which would call for visits to toilets in that area. 'They look like toilets in the South of the Soviet Union . . . ' This tipped the decision in favour of a helicopter.

Blix's paper on Thursday morning: 'International perspectives on an effective safeguards non-proliferation regime' provoked many questions, especially relating to the 'one-way traffic' between UNMOVIC and Intelligence. I was also able to discuss with Albright and Ms Keleher the relations between intelligence and international organizations. I learnt that morning that a Moscow theatre with 700 spectators had been occupied by some 40 Chechen rebels. This was the reason why an expected big crowd of journalists to see me that morning turned out to be a crowd of only two. As we went to the airport later in the day, we found one could not drive up all the way. We had to walk the last hundred metres or so.

MEETING WITH PRESIDENT BUSH. WEDNESDAY 30 OCTOBER 2002

Been to Washington and seen President Bush, Vice President Cheney, Secretary of State Colin Powell, Security Adviser Condoleezza Rice and Deputy Secretary of Defense Wolfowitz plus others . . .

It all came rather suddenly. On Monday I and Mohamed briefed the Security Council on practical aspects of the revised draft UK/US resolution. I pointed to a number of things I thought were helpful – demand for a declaration by Iraq, prediction of reactions if Iraq does not respect the resolution, immediate access to presidential sites, covering of Unmanned Aerial Vehicles (UAV) – and some that

I thought were doubtful or bad: urging us to select the best available experts as inspectors (redundant), taking Iraqis out of the country for interviews abroad. The impact of our combined briefs appears to have been strong. We evidently injected heavy arguments and had a lot of effect, especially on the E10.

On Monday evening (28 *October*) when I was at home, suddenly Colin Powell calls me and talks about the resolution and says it would be good if I saw the President ... He would keep in touch ... Later John Wolf (Assistant Secretary for Non-Proliferation and member of our College of Commissioners) calls and says I should see the Vice President – and maybe more – on Wednesday morning at 8.30. He said nothing about Mohamed ElBaradei, who I thought would fly back to Vienna on Tuesday.

Tuesday morning, I have a long breakfast with Dick Gardner going through a lot of points that might be brought up on Thursday evening in a programme – 'Can Inspections Do the Job in Iraq' – at the New York Council for Foreign Relations. As I come back to the office, I learn that it seems Mohamed is also going to Washington. So, I phone him and ask if we are both to see Cheney. He affirms this and says we shall also see Bush and Condoleezza Rice. Fine. In the afternoon I and my assistant, Torkel Stiernlof, take the shuttle to Washington. Directly to Hotel Marriott on Pennsylvania. Dinner with Mohamed, Jacques Baute, Torkel and John Wolf.

Wednesday at 08.30. Rainy morning. A van takes us all the way up to the West Wing of the White House. We do not have to get out and walk from the gate. Meeting with Vice President Cheney and Secretary of State Colin Powell. Only Mohamed ElBaradei and I. Cheney says he takes his starting point in the security interests of the United States. He does not talk about the world at large. Somewhere he says that the inspections cannot go on forever if they give no results. They are ready to 'discredit inspection in favour of disarmament'. He did use the word 'discredit'. Pretty straight way of saying that if we have not soon found the weapons of mass destruction that the US is convinced Iraq has (though it does not know where), the US is ready to say that inspectors are useless – as they have thought all along – and go for 'disarmament'. I say that we are aware that there are limitations on what inspections do: hard to find objects underground if you do not have intelligence, mobile objects, etc. Nevertheless, you can at the very least check their industries, military installations, get in anywhere, monitor the country. Afterwards I thought maybe I should have talked about the significance of multilateralism, but on consideration it might have been useless ...

Next, we – Mohamed, I, Cheney, Colin Powell and Condoleezza Rice – walk over to the Oval Office and PRESIDENT Bush. He makes a more boyish and less sophisticated impression than Cheney, whose appearance is that of a solid, self-confident – even overconfident – chief executive. Bush is effusive in the manner of an American host. Says he is 'honoured to receive you gentlemen ... ' He has Texas shoes (reaching up a bit on the calves). He looks thinner and less substantial than I had expected. He moves with agility and without any effort to attain stateliness or dignity, frequently changing his posture, sitting at the edge of the seat and spreading his knees, while Cheney moved in measured steps.

Bush explains to us that the US genuinely wants peace. (Yes, it is probably much less difficult for him ...) With some (well-known) self-deprecation he says that contrary to what is being alleged he is no wild Texan and the US is not gung ho on war. It will let the SC talk about a resolution, but not for long ... I think he mentioned the League of Nations ... The US has confidence in ElBaradei and Blix and will throw its full support behind us. I say something to the effect that we appreciate the US support, which is essential for success ... It is a shame not to have any note taker on our side. It is good, on the other hand, that it was both Mohamed and I. While one talks the other has time to think. It is harder to remember afterwards what the hell was said ...

It was not a substantial conversation. Was not meant by the US side to be one. Was meant to be, I am sure, a demonstration that the US (with Cheney, Wolfowitz and Rice lined up at the side of Colin Powell) for the time being is on the multilateral track, sincerely advancing with the UN. The impression – and I suppose the reality – was that this was not an exchange of views but rather an endorsement, an affirmation that the US is with us at least for now despite all the negative things that Mr Cheney and others in his administration have said about the UN path and inspection ... Well, Cheney is of the view that this is only for a couple of months.

The battle within the US administration goes on. Of course, if Iraq were to reject the resolution or if we have a clash in Iraq early (surely wanted by Cheney and co.) the war may be unleashed. Barring that and simply faced with an absence of weapons finds in Iraq it may turn out to be difficult for the War Party to pull the trigger. They will say that inspection has now been tried and found not to work ... However, others will then say: we have containment and that is enough for the time being ... It may turn out that the War Party lost the moment that Bush gave his speech in the General Assembly. Query how long the US threat will be real and keep the Iraqis compliant? When will Security Council fatigue on Iraq set in and Iraq begin to try to ignore the draconian requirements?

From the President we walked over to Condoleezza Rice's office and we were abandoned by Powell and Cheney. They congratulated Powell, who had celebrated his fortieth wedding anniversary. At Rice's office it was just she and her deputy and Mohamed and I. This was a real exchange of views. She was more open than on my previous talks with her. She expressed real understanding that we must maintain our UN legitimacy and that this is in the US interest as well. Even the one-way traffic of intelligence seemed in principle to be understood. However, she did put us on notice that the US had lots of ideas how we ought to go about our work and how we could be 'helped'. This, of course, was what Powell also told me at the Waldorf Astoria meeting. They suggest a 'top-down' approach. What they mean by this is that inspections should target the top (where registers with information are). Do I interpret this to mean that they have little or no idea where weapons are to be found, just asking us to find the map . . . ? They suggest we should overwhelm the other side with inspections. Perhaps double our size. Surprise them. They would like to have an exchange of letters with us. I sense she means some sort of agreement on how we shall proceed together and suggest that we might have something of a memo directed to several who want to help us. Perhaps I misunderstood her . . . Perhaps they want a letter exemplifying how they can help us . . . We shall see. The idea of a bilateral agreement is out of question.

My reaction to the sudden generosity is mixed. For nearly three years they have not been very interested (except in the beginning during the Clinton administration), gone along and accepted our reports. Now they turn around and say we shall have all support and at the same time tell us how we are to change our course. What is a bit disconcerting is that both Powell and Rice present these ideas and offers. Thus, it comes from the height of authority. Yet it must all be thought out at a lower level, in the National Security Council or in the Pentagon, probably the former. Have Rice and Powell thought it through? Probably not. They have other things to do and buy what has been served. Yet the same boys and girls who now know how we should go about our job are the ones who sent us the first US draft resolution in which they wanted 'coercive inspections' with P5 representatives on the inspection teams and armed security escorts . . . Perhaps it was a bearable compromise between Pentagon wanting war and no inspections and the State Department wanting to go with the system set up.

There remains one notable point from the Rambo project: the idea that as some interesting persons dare not be interviewed by us in Iraq, we should take them – facilitate their going – out of Iraq for interviews. I have said in the Security Council and repeated in Rice's office that I see 'practical difficulties' in this proposition. Do we expect the Iraqi government to cooperate with us to let some key witnesses defect? Expect them to let us take scientists and engineers and their spouses and families and associates to our aircraft to fly them out to be given asylum and green cards? If Iraq would be ready to cooperate to let this happen, why should it not go along with letting the persons speak freely in Iraq in the first place? And if Iraq will not cooperate in this, is UNMOVIC to undertake some military ruse to smuggle them out? Is that in our mandate? We do have the right to take out samples and equipment without search and restrictions, but Iraqi citizens . . . ? I sense in this provision the same military 'counter-proliferation' thinking as we had in the now-abandoned paragraphs. However, this one has been mentioned by President Bush in some speech. This seems to be the reason why it remains . . . Colin Powell explained to me that it was an authority, not a mandate. He probably understands.

After the fairly lengthy and substantial discussion à quatre in Rice's office we were joined by Wolfowitz, Jacques Baute, John Wolf, Torkel Stiernlof and others who could fit in the small office of the Security Adviser. We dwelt again on the interview paragraph and Wolfowitz seemed to think that you just tell the Iraqis that they will have to put up with our taking people out. I said I had my doubts that any interviewee would feel confident that he would get to the airport without any car 'accident'. I also asked if he thought we should call Tariq Aziz for interviews without witnesses ... I don't think we got any closer.

After the White House visit Mohamed, Jacques, Torkel and I had coffee at the hotel. Al Jazeera TV was there to interview Mohamed, and I, too, said a few things. Mohamed was also to do the BBC. His press people – Melissa Fleming and a Canadian – are very eager for publicity and to let the Agency be seen. So, they are much less restrictive than we are. They talk a bit loosely. But no great harm is done yet. And it is excellent that Mohamed is talking to the Arab world in Arabic.

Thursday 31 October 2002

Senior staff meeting to make all the key staff feel part of the drama going on. And to discuss distribution of work. Lunch with Tun Muyiat, the UN Security Chief who until recently was head of UN oil for food in Baghdad. In the afternoon long interview with Charlie Rose at a studio on Park. It was broadcast late in the same evening on Public Broadcasting. Sanmuganathan said he found it excellent and thought I was now very relaxed ... I always find it easier to have a talk one to one than when there are several persons in a discussion. In the latter case there is always a certain competition about who speaks.

After the TV interview Ewen Buchanan and I walked up to the house of the Council for Foreign Relations. Richard Gardner (Professor at Columbia) put questions to me for some twenty minutes and thereafter I took questions from the floor. The house was full: 2–300 persons. This is the cream of the foreign affairs crowd. I felt it went very well. Many of them were surely in favour of war rather than of inspections, but I think they recognized that I did not overstate the ability of inspection and that I knew most of my answers.

Friday 1 November 2002

Briefing the Security Council E10 (*elected*) members at 09.30. At the Syrian mission there was a lot of media outside. They had evidently learnt about my coming. Questions mainly about the meetings in Washington. I told the E10 that I am pleased to brief them. I serve the whole Security Council. I am sure they are glad to hear that, considering how they are mostly ignored by the P5 ... Yet in the case of Iraq they are important. The US would not have got nine votes for its first draft of the resolution. The Syrian ambassador told me that his foreign minister sent me an invitation to visit Damascus and Syria. My wife, too! I said I would be glad to come. They are rather close to the Iraqis so they might exercise some – uncertain how much – influence.

Interview with ABC. Nothing difficult.

Visit by Iraqi Ambassador al-Douri. He came with two associates. I told him about our Washington visit. He said he was convinced that the US is just talking about peace and inspection and have simply postponed the attack, which they have decided on, for some weeks. I said I did not think there was a decision. I explained that I thought the purpose of the invitation to Mohamed and myself was to demonstrate (with the sceptics Cheney and Wolfowitz present) that the US stands behind the draft resolution and inspections. I also talked at length about the declaration, which Iraq has to submit under the resolution. This is a chance for them to declare whatever they have. And when we do not have anything ... Al-Douri said, what are we to do? I explained that they ought to look deeper in the stores and stocks. A camel ranch? (*Allusion to Iraq revealing to UNSCOM its B-weapons programme documentation at a chicken farm*) If there remained nothing to declare, they needed to make this credible by documentation and testimony by witnesses. They were not believed now.

We did not say that the British intelligence paper (later called the dodgy dossier) was correct. But nor did we say it was wrong. Now, said al-Douri, if there is no more evidence? I said in that case we would not be able to exclude that anthrax and other things remained. We discussed the burden of proof question again and I said our ambition was to be judicious. We look for evidence. If there is none, we regrettably cannot rule out that some weapons remain. We are not in a criminal proceeding where they would be acquitted for lack of evidence. He intimated that Baghdad was respectful of our position and pointed out that the Baghdad reaction to our visit to Washington had not been to criticize Mohamed and me but rather to criticize the American attempt to influence us. Well, today he is authorized to say this. Tomorrow they might get back to telling the world that we are spies ... 'Truth' is what the leadership decides each day.

Per Ahlmark has succeeded in getting his vitriolic article published in the *Washington Times*. Previously in Standard in Vienna, Helsingin Saanomat and in a Dutch paper. (But not yet in Dagens Nyheter where he has attacked CNN for its 'romantic' reports from Baghdad.) I am pretty sure David Kay has helped to write the article against me. Kay is again singled out as the world's greatest inspector ... In reality, he is someone who wanted to become emperor and got stuck at the grade of lieutenant colonel. After his remarkable but few inspections in Iraq he has forever longed for the TV cameras ...

Today, Saturday 2 November. Cold. Almost snowing. Had UN security people here to 'sweep' the apartment and put in a new lock. Fell asleep after lunch.

Tomorrow, Sunday, breakfast with Walter Pincus and his wife, Ann. And in the evening dinner with the Gardners and a famous TV person, Barbara Walters. I have never seen her. She was at the Council for Foreign Relations and put a couple of questions. Danielle Gardner promptly organized the dinner ...

Next week more preparations for starting work in Iraq. The resolution could be adopted Thursday or Friday. There is much to prepare. Secure phones. Alice and

Brian have gone to Cyprus to rent premises. We need to meet the Americans and discuss their too ambitious concepts and see how we can get the right amount of help from them.

Sunday 3 November 2002

Walter Pincus and I had breakfast today. It is an awful time to meet. Nevertheless, at 9 the café was nearly empty and not until 10.30 did it fill up, so we had time to talk. He seems to think, as I do, that the timetable has been disturbed for the war gang. They cannot demand action in the early phases of inspections and that takes us into the new year, unless we have some incident ... If inspections do not find anything they will criticize us as ineffective, but it will not be easy to justify military action. We had better have some meaty objects of inspection, Republican Guard camps or presidential sites. I told him about the meetings in Washington and my interpretation that the President wanted to demonstrate that the whole of his team now accepts the UN path and inspection – for a time. Pincus feels that the drawn-out clash between Powell's adherents, including the joint chiefs and the CIA, on the one hand, and the Cheney–Rumsfeld–Wolfowitz group on the other has demonstrated that Bush was weak and undetermined.

Sunday night 3 November. Back from dinner with the Gardners and Barbara Walters. At Elio's restaurant on 2nd Ave. between 84 and 85 Streets. I must have gone by this restaurant on my way to Mas Mezcal on 86th several times but never noticed it. Now I know that Sunday dinner is the time when those who want to be seen go there. Next to our table there was Stephen Spielberg with his family. At another table was the family of Wolfinson, head of the World Bank. Others came up to us and said hello, mostly to Barbara Walters. The noise level was high which gives me some difficulty. In any case our conversation was all politics and a fair amount of Iraq. Barbara has interviewed Saddam Hussein on one occasion and she has recently interviewed Fidel Castro.

Monday Night 4 November 2002

Sir Jeremy Greenstock visited me today at my request. I wanted to ask him whether the UK supported the grand American approaches that now are surfacing as 'advice' to us: 'top down', i.e. looking for registers in ministries and administrations, doubling the inspector cadre, saturating the field with inspections and provoking the Iraqis if you can. I said we welcomed advice but would like to hear from the UK and others as well. Jeremy calmed me. We would need to be daring but our inspectors had not had field experience and it would be some time before they were accomplished. The Brits had patience. They were not in a hurry to get the results.

On the resolution he was rather hopeful. Friday or Monday for adoption. Possibly with unanimity. If the Russians voted for, the Syrians would hardly abstain. Today the text was placed before the 'principals' in Washington, i.e. Powell, Rumsfeld and Condoleezza Rice. Thereafter there could be a last round of calls in which Bush talked with other heads of state. The 'material breach' question was most easily solved by eliminating operative para. 4 on Iraq being in 'material breach' since 1991. It was unnecessary. It is future breaches that matter. An armed attack will not be undertaken because Iraq was in violation in the past.

I took up the question of UNMOVIC facilitating defection of people who would not allow themselves to be interviewed inside Iraq. He clearly understood the practical problems we see in this but noted that the paragraph would hardly be taken out. We could perhaps ignore it, but it would be unwise to appear reluctant. I was aware that I have had several goes at this paragraph publicly and that the US might be irritated by these criticisms. At the same time, I think it might be just as well to be on record if I won't use it in the future. Conclusion: enough said. From now just express satisfaction that the resolution 'strengthens our hands'.

Tonight, at Jean-David Levitte's farewell reception he sat down with me, and I thanked him for keeping me so well informed, sending me texts of resolutions, etc. I mentioned the interview-defection matter and he, too, thought it would stay. I said perhaps I had kept up my criticism too long. He said no, no. It served to underline our integrity and independence that I spoke up. I feel encouraged. A flock of journalists surrounded me, and we had a giggly conversation. I understood that they like it that I joke a bit from time to time. Cheers them up.

Tuesday Night 5 November 2002

Back from Finnish party for Jarmo Sareva. Lots of people. I learnt that the US/UK draft resolution on Iraq will be tabled tomorrow at an informal meeting at 10.30. I had better be there. The final text had been blessed yesterday in Washington at the meeting of 'principals'. Met the Chinese deputy permanent representative who is going to chair the meeting tomorrow. He was not sure whether China and Russia would vote in favour.

He asked me how I would interpret the word 'assess'. Clearly it is not the same as 'decide'. In the resolution, I imagine the Council will be asked whether a particular conduct of Iraq reported by UNMOVIC is 'assessed' to be a 'material breach'. I said that if the Council decided that the conduct was not a material breach it would be next to impossible for the US to go to armed action. On the other hand, if the Council decided that the conduct was a material breach, it would probably itself authorize armed action. However, the more probable situation would be that some assess action to be a material breach while others will not assess the action thus. The assessment would be determined by a regular vote, hence with a possibility of a veto. It is hardly a procedural question. The US could thus find itself in a situation where it could not get the Council to adopt a resolution which positively assesses a conduct as a material breach. (I do hope they have not asked UNMOVIC to report 'material breaches' to the Council . . .) Without such an assessment by the Council the US could evidently anyway unilaterally take action. But the same is true today of the situation in North Korea or Iran. It is not excluded that the US could take unilateral action. There is no explicit barrier to it happening – except the UN Charter. Why should they erect such a barrier in the case of Iraq when it does not exist elsewhere?

The Chinese deputy perm. rep. further told me that someone had asked him today why China had confidence in Blix . . . He had said that they had seen me at work for sixteen years in the IAEA. Nice!

The draft resolution must be on the table for twenty-eight hours before a vote. Thus, could be voted upon on Friday. It now seems certain the US could have nine votes. However, a divided vote would be a failure. We would say that the inspection part is supported by all. It is the sanction part that is dividing. Perhaps we could get the Russians and Chinese to say that? It could also be that the Russians would submit some formal amendment . . . It could be one that would be very attractive to E10 . . . Then we could be in the soup again . . .

Meeting at the *New York Times*. Invited to meet the editorial board and columnists. Nicholas Kristof, whom I like a lot, was there. It lasted over an hour. Went very well. Quite useful. When they write about inspection, they can now put a face to it.

Wednesday 6 November 2002

So, the Security Council met this morning in informal session and US ambassador John Negroponte introduced the revised draft resolution. I had received it an hour and a half earlier by fax from Jim Cunningham, so I had had time to study it with Torkel. Not much adjustment made as a result of our criticisms. The taking interviewees out of the country – organized defection service – was still there. The possibility for members to recommend to us how to conduct interviews and what data to collect and then to report it all to the Security Council was still there. The recommendation that we should select the most experienced staff remains (probably recommended by former UNSCOM staff . . .).

Lavrov, the Russian ambassador, started off with some criticism and promised that he would come back tomorrow. I think the Russians feel somewhat incensed at various articles which they find almost impractical, like one which might force Iraq to give us lists of staff in various weapons programmes from 1990 until now. Or to give us reports on all Iraqi peaceful programmes in chemistry – a country with a petrochemical industry . . . Jean-David Levitte, the French ambassador, followed in a rather positive vein, arguing that there was now no doubt that violations by Iraq would be followed by a reaction in two phases: first assessment of whether there was a 'material breach', secondly consideration of consequences.

What is not stated is that if the Council does not manage to agree on consequences the US will feel free to decide for itself which consequences it will give.

Levitte suggested that the Council should ask my comments. He characterized me as the 'barometer' on the practicality of the provisions on inspection. When I was given the floor after the member states, I said I hoped the barometer would point to fair weather ... It was good to speak already today. Greater chance that my suggestions might be acted upon. One suggestion was acted on immediately: they had talked about privileges and immunities simply in accordance with the two conventions, forgetting to state that we should have immunities like 'experts on mission'. On several points I avoided asking for any modification. Just said that I would interpret them as follows ... If they don't contradict me, I shall do as I said ...

Now hoping that the resolution will be adopted on Friday. We need to sign the contract on the airplane service and ask for permission to fly across Syrian territory. If media have been intense on us in the past, I fear they will be even more intense in this coming period, as we start to set up the inspection regime.

Lunch with the ambassador of Cyprus. Celebrating the agreement on the field office in Larnaca. I am very pleased with it. The place is much nicer than Bahrein and the regime friendly, lots of UN in the area and they are used to UN. The ambassador promised to try to arrange for me to meet the President on my return from Baghdad. Benon Sevan was at the luncheon. And Mr Mavromatis, a Cypriot who reports on human rights in Iraq to the GA. These reports are shocking revelations. I asked him why Saddam let out the prisoners. He said the prisons were so horribly overcrowded that they must do it. He thought the Iraqis might be 'cooperative'. Probably, but will it comprise also admissions on the weapons issues?

Tomorrow the Council discussion continues on the revised draft resolution. It will be interesting to hear Russia and to see if the US will make any modifications. It would not cost them much to show a bit of generosity to the Russians.

Thursday 7 November 2002: Battle in the Security Council Is Over

By this morning the representatives in the Council had their instructions and could better comment on the draft resolution. The US and UK had also made some minor modifications to ensure that any material breaches would be considered by the Council (while they did not preclude the US acting unilaterally). Mexico, Ireland and some others pleaded for a mentioning of a nuclear weapons-free zone and for a lifting of sanctions in case Iraq complies. However, while earlier the resolutions promised carrots (lifted sanctions) for good behaviour (disarmament) and got nowhere, this text promises sticks (armed action authorized by the Council) for bad behaviour (continued stonewalling on disarmament).

The Council reconvened at 18.00 and the statements by Russia (Lavrov) and France (Levitte) showed that they were likely to vote in favour.

The US undertook two minor modifications pleasing respectively the Russians and the French. The Syrian continued to press for a vote on Monday rather than tomorrow. He even indicated that he was unable to participate in a vote tomorrow, partly because they start celebrating Ramadan tomorrow. Nevertheless, the US insisted on a vote tomorrow and I think the Syrian was very pleased because like this they are off the hook.

I really feel somewhat tired. Again and again I am about to fall asleep at this computer. How nice it is Friday tomorrow! Today we had a senior staff meeting, which is needed to keep the central people aware of what the organization is facing and make them feel that they are part of a collective effort. I also had a long interview with the Financial Times and a chat with the ambassador of Pakistan who will be on the Council in the new year. Tomorrow lunch with Jarmo Sareva, several interviews.

Saturday 9 November 2002: Resolution (1441) Adopted by Unanimity Yesterday 8 November

It appears that the two minor modifications undertaken had been enough to secure positive French and Russian votes. Perhaps they had intended to vote in favour anyway but were given these modifications better to justify their votes. For the French there was a change of an 'or' to an 'and' in operative 4. I would have read it as meaning that although individual members of the Council may report Iraqi violations before the Council, the latter will only assess whether a 'material breach' has occurred if UNMOVIC or the IAEA have submitted a report. Amb. Cunningham said to me privately that the change made no difference and this was also the reading of Negroponte when he introduced the text. However, after the meeting adopting the text France, Russia and China issued a statement, which apparently (I have not seen it) registers their joint interpretation.

For UNMOVIC, the US construction would almost be better because if the US were to judge something happening as a violation and we did not, we could simply ask the US to table it alone. If our report is indispensable, the pressure might be the greater that we go ahead and we would be seen as acting under pressure. The US construction is, of course, an indication that they do not wish to be dependent upon us. However, our judgement could in any case become crucial, as we would be seen as an independent judge. It could heavily influence members of the Council in their attitude to judging something as a 'material breach' and authorizing armed action.

The other last-minute amendment was to say in the last operative paragraph that action could be authorized to 'secure' peace rather than to 'restore' peace. The latter expression would have implied that the present premise is the existence of a state of war – which the Russians object to and which is a legal notion (as no fighting has taken place since 1991).

The big surprise was that Syria voted in favour after having said the evening before that it would not be able to participate in the vote. Kofi Annan told me that he and Chirac had talked to Assad in the meantime. Someone claimed that the US had also promised that Syria would be allowed to export wheat to the US in return ...

I suspect that a number of other Arab states had been contacted by the US to persuade Assad and with such support and with Russia and China as company he dared to displease Iraq.

The unanimous vote is seen as a major victory for Powell, who is seen as the one pushing Bush to the UN path. However, if inspections are met with no resistance while yielding no results, the hawks will scream that the world is being both fooled and trapped. The US will urge ever more provocative actions by the inspectors in the hope of Iraqi non-compliance. However, if such actions were undertaken, we would lose credibility. In the coming week the Americans are coming up from Washington to see us and offer 'advice and support'. ...

In the papers today some say I have the world's most difficult job! Yes, I may come in for squeezing. The hawks are already writing things. *Washington Times* came yesterday with an article accusing us of holding back information that Iraq had hidden some 8,500 litres of anthrax. Information which had been supplied by US intelligence. Well, I have said that if I had 'solid' evidence of WMD in Iraq I would report it to the Council. In this case the evidence is not sufficiently 'solid' for a standalone report. It was also *Washington Times* that published Ahlmark's article. Probably with a bit of help from David Kay and perhaps others in the US intelligence community. In the future it will probably rather be accusations about slowness or timidity.

How will Iraq respond to the resolution? The article which originally called for their acceptance within seven days was somewhat redrafted to ask them to 'confirm' within seven days that they intend to comply and implement. The guess is that they will do that. They would be unwise to attach any conditions or interpretations because this would be seen as renewed wriggling and be to their disadvantage. At least at this stage it would be wiser for them to look angry, incensed, unfairly treated but cooperative. I had asked al-Douri, the Iraqi ambassador, to come and see me at the end of yesterday, Friday. He had already received notification of the resolution from the SG's office. I told him that we planned for twenty to arrive from UNMOVIC and ten from the IAEA on Monday 18 November from Larnaca. I asked him to urge his government to speed up the necessary approval of the flight into Iraq and return flight on 20 Nov.

He seemed surprised that we had decided to come before knowing what the Iraqi reaction would be to the resolution. I explained to him that if they came with no reaction, we would be ready to come anyway. But, of course, if they rejected the resolution we could not come. Theoretically, they could say that they will continue to ponder the resolution but meanwhile they invite us. However, they should answer by Thursday evening. If an ambiguous reply comes there could be time for the Council to meet informally on Friday ... Also there could be a chance for us to go to Baghdad and discuss. No inspectors are going in at this stage. What if they suggest that they want to discuss 'practical arrangements' under the new resolution before confirming their intention to accept it? We could do that, but they would have to be short. On balance, I doubt they would dare to do any of these things. They would be seen as starting tricks again.

The ambassador said he was convinced that the US was against our deployment of inspectors. Hence his surprise that we intended to go even if the Iraqis were not to answer in time. I said I thought he was wrong about the US. They want inspections now. (For how long is another question.) If the ambassador's reaction is any indication of what the leadership feels, they are disappointed and feel let down by Russia, China and France. They had had hopes for vetoes, etc. They seem so convinced about their being victimized. Al-Douri said he had been a professor of international law (pupil of Mustafa Yasseen) but he had now concluded that there was no international law ... I tried to show him that for instance the expression 'material breach' came from the Vienna Convention of 1969 on the Law of Treaties and that the definition in the convention had some relevance.

Thursday 14 November 2002

Preparations for Baghdad and media. On Monday Mohamed ElBaradei spoke in the General Assembly and I went to listen to him as a courtesy. The speech was fine. Actually, it struck me how similar in components it was to the ones I used to give: the need for nuclear power and the encouraging signs, a piece about environmental threat and about *nuclear power being the only factor that really could do much*. A piece about nuclear safety improving and about the need to show in action that nuclear waste can be handled. A few pages about the use of radioisotopes for non-power purposes, like cancer treatment, sterile insect technique (now in Ethiopia and Mali). And about non-proliferation. Safeguards agreements and the poor adherence to the additional protocols. However, things move, albeit slowly. The tripartite agreement between Russia, US and IAEA has not moved much ...

Mohamed manifests his wish to handle the nuclear inspections in Iraq on his own and a little differently from UNMOVIC. OK. He had concluded that the Agency should not wait for forty-five days to declare that it had 'resumed inspections' in the terminology of Res. 1441. Better prove to be 'proactive'. If this moved up the date when IAEA would have to give its updating to the SC – OK, said Mohamed. We need not report on the same day. That's true. I always held the same, when I was at the IAEA. However, we rallied to his view, and we shall both seek to let our teams 'resume inspections' on Wed. 27 November. Report sixty days later: 27 January. Mohamed did not seem to feel that we should have anything but protocol meetings with the Iraqis and let our colleagues work on the logistics and thereafter let the inspections move on. I feel this is too lax and I am inclined to bring up a number of issues for joint conclusions:

- Agreement on how we shall handle media in the context of inspections (no circus please ...).

- Timelines under Res. 1441. Early measures needed: Office in Mosul. Implementing legislation. Checking that measures in our letter to al-Sa'adi are accepted, including U2 flights.
- Safety in flying in no-fly zones.
- Abolish boxes for helicopter flying.

Today I spoke to Mohamed who was in Washington. He did not sympathize with our intention to have a media man stationed in Baghdad. His inspectors would refer to Vienna for comments ... OK. But there are tons of journalists in Baghdad and I don't think we can simply stonewall.

We have not yet heard about Iraq giving us permission to fly over its territory into Baghdad. The Syrians have granted their permission. Perhaps the Iraqis want to try to rattle us. I think we will take it coldly. Simply wait. But perhaps a reminder to the Iraqis here in NY tomorrow.

On Tuesday 12 Nov. we had briefings at the US mission about intelligence conclusions (not evidence) regarding the three disciplines. Then a rather sharp exchange about how they would like to beef up our plans and help us to achieve what they see as the right capacity. The benign negligence is now turning into an overwhelming embrace. The Pentagon must be behind it. When we resist some of this, they will later be able to say that we failed because we did not accept their assistance. But if we swallowed all, we would be again like UNSCOM, a remotely controlled body of the US military.

In the afternoon I had two heavy TV programmes: BBC's *Panorama* and NBC's *60 Minutes*.

Wednesday 13: All-staff meeting first thing in the morning.

As I was leaving to take the elevator from the thirtieth floor on Wednesday a young man and a young woman came from the disarmament department, evidently interns of some kind. They recognized me (from TV) and we talked. I told them that in 1950 I had had a month at the UN as an essay-contest winner and that it decided my choice of career. Today, as I walked out, they caught me and handed me two candles and said they wanted me to have those for a candlelit dinner with my wife. How sweet! I should have told them that this very day I was called by one other member of the ten-student group who were here in 1950. He phoned me from Canada and wanted to wish me well.

The big event on Wednesday was the 'Iraqi acceptance of Res. 1441'. A horrendous letter of some eight vitriolic pages and a few lines that people choose to read as acceptance. Actually, it only says that they will 'deal with' Res. 1441 ... They expect the inspectors to verify that they have made no WMD since inspectors left in 1998. They talk about inspectors being 'supervised' ... What is meant? I did not at first think that the US would consider this tolerable. However, the Council had not asked that Iraq should 'accept' the resolution. Only that it should confirm its readiness to 'implement'. Some seem to think that Saddam himself has dictated much of the letter. It is very rambling and somewhat vulgar in style.

Visit to Kofi Annan at 6 p.m. Took Dimitri home with me to finish they day with a few sandwiches and a beer and a 'gammel dansk' (*aquavit*).

Thursday 14 November. Interviews with Le Monde, Itar Tass and the main Chinese agency. Yes, we must cater for the world. Not just for the many huge American bureaus. I have done rather well internationally. Also Polish, Swedish radio, the UN, tomorrow a Greek one.

Tomorrow, Friday, will be tough. Health control in the morning. Then senior staff meeting. Then joining the UN daily press briefing (to put in an appearance . . .). Collecting all my papers and departure from home at 4.30 for JFK. Going to Paris to meet the French foreign minister on Saturday. Then on to Vienna in the afternoon or evening. Sunday to Cyprus. Monday to Baghdad . . . Next week: back to Cyprus. Then to London for the Chernobyl Shelter fund and meeting with 'beards' (*intelligence people*) . . .

Friday 22 November 2002. Back from Paris, Larnaca, Baghdad and London

Tired and with a stomach that has rebelled for two days, I am back in New York on a Friday evening. Looking forward to decelerating, though there is much to do during the weekend, much to write and to prepare. Briefing the Security Council on Monday afternoon. Excellent. They should not have the reports through media.

So, on Friday 15 November, Torkel and I enplaned on Delta for Paris. Already in the NY business class lounge we were found by Mr Roth of CNN and a photographer. They accompanied us to Paris, to Vienna and to Larnaca. Just to shoot a few feet of us checking in, waiting for my – nearly lost – suitcase in Paris, checking in at Vienna airport, etc. I have coined the expression 'material news' for news of some substance, contrasting it with soft news or 'non-material' news. Much of what I have experienced on this trip has been 'non-material' news.

The French had sent a car to the airport to take care of us during the day on Saturday 16 and we went to the (very) modest Hotel de France where we had rooms for the day. Showered and rested a bit before we went for the 12.30 meeting with the French Foreign Minister, Villepin. This time we did not enter via the personnel entrance but the grand staircase! The ministry, at least the brass, seemed to be working although it was Saturday. The meeting was good. Villepin speaks English and so does the whole crew. What a change in ten years . . . The outgoing UN perm. rep., Jean-David Levitte, was there (he has been moved to Washington, much to his chagrin) and so was his successor. Pagano, the head of the UN organization department, was also there. Villepin expressed his satisfaction with our contributions in helping to bring about Resolution 1441 and we reciprocated by stressing the central role France and Levitte had played in getting unanimity.

The French stressed that they did not think an Iraqi false statement or omission in the declaration was per se a 'material breach', but rather a matter to be investigated by UNMOVIC. Well, if the evidence of the omission or of a false statement is solid, I don't see why we should need to investigate first. However, in all likelihood the evidence will be circumstantial and in that case assessment of the evidence is in place. Excellent lunch: partridge (with one pellet). After the lunch, car to the Mexican residence and meeting with the Mexican foreign minister, Castaneda, son of Jorge Castaneda, my old international law friend and former foreign minister (who visited me officially when I was Swedish foreign minister in 1978). We discussed what could persuade Saddam to declare and give up his presumed arsenal of WMD. A possible argument could be that he should save not only Iraq but all Arab states in the region from war ...

Trip to Vienna and overnight in a small hotel GRABEN in Dorotheumgasse. It was OK. We arrived so late that we did not go out even for a beer.

Sunday 17 November 2002

Joined by Mohamed ElBaradei and his crew and by Dimitri we enplaned on Austrian (*Airlines*). Media were at the airport to film our checking in! And as we all gathered in the business class lounge the CNN young lady came in and asked if she could film all of us together. Sure ... Four hours' trip to Larnaca. Met by huge press gathering. Short statements by Mohamed and myself and answering some questions.

On Monday 18 November the flight was set to 10 o'clock. It worked fine. A bus took us right up to the four-engine turboprop Hercules L-130. The media transport was somehow delayed so we hung out for a while before we mounted the craft. Each person identified his/her suitcase before it was taken on board. The plane is a transport vehicle. Mohamed and I sat together in the front row. No windows. Two toilets parked in the front of all the passenger rows. A curtain was fixed to be pulled around them when they began to attract visitors. Not elegant but functional. A sandwich and juice were served to avoid any need for lunch on arrival in Baghdad. They had received permission to fly the most direct route, i.e. across Syria. About two hours. Rather noisy. We have a UN limit of thirty passengers, linked to insurance requirements. With me there were: Dimitri, Torkel, Surya Sinha, Ewen, Hiro Ueki, Mullady, Gregoric, Sam and technical people and UN security guards.

Baghdad Visit November 2002

Landing in Baghdad. Mohamed was all the time eager that we should see Saddam Hussein himself. I remained sceptical both on the chances and on the value. As to the chances: he has never seen Ekéus or Butler and he regards the inspections as an insult by the Security Council. I would also wonder whether he would feel it below his dignity to tell lowly dignitaries a lie about Iraqi WMD ... As to the value, what would we say? We would be bound to urge him to make an effort to find any WMD and declare them. Stress the risks of not declaring whatever they might have and impress upon him that the demanding opinions we see at the UN are not only those of the US and UK. In short, we would seek to inject some insights into the real world in the awareness that he might not have been fully informed. Not easy. Mohamed made repeated attempts for us to be received at the 'highest level' and he said to me that he would think it a bad sign if only General Amin from the NMD met us. Well, that was what we got! Our opposite number would be General Dr al-Sa'adi, claimed to be of Cabinet rank. At his side were, as in Vienna, General Amin and Ambassador Hasan (former UN ambassador, a weak but well-connected number ...). I have no complaints. It would have been awful to have foreign minister Sabri or Tariq Aziz as counterpart. They just drool out State of the Union propagandistic lines. I have high regard for al-Sa'adi. He is very skilled, business-like, unemotional. They did arrange for us to see foreign minister Sabri for a short talk on the second day before we started our discussions with al-Sa'adi. We had to wait about a quarter of an hour before we were asked in. Whether by design or not, I do not know. Sabri seemed tired and somewhat bored. He had just had a meal and broken his *Ramadan* fast.

There was total media circus on our arrival. One would have thought that there would be order in a totalitarian state, but they evidently allowed media to mill around almost as they liked. They had prepared a stand for us to speak at, but media assaulted us long before we got to it. The combination of Mohamed and me is good. Many media were Iraqi or Arabic and Mohamed could reply in Arabic.

This was in the middle of the day and General Amin proposed that Mohamed and I and our policy groups should stay at the Al Rasheed hotel, where we were their guests. We should meet in the evening and later they invited us for joint supper. Fine. The UN security guards took good care of me and my luggage. Mohamed and I got suites on the thirteenth floor in this Skanska-built former luxury hotel. Good taste. After we had settled in, we took off for the CANAL hotel, where UNOCHI and UNMOVIC are located. We had talks with the UNOCHI head, a nice Portuguese. We walked around his floor and later opened the sealed third floor that belongs to UNMOVIC. Thick layers of dust and grime. Innumerable tracks of mice, but none of pigeons. Evident that UNSCOM had left the place in great hurry, when they evacuated in the space of an hour in 1998 before the bombings started. A bed was unmade and a desk had diskettes strewn around. We had brought a number of vacuum cleaners with us for the cleaning. Dimitri later opened the room in which they had run the electronic eavesdropping. There was still some equipment. Should we hand it back?

The talks on Monday evening dealt at length with the requirement that Iraq submit a declaration of all WMD and non-weapons-related programmes in the nuclear, chemical and biological fields. They asked us how they could cover such a huge area. We said we were not authorized to interpret the resolution but stressed that surely the WMD part was the most important. They should really look into stores and stocks. If they declared zero, they would need to present more documentation. As to non-weapons programmes remote from weapons maybe they could list them with indication of site and a note that more information could be had on request. While Mohamed was not keen to bring up any items, I had prepared several points. After all, we do not meet that often and we were now to get going. So, I put them on notice that we would want to set up an office in Mosul very soon. I reminded them that implementing legislation was a subject we had talked about and it should not be too difficult for them to move on it. I said we would need expansion at BOMVIC. I took up the issue of media and said we would not tolerate any media at the site or area of inspection during inspections. We could not have a media circus. They accepted this position but said they would allow media in after the inspectors had left. We did not raise the issue of aviation in no-fly zones because we are not ready with it ourselves.

Supper around 10 p.m. in a rather luxurious area. It started with the typical Middle East hors d'oeuvre dishes of olives, etc. and excellent newly made bread. Then came a huge and beautiful fish of which large chunks were placed on our platters. I thought this was the end, but no, shish kebab and rice followed. For dessert fruit. I had a kind of sweet lemon which I had never met before.

On Tuesday: diplomatic corps was invited to Canal Hotel for us to brief them. There must have been about 100. I began and Mohamed followed and there were lots of questions. The most insinuating (and ignorant) came from the Ambassador of Egypt. Either he wanted to appear pro-Iraq or he was an idiot. Mohamed concluded the latter. In any case the interest was lively, and I think they got some food for thought. Mohamed had initially told me it was quite unnecessary to address the diplomats. I think he changed his mind when experiencing. He has also been cold to the idea of having any media person in Baghdad and said that we should handle all that from capitals. However, as we brought both Buchanan and (the new man) Hiro Ueki, Mohamed felt constrained to bring his Canadian head of public information. In fact, this fellow and Melissa Fleming are both very media hungry. Dimitri is irritated but so long as they do not put their feet in their mouths too often (and it has not been too bad) I think we should be generous. Indeed, Mohamed is being matched by them and I think his prolific addressing of Arab media is a great asset.

After the diplomatic corps we addressed UN AGENCIES in Baghdad. There were perhaps forty people. This, too, was most useful. I could assure them that we felt like members of the UN family. Peace is a basic condition for development. Doing away with weapons of mass destruction is a humanitarian task ...

On the Tuesday 19 November we had a meeting with foreign minister Sabri, who was more political. He was 1,000 per cent convinced that there were no more WMD in Iraq. Then further talks with al-Sa'adi and the large Iraqi delegation. They said they were sorry we stayed for such a short time and asked whether we could not come once a month. I said I thought we had settled most matters pending and that we could come when there was a need. Perhaps January might be a convenient time.

After the talks we had a press conference in the Cafeteria of the Canal Hotel. This was organized by our own people. There was a roped-off atrium in the middle and room for the media all around. A platform and two mikes on one side. We both made statements and thereafter Mohamed took the questions from the left side and I took those that came from the right side. It was fairly well organized. Our spokesmen picked the questioners for us. It was here that I managed to deliver the line: 'producing mustard gas is not like producing marmalade. You kept track of how much you make and what happens to it ... '

In bed by midnight. Ready for departure at 7 a.m. Mohamed grumbled no end about this early rising, and I did not like it, but if we were to see the President of Cyprus I had thought we would need some margin. In any case my kind and attentive UN security men (Eric was one of them) secured breakfast for me.

On the Wednesday morning we left Baghdad. General Amin rode with me and we talked about the Mosul office and various other things. He seemed to plead for one hour's grace time at presidential sites and said that 'he might be there ... '. I only responded that I heard what he said, indicating no reaction.

Some media at the airport, but most had been said at the press conference the evening before. The flight to Larnaca took an hour and a quarter. More media. Visit to President Clerides. We rode in two cars to Nicosia and to the presidential mansion on the top of a hill. It had been the residence of the British governor. Modest style. Plenty of modern Cypriot paintings. The president was a fighter pilot during the Second World War and is now some eighty-plus years old. A small genial fellow. We talked mostly about the ongoing talks about the reunification of Cyprus. He was worried about the timetable. His Turkish counterpart, Denktash, had recently had open heart surgery in New York and complications were delaying his return to Cyprus. Clerides' term as president was soon expiring. There was uncertainty whether the newly elected Turkish Muslim government would be positive to the basis for discussions which had been prepared by the UN. The Greek government was positive and so were the Greek Cypriots.

Lunch at Flamingo Hotel. Our friendly hotel manager invited Dimitri, Jacques, Torkel, Ewen, Sam and me for a fish lunch. I was not prudent and ate of the salad plus all the oily fish, octopus, etc. I was punished eight hours later in London by a running stomach ...

MEETING WITH PRIME MINISTER TONY BLAIR, 21 NOVEMBER 2002

London. Wednesday evening Vince Novak comes to the Lancaster Royal Hotel to brief me for the Bank meeting about the Chernobyl Fund. On Thursday morning I dare not eat anything. However, I manage to run the meeting at the Bank. Eating Imodium and feeling at least the consolation that I should be losing weight ... In the evening I felt so well that I ordered a triple decker and tea. I had been overconfident. Woke up early in the morning with stomach running again ... Checked out and was taken with Dimitri and Torkel to see British intelligence. Very useful briefings. More Imodium ... Then on to 10 Downing Street and half an hour with prime minister Tony Blair. I was not in the best of shapes, but I think it went reasonably well. I cautioned him that the Americans have somewhat grandiose ideas about scaling up our inspection operations and that we worry that confusion could result. Actually my earlier interlocutors this morning had no sympathy for the US approach. Blair seemed to foresee that the Iraqis would not declare very much on 8 December and that it would fall to us to look and that we might well be back in cat and mouse. He did not say that this would lead to triggering war. I suspect that if there is nothing flagrant, just an absence of any substantial admissions, it might be difficult for the US to go to war. Won't they need some tangible *casus belli*? More than just claiming that Iraq is lying ...

Saturday 23 November 2002. And Monday. New York

I was lucky that Gustavo, Mohamed's man in New York, phoned me to talk about my briefing of the Security Council on Monday morning. I had tried in vain to reach my doctor. But Gustavo had an Argentine doctor whom he mobilized. The kind soul came within an hour and prescribed Doxycycline (same as for anthrax and borrelia), an antibiotic with a broad spectrum, and something even stronger than Imodium. Well, this helped me. I lived on soup and toast for a while. On Sunday I prepared my brief for the Security Council, gave it to Gustavo Monday morning. He read it to Mohamed over the phone and had a few minor suggestions which I accepted. So, I could deliver it on behalf of both of us on Monday afternoon. Lots of media for me after the meeting, which went very well. Saw both Fedotov (now deputy foreign minister of Russia and our commissioner) and the Iraqi ambassador al-Douri before I went to the Council.

Tuesday 26 November 2002: College of Commissioners

I reported on the trip to Baghdad and on the various interpretations of Resolution 1441 and on suggestions to accelerate expansion of our inspectorate in Baghdad. (US view.) Several members warned against any crash programme. All inspectors must have about the same training. No different categories of inspectors ... Useful notes for John Wolf.

Thursday 28 November 2002, Thanksgiving

Today is free and I enjoy going at ultra-slow pace. I was rather exhausted last night after a period of much work pressure, media pressure and political pressure. In addition, the stomach infection lasting from Thursday a week ago (London) to last Sunday (NY) cut my strength a bit and it was followed by beginning of a cold, which fortunately subsided (at least for the time being . . .). Tonight dinner with Göran and Bozena at a French restaurant down at 20th Street, Fleurs de sel. (Turned out a nice evening with reasonably good food.)

Yesterday, Wednesday 27 November, had two major elements. A several hours long 'working lunch' with the US at their mission. John Wolf, the assistant secretary for non-proliferation, was there with a number of colleagues. Secondly, a substantial interview for CNN with its international star reporter, Christiane Amanpour. First the US discussions. They discussed a number of inspection concepts with us:

- The top-down approach: we know Iraq has WMD. The leading figures must know where things are. Go and look at their files. Fine. Am I to draw the conclusion that you only are convinced they have the WMD but really don't know where they are? I could have figured out myself that the tops might have some clues but thank you for the idea . . . I suppose you don't mind if there is some provocation at the same time. At least there would then be some result. The 'testing of cooperation' would occur. Iraq would be pressed relentlessly until it would tolerate no more. Then it would balk. Cooperation would have been tested and – eventually – denied. The report to the SC would be due. I don't know where we could expect the Iraqis to balk: at Saddam's bedroom or his mistresses' quarters? The question would arise if we really would have the Security Council with us in a tactic of provocation. Or would the sympathies in media and public opinion swing to Iraq? This is what happened to UNSCOM. I have stated that we are not in Iraq to harass but to perform inspections. There *could* be reasons to inspect women's quarters (by women inspectors) to look for documents which their husbands might have taken to hide at home but there ought to be specific suspicions. It cannot be done with the simple purpose of provoking. A further sobering thought is that UNSCOM tried the top down a good deal but did not catch any fish. Once Iraq has learnt that documents and diskettes are prize catches, they have mechanisms to quickly whisk them away.
- The saturation – or trawling fish – approach of inspections. Go to a lot of different sites at the same time. Some people will be caught off guard. OK, but do we have the resources of planning and doing, ourselves?
- Expansion of staff. Instead of 100 inspectors in Baghdad, why not 200? Then you can do the trawling. We have difficulties in welding together and organizing the forces we now gather and providing them with equipment. Don't push us to an unmanageable situation. That would be embarrassing.
- Interviews. It was conceded that we would neither kidnap nor organize defections. Fine. If interviewee after interviewee declines to be interviewed alone, we could report that to the Council. OK. It would be for the Council to assess

- whether it was caused by the individual's fear of being misunderstood or by their fear of their own authorities.
- We can invite an interviewee and his family and if he says they want to leave for interviews abroad, just demand it! If Iraq refuses to let them out, threaten immediate report to the SC. Is the US ready to go to war to enforce the right to interview? If so, I would be ready to try. But if Iraq refuses, alleging, for instance, that the family needs an exit visa, where does it leave the family? At the BOMVIC? We have a chartered airplane to transport UNMOVIC/IAEA personnel. What if the Iraqis say we do not have any right to take Iraqi passengers who are not our personnel . . . ? Am I to draw the conclusion that you can (try to) offer them safe passage out (to an awaiting green card) because they would not dare to speak in Iraq and remain there.?
- Offer of some forty new US candidates, mainly from highly qualified US military. They could not have the ordinary UN contracts. OK, we shall look at them. Alice said their CVs were extremely good. Whoever we take, we shall want them to take part in the next training course, i.e. 20 January and three weeks on. We would need to balance any increase from the US side by increases from other sides.

The interview with Christiane Amanpour. The moment was right. But I was tired . . . And it was in the crammed CNN studio on the fourth floor with technicians hanging in cameras and cable near us. It was hard to get the feeling of a closed conversation (as I felt with Charlie Rose or even with CBS at the Millennium Hotel recording). She was also more in questioning than conversation mood. And I did not feel that she had prepared herself very much. She asked about my concerns about 'interviews' and about the difficulty for Iraq to declare its chemical programmes in thirty days and about the IAEA' s visiting Iraqi fissionable material only every six months rather than every six weeks if all the material in the country had been added together. These points she must have picked up in some recent articles. (Clearly from Gary Milhollin's article in the *Wall Street Journal*.) She had thus done some shallow fishing to find something to grill me with. Some of these questions, of course, become almost standard and I ought to work out standard replies. Here are some attempts.

With the criticism that we have heard about you, we must ask 'are you the right man for this job?'

This criticism of my role at the IAEA has come exclusively from some private individuals. I was re-elected three times at the IAEA and could have been re-elected a fourth time. I did not apply for my present position at the UN. I was drafted for it and the Security Council unanimously supported me for it. I believe I still have the Council's confidence.

Yes, Ahlmark is spreading this in an article, which he publishes all over the world. He claims he has known me for forty years.

The reality is that Ahlmark and I have not met for some twenty-five years. He has no first-hand knowledge of my work at the IAEA but bases himself on slander from someone who worked for me and did not get the promotion he wanted. He wants to give this fellow the Nobel Prize for peace. For someone who pretends to be revealing truths, Ahlmark is scandalously uncritical of the sources he relies on.

Monday 2 December 2002

It was a relief to have the weekend. Friday night I was tired. Left the office shortly before seven and was invited for dinner to Andrew and Pamela Jacovides. Relaxing.

During the weekend reading Sven Hedin's *Babylon, Nineve and Baghdad*. A bit more interesting as he gets down to Baghdad after having described every turn and village on the Euphrates passage by raft.

Shopping a bit on Sunday: pyjamas at Bloomingdales and a book by Bob Woodward on Bush and the war.

Drafting a letter in response to Colin Powell's letter of 13 November to me.

Today a talk with Condoleezza Rice at the US mission. Pleasant and relaxed, but she seems fixed on the idea that we should take Iraqis out of the country and interview them, say, in Cyprus. She admits we cannot force them out. And if they all say no? Just report it to the Council …

THE IRAQ DECLARATION UNDER RES. 1441

Much of the week was about how the Iraqi declaration under Res. 1441 (2002) was to be submitted to the Security Council. In the past the so-called full final and complete (FFCD) declarations were always submitted to UNSCOM and the IAEA. This resolution adds that the Security Council should also have the declaration. To be sure the US wanted to have access to a text and to be able to declare Iraq in material breach if it did not declare things that the US claims to have evidence of. However, with the proviso that the Council should get the text, it had also created the problem that parts that might facilitate proliferation would get into the hands of other states than the P5, which already have experience of BC and A weapons (already live in sin, as I say …). Syria, for instance, is a member of the Council.

We had told the Iraqis that as a service we were willing to receive at BOMVIC (*Baghdad*) the text of the declaration intended for the Council. This gave them a couple of days' extra to work in the declaration. It was to be delivered to the Council on Sunday 8 December. We received it in Baghdad on Saturday 7th in the evening. Surya Sinha took it to Larnaca on Sunday morning. He was accompanied by Eric, a UN security guard. They shared the two hand luggage bags. Took Lufthansa from Larnaca to Frankfurt and then on to New York, where the UN had arranged to meet them on landing and took them by car directly to the UN. Dimitri and I came at 8.25 p.m. to the UN building where lots of media and cameras were assembled to interview me. Fortunately, Surya arrived before I had run out of interview stuff and his bags became the centre of attention. We went up to our thirty-first floor. By nearly 11 p.m. the President of the Security Council, Ambassador Alfonso Valdivieso of Colombia, arrived with advisers and Adam from the UK mission, representing the current coordinator of the P5, and Duffy from the US mission.

I formally handed the hand luggage bag to Valdivieso and he directed me to hand it further to the UK/US, which were to copy it and spread it to each of the P5 to the fury of the elected 10. Here was the background:

On Friday morning 6 December I was in the Security Council private meeting and presented my routine quarterly report on UNMOVIC. During the question period Lavrov noted that the declaration to arrive would contain proliferation-prone material and the Council had to take care not to spread it. He inquired whether UNMOVIC could be of help to purge risky material before the declaration was distributed to the Council. I responded that we would perform whatever service the Council wanted, but it would take a bit of time. After much wrangling the President concluded that UNMOVIC should receive the bag on the Council's behalf and distribute a purged version to all. Greenstock made feeble attempts to suggest that we might want to have help from the P5. I did not respond to this, but Gustavo Zlauvinen declared on behalf of the IAEA and Mohamed that the IAEA would call for such help ... US Cunningham acquiesced in the solution. This nearly cost him his head ...

On Saturday all hell broke loose. Hawks in Washington realized that they had joined in asking the inspectors of all people to censor what Washington should read! Colin Powell got into action at the ministerial level. Negroponte worked in NY. Saturday afternoon I talked with Greenstock and Negroponte and the Mexican foreign minister, Castaneda. First Greenstock tried to get me to ignore the Friday conclusion from the Council and give the P5 the whole declaration; I explained that I had no authority to do so. They could call a new meeting of the Council and change the conclusion. This was not to their liking. I said that I would do whatever the President told me was a new sense of the Council. So, they roped in all the members, mostly via capitals, and got their consent that the Council President should allow the P5 to get a copy each to read and to advise UNMOVIC and the IAEA as to what they should purge. In reality it was all about Washington wanting to see every sentence ... Only Syria formally objected to any change in the Friday conclusion, and they (and the President) decided to ignore it.

On the Tuesday thereafter I was to brief the Council at a luncheon as to how we were to handle the text, and our purging of it. Feelings were furious. Even Norway felt indignant at this unequal treatment of Council members. Lavrov said that the procedure had been wrong, but the substance was right. Well, did the P5 really want to advise us on the purging? They have since stated that they will accept our conclusions on the purging. What they really wanted was to see for themselves the whole text ... All right, the US, France and Russia have given us their advice and that is not bad. Query whether the UK will. I doubt the Chinese will come in time. Tomorrow we must freeze the text and have it in at least fifteen copies. As the text to multiply is about 3,500 pages, a day is needed for the copying ... On Thursday Mohamed and I are to present preliminary assessments of the text. Right now, the problem is the final purging and the reasons given for purging. We are omitting not just passages which can contribute to proliferation but also passages about suppliers and individuals.

Friday 20 December 2002: *What a Week behind Me!*

During Monday our analysis people finished their analysis of the 10,000 pages (actually, 3,000 pages in the main body and 5,000 pages supporting documents in Arabic, which have not been translated) and checked the advice we had got from the US, the Russians last week and the Brits and the French on Monday. The censoring was not too difficult on the cookbook (for weapons of mass destruction) side. The deletion of the names of suppliers and persons could be more controversial in the eyes of media, which love to find culprits, and in the eyes of lawyers in the US, who want corporations to sue for illness sustained by people they claim came in contact with chemicals in Iraq.

Our people led by Jean-Louis Rolland finished their work late Monday evening. The President of the Council, Ambassador Valdivieso, came up at the end of the day and I received from him the instruction that we should make fifteen copies to be distributed at the end of Tuesday when they would be ready. So we did. (Later we got instructions to make five more copies for the new members of the Council.) Igor Mitrokhin is an excellent organizer. During Monday I spent a lot of time on the covering note to the material, which was to be distributed. The production of the fifteen copies took the whole of Tuesday and all members were invited to pick them up at the end of the working day. Most did, but not all.

So, the ten elected members got only one day to study the purged text (the 'working version'). I had spent part of the weekend drafting the first parts of my speech for the Security Council, Thursday 19 December. I had drafted one part describing the inspection build-up in Baghdad and a second part describing the results of the first few weeks of inspection. The third part was to describe the preliminary analysis of the declaration. Now on Wednesday 18 December I worked into my draft a big and good chunk prepared by the Australian Rod Barton and reworked a final page drafted by Dimitri on where we go from now if Iraq fails to provide evidence. All in all, about ten pages.

Thursday 19 December 2002

Mohamed and I went to see Kofi Annan at ten in the morning – before the SC meeting. I thought I had found a good last page for my speech. I ended by saying that one could not promise to find every last bolt, but new techniques were now available, and Iraq would find it harder to hide in the long run. After our discussion with Kofi, I felt this was perhaps too defeatist in tone. On the other hand, I don't think it is becoming to promise more than we can deliver. I don't want to oversell inspections.

There was not really a discussion in the Council. No one expressed satisfaction with the Iraqi declaration. It had become clear to all that the Iraqis have copied large parts of earlier declarations and added bits here and there. The US has tried to declare that this declaration amounted to yet another 'material breach'. Well, if you are convinced that you have evidence that Iraq is concealing something, a non-mention of this something becomes an omission. Someone not in possession of evidence cannot tell whether there is an omission, but the result of the lack of evidence is that no confidence can result.

When the Council was over, Mohamed and I spoke to the numerous press people outside. Mohamed is much more relaxed than I. Later in the afternoon after the Council, I had the BBC and Canadian television. Japanese TV and the Jim Lehrer show. I did not feel it went very well, but no one has told me so.

Today a briefing of EU at their mission. Useful. Not too difficult. Then I had CNN, which was not too good. Before I spoke, I saw Mohamed on the screen. He was interviewed by Christiane Amanpour. I find that the setting of a studio affects me. At CNN in the UN building, it is all cramped and crowded. I much prefer sitting at a table. When you sit in a chair with nothing between you and the camera you feel sort of naked, defenceless. You have to keep your legs under control. Not move them. It was Richard Roth, the station head who interviewed. He is mild and soft spoken in private but loud and 'aggressive' when the cameras are on. A relaxed calm response becomes harder. I sort of adapt to the tone of the interviewer. Should not.

Today there is a picture of me on the first page of the *New York Times* and further into the paper there is a long excerpt from my speech in the Council. Does not happen every day . . . The main editorial of the Times was about Iraq's Declaration, and we came out quite well. They termed me the 'cautious Swede'. All right, I don't mind that. In the UN building, more and more people now recognize me. Outside in the streets people do not. In restaurants a few do.

Saturday 21 December 2002

Kofi Annan called me. He had been in Washington yesterday attending a meeting of the so-called quartet on the Middle East. It consists of Kofi, Powell, the EU and Russia. They had also talked about Iraq. Colin Powell had been quite pleased with the processing of the Iraqi declaration in the Security Council. He had praised me and Mohamed and said that Blix was as reliable as a Volvo . . . Considering that he loves Volvos and spends free time (does he have any?) poking around in his stable of old Volvos I think this was high praise. In retrospect I think my comments came out in the right balance.

I talked to Dimitri this morning. He was awaiting Regina and Alexandra today. He sounded a bit better. Had got his voice back. I commented that the NYT today reports that the US is planning to give us intelligence soon. Talk is about giving satellite images! What the hell, we buy those commercially ... I hope they mean something more serious. They talk about their concern for leakages and say that UNSCOM leaked. Well, they have had two years during which they could have discussed security with us ... I think we might have more concern that they misuse us than that we leak. They can evidently not have a conversation with us in New York about intelligence without this being talked about in the NYT the next day! Above all they speak about the importance of taking scientists out of Iraq. Is the CIA behind that? Is the main purpose getting some potential defectors out? Or is the main purpose getting an Iraqi refusal of letting people go and thus a 'material breach' of the resolution? (I imagine that many Iraqis would not all by themselves like to go to Cyprus for an interview.)

Friday 27 December 2002. At Les Carroz

I left NY almost one week ago by Lufthansa via Frankfurt to Geneva, where Eva and Mårten met me on Sunday 23 by 2 p.m. Had bought booze and an electric plug adapter in Frankfurt. A hostess on the flight Frankfurt–Geneva recognized me and told me that her mother had worked for the IAEA Maritime Radiology Lab in Monaco! She was nice and gave me a bottle of wine as we neared Geneva. I sent my greetings to her mother. The adapter I had bought turned out was for adapting European to US sockets rather than one for US to European ones. Cost four and a half Euro! (In Carroz I later bought the right one in M. Martin's shop for one and a half Euro.) No snow in Carroz but some rain. Xmas menus begin: herring, ham with Swedish mustard and apple mousse, aquavit and beer.

We have been on the phone a good deal. Dimitri has phoned me from New York. He has got over his cold and Regina and Alexandra have joined him. They go to St Martins for New Year. He has had talks with the US intelligence and military. I and he are sceptical about any US assistance to us by the Predator drone. One was shot down the other day by the Iraqis. Imagine it had been one marked UN, working part time (though ostensibly full time) for us! The US says they can let us have one exclusively for us ... However, the pictures it gives must be relayed through US centres. So, I fear there are no exclusive uses. They are big and can operate many hours. The corresponding French and German machines are smaller and operate shorter hours. Politically it would be better to have a German one, provided that the manning and operation is free of charge. Inspection must be, and be perceived to be, an alternative to armed action, not a prelude (precursor).

The fuss about interviews with Iraqi scientists abroad continues. Washington Post reported that the IAEA had 'initiated' a new investigative phase by interviews. It suggested that the Agency thereby was well ahead of UNMOVIC ... Nothing like a little friction to report ... Well, it turns out that Mohamed had said in some interview from Sri Lanka (where he vacations with his family) that the IAEA was starting interviews – but not saying it was abroad ... So Gwozdewski (his public info man) goes out and does one better, while the reality was that they had asked one Iraqi for interview in Baghdad and this chap had insisted that there be an Iraqi minder present, which the IAEA had gone along with. So, there was nothing new – except possibly that there apparently was no recording machine.

There seem now to be nearly 100 UNMOVIC inspectors in place and some 6 from the IAEA. As we have to give an interim report to the Security Council on 9 January, I am beginning to think what elements should be in it. We must talk about the 81 mm aluminium tubes which Iraq declared to us and we have now inspected and which the US is claiming are for uranium centrifuges. We have to report on the air force document from the period of the Iraq–Iran war, now transmitted to us. About our demand for implementing legislation and for beginning interviews ... The planning of a second trip to Iraq is now firming up. Mohamed and I would fly from Larnaca either 18 or 19 January and spend a few days in Iraq, perhaps make a trip up to Mosul? The Iraqis aware of the criticism against their 10,000-page declaration are eager to be seen to meet us and to explain any questions about the report. I think they could jolly well give such explanations publicly and in writing. They know what is fishy and needs to be clarified or amplified. A trip around the 19 January would fall suitably before the 27 January, when we have to 'update' the Security Council. Media try to play up that meeting as a big event. As the occasion for a final report, while it is an 'updating'. Perhaps the increasing media attention will make the meeting into the event they want it to be ... The US would probably want to advance the view at that stage that there have been more 'material breaches', laying the ground for possible armed action in February when their preparations are ready. However, query whether there has been much drama before 27 January. If we were to get information leading us to some hidden sites and the Iraqis stopped us there, this would certainly be a big thing. But Iraqis refusing to be interviewed without minders present would hardly be big.

Sunday 29 December 2002. Rainy Les Carroz

I was reading Bob Woodward's book about Bush at War. It is impressive intrusive journalism about the reaction to September 11. But query whether its popularity does not chiefly rest on its thrill and entertainment value. It is indulging in the day to day, even hour by hour, development of collective thinking and action. It is more chronicle than history and analysis.

I am also reading Joseph Conrad's 'Victory', which I had never read before. The intrigue is more tense than in most of his writings. Action is not slow but grips you from the first page. Yet it is his mastership in describing the soul – without psychoanalytical paraphernalia – that grips you the most.

I have read a book containing a long interview with Scott Ritter on Iraq. It confirms my impression of him as a sincere but not sufficiently critical player. He is probably truthful in his account of events. Among the noticeable points is his saying that he had CIA staff on all his teams and that they were excellent and indispensable. Only when they began to 'call the shots', decide, did he react. The objective was no longer exclusively the mission given by the Security Council, namely, doing away with the weapons of mass destruction, but also spying on the whereabouts of Saddam Hussein. OK, but I think UNSCOM should have put its foot down long before that happened.

From the very outset of operations in 1991 the CIA was part of UNSCOM's operations and through UNSCOM probably also part of the IAEA's operations. UNSCOM asked to have representatives on our teams. I did not suspect at the time that they were CIA. I was just irritated that they wanted to have what I thought were 'chaperones'. As UNSCOM was responsible for all logistics and intelligence and designation of sites to be inspected it was hard to resist their having people on our teams. I only reacted sharply when I once in the early period discovered that Ekéus was in full swing asking missions in New York to name inspectors for what was to be an IAEA inspection. Ekéus became so unpleasant that I preferred to let *Mauricio Zifferero (head of the IAEA Action team for Iraq)* handle it without much participation from me. In retrospect, I might conclude that I stood for the independence of our mission and having failed to sustain it left it to the more 'pragmatic' Zifferero to run our part of the show – which he did very well.

Tuesday 31 December 2002. At 22.40. New Year's Eve. Les Carroz

UNMOVIC is presently headed by Rachel Davies. Dimitri has gone to St Martins somewhere in the Caribbean without possibility of cell phone contact and, unacceptably, without other telephone link. This afternoon a problem arose in the box set by him for the helicopter flight linked to an inspection mission tomorrow. Iraq had demurred and said they could not guarantee the safety of the flight. At the recommendation of Rachel and Surya Sinha I agreed that we should cancel the flight and let the inspection be only by ground action.

End of the year. From May when I joined the Secretary-General's 'dialogue' with the Iraqi foreign minister, it has been an intense and tense year. The inspection path must be and must be seen as an alternative, not a prelude, to armed action. I do not think that the US has made up its mind to go to war even though they are taking all the steps in that direction. It serves to scare the Iraqis. And should the Iraqis not provide maximum cooperation the US might determine that the inspection path is hopeless. There is presumably a momentum built into the great build-up of troops. Can Bush refrain from letting the coiled spring jump without losing face? He will need some manifest action by the Iraqis to hold the spring down. Will the Iraqis reveal something in January before the Security Council meets on 27 January? So far, they are simply repeating what they have said before, namely that they have nothing and have no more documents. There is no evidence available to us that solidly contradicts that. However, the British, German, French and US (not to speak about the Israeli) security services seem convinced that Iraq is hiding weapons of mass destruction. (Indeed, the suspicion that they may have chemical and bacteriological weapons is vastly complicating the US preparations for war.) Mohamed and I shall go to Baghdad around 19 January. It is a strategic moment just before the Security Council meeting on the 27 January. But in ten days' time, on 9 January, we have another meeting with the Council. I am preparing ideas to advance at that meeting. The US is seeking to contend that Iraq is in 'material breach' if it does not provide conclusive evidence that it does not have WMD. The burden of proof is on Iraq. OK, we don't have to prove that they still have such weapons. But are they in 'material breach' if they don't? I would rather say that they have not fulfilled the criterion for the lifting of sanctions laid down in Resolution 687. That is different.

Year 2003

Friday 3 January 2003

A rather full day. Home by 7.15 p.m. The British Ambassador, Sir Jeremy Greenstock, phoned and suggested I visit the British PM, Tony Blair, on my way to Baghdad around 17 January. He recommended I also visit the SG of NATO, Robertson, if I go to Brussels to see Solana and others. I wonder if the French Foreign Minister will not also want to see me in that round ... What will Russians then say ...

The media pressure will rise as we get closer to the speculated time for a US armed action. Already the 'updating' we are to do in the Council on 27 January is billed as a 'report' and possible grounds for US action. The non-aligned have written to the President of the Council and asked that the meeting in which we report (update) be open to all members. I understand there is a procedure under which a meeting of the Council is open to all but only members can speak. We'll see if this is the mode the Council will choose. It does not like to be seen as exclusive and closed. If they allowed members to speak there would be a stampede of states arguing against armed action.

Our updating is seen as relevant for the question of peace and war. If we find severe errors or omissions in the CAFCD (Current Accurate, Full and Complete Declaration) this will weigh as breaches. The US will argue that even the non-presentation of evidence is a breach. That will be hard to maintain.

Already this morning there were journalists and photographers near the elevators as I came from the long corridor to the conference building and some news lines resulted from the few things I said: that we would ask for clarifications on some points in the declaration, that our inspections cover ever-larger areas, that we are considering how to move on to interviews and that we planned to go to Baghdad ...

During this weekend, I need to draft a first outline of my presentation for 9 January. We are set to go to Baghdad on 18 January. Mohamed should be free.

Saturday 4 January. 2003

With increasing attention being given to Iraq I seem to land in the limelight, whether I speak in interviews or am invisible. Sergio Gonzalez Galvez phoned me yesterday and said he had seen me on TV in a white coat and a silly white cap walking into a North Korean nuclear installation. It must have been from 1993! The fact that my name is so easy possibly also plays a role.

Kofi Annan phoned me a little while ago. He was planning to be away next week and not be present in the Security Council on 9 January. OK. He relayed again that Colin Powell seemed very pleased with our way of operating. We talked about the interview business. He was aware of the IAEA debacle of conceding an interview with a minder when they had first asked for it to be private. He even knew that the spokesman (Ueki) had had to backtrack a bit after the interviewed scientist had protested. I said I was thinking about asking for three kinds of interviews: with minder, without minder and perhaps also in Larnaca.

We talked further about North Korea, and I said one ought to explore the question of guarantees against any violation of DPRK's borders. They are paranoid. I also mentioned the evident case for the several great powers to act together. Kofi said he was sending Maurice Strong to the DPRK for an exploratory mission. He suggested that Maurice might speak to me. I noted that if inspection were needed, the IAEA were the ones to do the nuclear, but if they needed inspection of missiles or biological, UNMOVIC was the only one with experience and present capability. I said we had no need for further work, though. Financing would also be difficult. Later in the evening I had direct contact with Maurice Strong. He told me that the DPRK was very touchy about any intermediaries. They wanted direct settlements with the US. However, the UN had played a big role (through the World Food Programme), and he, Maurice had been sent there to discuss long term economic questions, including energy. So, this time the humanitarian (*aspect*) was the entry ticket but an extension was provided. Maurice had had a bypass operation in the past year and felt like a new dog ... He praised me warmly for my Iraq work.

Sunday 5 January 2003

Korea and Iraq. The Korean crisis disturbs the US Iraqi strategy. The DPRK has thrown out the IAEA inspectors, may have two nuclear weapons and may start producing more plutonium and the US says it can all be solved by diplomacy. Iraq has been open to the inspectors everywhere (so far) and has no bomb-grade material and a major invasion is said to be inevitable ... Well, the latest noise from Moscow is hopefulness about a diplomatic solution ... Nevertheless, the comparisons make a US belligerent line in Iraq no easier.

Thursday 9 January

Security Council meeting today. ElBaradei and I briefed the Council on the current inspection situation, which was not difficult, but also on how the Declaration by Iraq does not respond to the many questions in the Amorim Report and the UNSCOM document 1999/94, which was more difficult.

Many members of the Council have only been there a short time (as of 1 January, Germany, Spain, Chile, Angola and Guinea are new) and do not seem to have any idea of Resolution 1284 (1999). All they have focused on is the new (American) resolution 1441 (2002). It is that resolution which requires that we shall 'update' the Council sixty days after the start of inspections, i.e. 27 January. As the US military prefer to start an armed action by the middle of February, if such action is to take place at all, they would not mind a dramatic meeting of the Security Council on 27 January. However, it is doubtful that an international alliance can be cobbled together by that time. More likely an alliance against armed action.

I had occasion to remind the Security Council today that inspection aiming at disarmament did not start in Iraq on 8 November 2002, the day of the adoption of Resolution 1441, nor, do we hope, will the task stop on 27 January, when Mohamed and I are to give the Council and 'update'. Rather, under Res. 1284 we are obliged to define 'key remaining disarmament tasks' around the end of March. The Council is to consider and approve our selection and 'programme of work'. Resolution 1441 continues with the strong powers it confers upon us.

There may be difficulties ahead for the US. If we have a denial of access or if we stumble upon some stock of *the nerve agent* VX or anthrax, then the material breach will be easy. However, if nothing dramatic occurs it will be hard for the US to garner support for armed action. I doubt the US, if it tried, would even get a majority for a resolution authorizing armed force. And if it did not have such a resolution, going it alone would have much less support in American opinion and might not allow the US to deploy from Turkey or Saudi Arabia.

Friday 10 January 2003

The *New York Times* today had extensive reporting of my and Mohamed's reports yesterday to the Security Council. NYT even carried long excerpt from our speeches! It is an incomparable newspaper in coverage; it also had its chief editorial on our subject and advocated continued inspection unless some smoking gun turns up (or the US presents the evidence it claims it has).

The build-up on the Iraqi issue for 27 January continues but the UK and others try to play it down a bit. Many begin already now to suggest that the inspectors should be allowed to perform their work, to take their time ... Mohamed has been saying that a few months will suffice for a thorough investigation. I don't understand how he dares to say that ... even though I realize it is less far-fetched in the nuclear sphere than in the chemistry sphere. After all, Res. 1284 does not put any end to inspection, only to sanctions – provided that key remaining DA tasks are solved.

11 January 2003: Possible Perspectives for Iraq

Alternative A: The US build up in the Gulf will be around 100,000 men by the end of January. There may be a momentum in this very build-up. How can you build it *down*? So, there will be pressures for striking in February. But there are considerable counter-pressures. Unless something dramatic and flagrant happens hardly any country in the Security Council would support armed action. The US would have to bypass the Council to avoid showing how isolated it would be. However, without SC endorsement the US would hardly get permission from Turkey to attack through Turkish territory and it would have a lot of other obstacles in the region. There are other significant obstacles. Wall Street does not like the prospect of war and the oil price may be affected, especially now that Venezuela is out of production through strikes. The popularity of war in the US is also highly questionable. Media speak much about the build-up and about the inspections but not about more evidence of WMD. On the contrary, the aluminium tubes for centrifuges that were held up as evidence of an ongoing nuclear programme seem to have been written off by the IAEA and we hear no more about the import of yellowcake (*raw uranium*) from Africa.

Barring dramatic discoveries or standoffs, I think there will be a low likelihood of US armed intervention. What is then the outlook?

First, the timetable is indicated by Res. 1284, i.e. UNMOVIC/IAEA are to submit a work programme by 27 March and that programme will identify the 'key remaining disarmament tasks', which will have to be approved by the SC.

Will the Council wait until 27 March for this list? Will it be tempted to hold that we have 'started to work' (not only 'resumed' inspections) long before 27 January and that, hence, the work programme should be submitted earlier than sixty days after 27 January? Possible, but not very likely. To be sure, we have gained a lot of insight and shall have done a lot of re-baselining by 27 January. All this will, indeed, help us to draft the work programme and to identify key disarmament tasks.

Already now one gets some gut feelings as to where the Iraqis are: on missiles they must have made much progress, deploying missiles with a reach somewhat over 150 km and ready with missiles that reach that target with a very big payload. Lastly, they may be ready with a design of a longer-range missile, perhaps they have even produced it and are hiding it now. In the chemical area they have probably mastered how you undertake industrial level production of VX. In the bio sector, the anthrax-freezing techniques should be ready. They probably have stores of old anthrax and ability to step up production.

Outlook: Long-term monitoring that will make it impossible for Iraq to undertake major industrial production of proscribed missiles and large-scale production of chemicals, or, indeed, nuclear. They would run risks of detection constantly due to espionage and defectors. Provided that the Security Council remains agile and ready to back up inspectors.

Alternative B: If, in the next two weeks, we were to discover some prohibited items, weapons of mass destruction or proscribed missiles we would immediately report it. This, to be sure, would be a material breach, but what advantage would there be in an armed invasion? The hawks in the US would confirm that Iraq cannot be trusted and that only regime change is meaningful. Others will say that Iraq must now declare everything else they have ... Or, they will say that the case showed that inspection could be relied upon to reveal hidden objects ...

Dimitri Perricos was here for a moment this afternoon. He is going to Baghdad now. Will arrive there on Tuesday and lead a number of inspections.

Wednesday 15 January

Off to Brussels (EU – Solana, Patten; Paris: Villepin and Chirac; London: Blair at Chequers; Larnaca, Baghdad; Athens, New York). Back next Tuesday evening and report to the Security Council Monday 27 January.

A hectic period. The US govt is warming to war. Over 100,000 men in the Gulf area. Nothing has happened to precipitate, but with such a build-up most people will find it hard to believe there will not be armed action. Or is it just pressure? I am not hopeful that the Iraqis will crack and put some weapons on our table. Either they are gambling or they have very little. We don't know.

SECURITY COUNCIL MEETING ON 27 JANUARY 2003

Monday 27 January 2002. So, for 12 Days I Have Made No Notes!

Today was the big day. Someone said 1,000 journalists were accredited to follow Mohamed's and my speech in the Security Council! A report stated that the Dow Jones was falling as I was speaking! My critique of Iraq was interpreted as supporting those who want to go to war against Iraq and this is not deemed to be good for Wall Street ... Well, I am not keen on the war, but I have seen it as my duty to give a straightforward assessment of the current situation. A landscape painting of simple naturalism, no romanticism, nor surrealism ... I have said to the media that my answer to those who have said my speech played into the hands of those who want armed action has been that I do not play at all ...

I think I did give a straightforward picture. And it does not come out too nicely for Iraq! In a central part I was saying that it appears that a decision has been taken in Iraq to be cooperative on process and that a similar decision is needed to bring about the cooperation on substance that is indispensable to bring about disarmament by the peaceful method of inspections and long-term monitoring. After our visit to Baghdad and the various points Iraq has resisted (U2, private interviews, access to private houses) and the various forms of harassment against our inspectors (incident with inspectors sightseeing a mosque) they have put up, I cannot imagine that they would have expected a very positive note. Maybe what I delivered was more severe than they had expected. I was told that the Egyptian Islamic press bashed both Mohamed and me.

I was trying – as always – to give an accurate picture of the situation. The world being such as it is, it is not difficult to find good and bad marks for most relevant players.

The production of the 'update' (report) was quite an effort! I began writing bits in (*our chalet in*) Les Carroz (*France*) during Xmas and New Year. Little of that proved eventually useable but it was a kind of warming up. I had thought I should make it clear that Resolution 1284 (1999) was still operative and that just as we had delivered a report by 1 December to the Security Council, we should deliver one on 1 March. In the plane on the way back from Baghdad (Athens–New York) I wrote some notes on the subject of private interviews with Iraqi scientists, on the inspection of private homes and on the find of twelve chemical weapons warheads. Then, of course, the discussions in Baghdad and our ten-point Joint Statement had to come into the text.

Serious writing began on Wednesday 22. That day I also called in Rod Barton and Geoff Forden to be responsible for the principal section that was to be devoted to unresolved disarmament issues, like VX, anthrax and al-Samoud missiles. The next time for writing was Friday afternoon, when I stayed in the office. Saturday at home writing and then to the office by 4 o'clock, staying, myself, until ten in the evening. On the Sunday I worked the speech on the computer at home until 4 p.m. Thereafter at the office where I stayed until nearly ten. Torkel, Ewen, Rolland, Perricos, Rod Barton and Geoff Forden plus Surya and Jean-Louis were gathered. We had to divide the work somewhat between us.

The production of a speech (this one fifteen pages) is an interesting process. I often feel a little like a sculptor facing of an amorphous clump of clay. One has certain ideas that sit in various clumps. They have to be fitted together. Then one has to consider the total length and the order in which the ideas are presented.

This one had a first part describing the development and thrust of the three main successive resolutions: 687 (1991), 1284 (1999) and 1441 (2002), finding the requirement of cooperation to be the continuous thread. And noting that Iraq did not seem to have genuinely determined to cooperate on the substance of disarmament, which is required to go the peaceful path through inspections. A second part explained that there is cooperation on substance and on procedure and that the latter – access, communications, infrastructure – had been positive and that the former needed a decision of the same kind as they had undoubtedly had on process. Then a long section about a number of open issues like anthrax, etc. The third part specified how Iraq could provide cooperation on substance, namely, by providing proscribed items (as *UNMOVIC now identified* 122 mm chemical warheads), providing documents (instead of our finding them in private homes), providing interviews (rather than individuals who refuse to talk without minders present). The fourth and last part described our accelerated build-up and our readiness to serve the Council.

My report sounded much more critical than Mohamed's. He reported progress and said, as usual, that he only needed to confirm that nothing had happened between 1998 and now and that there were only a few open questions. He pleaded for some additional months for inspection and said this would be an 'investment in peace ... '. I was asked again and again why I did not plead for more time. My first reaction was to say that with the unsatisfactory situation on cooperation on substance, where Iraq does not seem to have developed any determination (the 12,000 pages report did not solve any questions), I could not in good conscience assume that a few more months would help. Later comments added that if I were given some more months by the Security Council, I would certainly welcome it. With eight years of inspection, four years without inspection and now only two months with renewed inspections one wondered whether it was not rather early to call it a day ...

Saturday 1 February 2003: A Tough Week Is Gone

The past Iraq week. On Tuesday 28 we had a little breathing space. I had a video conference about the Iraq situation with people in the European parliament. A luncheon with the EU ambassadors (at the Greek Ambassador's residence). TV interviews with Reuters and al-Jazeera. On Tuesday night President Bush gave his State of the Union Address and I did watch the whole thing on TV. There was a long piece about DPRK and Iraq at the end. He sought to highlight the economy by beginning with it and filling most of the speech with it, but the culmination was on the international twin problems. Most readers interpreted the speech as meaning that the decision to go to war had been taken. I doubt that. He did not say and think they still hope for a last effort.

On Wednesday the Security Council met for informal consultations based on our updating. No criticism of my rather sharp speech.

On Thursday evening a letter arrived from al-Sa'adi inviting ElBaradei and myself to Baghdad to discuss transparency, implementation of our joint statement, etc. Mohamed was already on the way to the airport when I got it. I succeeded in reaching him on the cell phone and we had similar reactions, namely, to respond by clarifying that the central theme to discuss would have to be cooperation on substance. In addition, Iraq would have to act on the issues, which had not been solved in Baghdad, namely, the use of U2 planes, interviews in private and implementing legislation. I talked with Kofi Annan, and he went along. He thought it would be unwise to ask for confirmation that Iraq is going along with our proposal. We might risk that they would come back with something woolly. I put nothing in our text about a wish to meet at the 'highest level'. This is Mohamed's wish. I don't know if it is meaningful. At any rate I don't want to have a request turned down.

Saturday 15 February 2003. Colin Powell's PowerPoint Presentation to SC

Two intense weeks. Let me take it chronologically. We sent our reply in accordance with the above. On Wednesday 5 (*February*) the US Secretary of State, Colin Powell, came to the Security Council to convince it through a PowerPoint show that Iraq was not complying and that it was hiding weapons of mass destruction. It was a good, well-rehearsed show. Powell told us that he had spent four days at the CIA to go through the material, select what he wanted, secure the declassification of it and put it in shape for presentation. He presented it very well, but for the experts it was less than compelling as evidence. That evening of 5 February, I and Torkel Stiernlof, my special assistant, and Ewen Buchanan, took British Airways for London to see the Prime Minister the next morning. We are now given royal treatment at JFK. BA checked us in at the Concorde lines (while CNN who trail us have to be in ordinary business-class lines ...) and we were able to have dinner in the departure lounge and thus avoid spending hours over a meal rather than sleeping on the plane. Our departure was at 9 p.m., so there was no difficulty. Perfect arrangement. On the plane, Fox television came (with a Swedish correspondent) to interview me and so did the CNN journalists (Richard Roth and the nice Liz ...). People took us to the FCO, where we were shuffled into the Ambassador's waiting room. A Dickensian character from the non-proliferation unit looked after us: Mr Spoor? He wore a ruffled suit, unkempt hair and unbelievable shoes. We thought we would meet the foreign secretary, Jack Straw, first but we were mistaken. This was just waiting. Shortly before 11.30 we were walked over to 10 Downing Street, where some 100 journalists were waiting across the entrance. We entered without any interviews and realized that Mohamed ElBaradei was already there. He had been taken into a separate room with Jack Straw. I was met by Tony Blair, photo opportunity and then shuffled into his office (the same as I had met Margaret Thatcher in years ago). Somehow it all went so fast that Ewen Buchanan was shuffled in with Mohamed to be with Jack Straw. Torkel Stiernlof somehow was left behind and missed both audiences! He probably thought that the arrangement was one to one ... So, I have no notes from my talk with Tony Blair this time ... After about half an hour I moved over to talk to Jack Straw and Mohamed moved to talk with Tony Blair. I understand that Mohamed used the occasion to talk more broadly about the Middle East. Blair had recently hosted a conference with Palestinians so it was most appropriate.

We had lunch at the Royal Horseguards hotel with FCO and intelligence people. For the first time we had some discussion of what resolution might be forthcoming: an ultimatum of some kind. It was in any case not just a text that would directly authorize the use of force, but it would demand something and if Iraq failed to deliver that there would be green light for military action.

On Friday morning 7 February, we flew to Vienna, went to the VIC (*Vienna International Center, the UN complex in Vienna, Austria*) and I gave a one-hour pep talk to the participants in our seventh training course. I had no manuscript this time but talked about the current situation, which probably interested them most. I am glad I showed up.

After the lecture we checked out and then went to the airport (by taxi again) and adventures began. We got all the way to the Tyrolean plane for Budapest and were even seated in that plane when the captain announced that there was something wrong with the computer... Back we went to the terminal and began to ask about alternatives. We were first told that we could take a plane for Prague where we could change for Cyprus Airways and arrive at Larnaca by four in the morning... After discovering Laura Rockwood (a legal adviser at the IAEA) and all the big TV correspondents, Austrian Airlines wisely laid on another plane to take us to Budapest and the kind Cyprus Airways waited for us almost two hours. So, we arrived rather late in Larnaca. I went directly to Mohamed's hotel, to sit down with him. We used the occasion to talk also about the DPRK. Having sat in the plane between London and Vienna next to the Iranian foreign minister, and having talked to him about an NWFZ (*a nuclear weapon-free zone for the Middle East*), I had the idea that Iraq could cut a reformist profile for itself if it came out and urged that a NWFZ should be the vision for the future and declared that Iraq's disarmament was a step in this direction. It could declare its willingness to adhere to the Chemical Weapons Convention and to accept the Additional Protocol for IAEA safeguards. It could declare itself a test ground for bio inspection – which has not been adopted under the biological weapons convention because of US resistance. Mohamed shot down all these ideas and said they would be seen as a circumvention of the essential acute problem, which is Iraq's implementation of UN resolutions. I felt he was right and that it was good to have him to talk to.

While I accepted Mohamed's argument on this point, I did not go along with his thoughts on another matter. He is trying to push me all the time to sit down with the Iraqis to discuss the concrete weapons issues. It has looked a little like al-Sa'adi's wish to settle things by conversation at the table. Iraq holds that they have no weapons, and they just need to convince us of that, which can be done in dialogue. As we hold that they have to produce evidence on remaining items, discussion is not what we are looking for. Listen, yes, at any time but not discussion. I do tell Mohamed though that our document describing the open arms issues as we see them against the documentation of today, will soon surface. It will be in March and the document – the so-called Cluster document – will be used as a basis for the selection of 'key remaining disarmament tasks' which is supposed to be made toward the end of March.

When I returned to the Flamingo I was met by the owner, and Gregory Patilis and a few more, and the owner invited us to beer and cheese toasts. It was a nice relaxation after a long day.

BAGHDAD VISIT FEBRUARY 2003

Saturday 9 February Larnaca–Baghdad

We left Larnaca by our own Hercules L-100 plane at 9 and arrived – with one hour's time difference – at 12.15 in Baghdad, where Amir al-Sa'adi met us. There was a demonstration outside the airport, and I could see two placards, one reading WAR NO, the other reading INSPECTION YES. Not bad. Government welcome?

Talks from 4 to about 8 in the evening. Al-Sa'adi presented a lot of answers to questions which IAEA had put to them. He turned to us and said they had prepared 'papers' on some central issues like anthrax, VX and missiles. He explained them and we agreed that we would bring some experts the next morning to see what further clarifications we wanted. So, I did not move to some kind of negotiation but solely to talk to get maximum clarity. Our experts got the papers immediately and studied them till late in the night; they met the Iraqi experts in the following morning. Bovallius' comments were that, it was useful, but no, there was no more evidence ...

Al-Sa'adi further proposed that we might jointly try to examine whether some kind of quantitative analysis could be achieved through drilling into the ground where the Iraqis had poured the anthrax and the VX. They had made some test drillings and thought you could get some quantitative assessments by looking at a large area and seeing what it yields. There was a rock foundation under the earth where in 1991 they had unilaterally poured the chemicals and biosubstances ... Our experts were not very hopeful that this would work but we might not have great difficulty in getting the necessary advanced equipment needed.

We discussed the U2 flights, and I discovered that it might be less difficult for them to accept such flights if we also had non-American planes, notably Mirages and Russian Antonovs. I said I thought we were interested in that (the Russians had recently told me that we could have Antonovs without any charge, just like the US and France). Nevertheless, they insisted on US/UK stopping fighter planes in the no-fly zones while the U2 was in the air. This we would not agree to. I made it clear that we would not have any joint statement but preferred our separate press briefings. Yet we should compare notes to avoid our statements going in different directions.

The Iraqi side announced that General Amer Rasheed had been appointed chairman of a Commission to scour the country in search of documents providing documentation. The commission appointed earlier to look for any possibly existing proscribed further chemical warheads had had its mandate expanded to cover any proscribed items. The chairman, Mr Mohamed Shaker, was included in the Iraqi delegation. Both developments were to be welcomed, provided they lead to results ... and are not just manoeuvres ...

Mohamed had, as before, pushed for a visit to Saddam Hussein but, as before, this was not granted and we were, again, invited to see the Vice President, Ramadan. (Actually, on the Sunday.) He is a short fellow with a revolver in his belt and a beret on his head. Perhaps sixty. He was evidently not very happy with my report on 27 January in the Security Council. He talked a little ominously about how one can become a statesman but also how one can lose such status and become like a Butler (my predecessor) very quickly. I said one had to follow one's conscience, to which he agreed. It was calm discussion. Mohamed preached the need for a 'change of heart', and early adoption of legislation implementing the UN bans on weapons of mass destruction. When Ramadan replied that legislation took time, Mohamed noted that they had had twelve years. He also tried to impress that time is running out ...

We had dinner, offered by the Foreign Minister Naji Sabri. Same flat fat fish as last time. Beautifully grilled over charcoal but fatty and you only nibble a little. I dare not take the fresh vegetables. The shish kebab is ok. This time we were offered red wine. I think I took Naji Sabri with surprise when I said that I was aware that he was going to Tehran the next day (I had learnt it from the Iranian foreign minister in the plane when we talked ...). Sabri said it was not public, because last time he was to have gone there, it had to be cancelled due to demonstrations in Tehran. He did go and I read that some members of the Majlis had tried to impeach Karchai (the foreign minister) for inviting Sabri ... Sabri was minister of information earlier, so he is well versed in the propaganda. Al-Sa'adi is much preferable.

I had *some* side meetings. *One* was with a small delegation from South Africa, led by their Undersecretary of State for foreign affairs, an intelligent man of Indian extraction. They had come to urge the Iraqis to open up, as South Africa had done, gaining the confidence of the world. They told us they were acting in line with the UN resolutions and Mandela is running his own show, which is more linked to NGOs.

On the Sunday 9 Feb. we had further discussions with al-Sa'adi and his delegation. Our experts had had talks with theirs on the basis of the papers they had studied during the night. On one point al-Sa'adi scored a small triumph. We had complained that the list of personnel they had sent us was defective and too short and we had given examples of names which we had, ourselves, and which we were surprised were not in their lists. Al-Sa'adi now went through the examples we had given and showed that most of them were, in fact, included in their list. Exceptions were some 'technicians' ... Well, well, I thought an angry thought about the need for quality control but also realized that there could be difficulties resulting from different transcription of Arabic (this turned out to be the case).

We talked about interviews, and we insisted that we decide whether we want to be without minders and tape recorders. Regrettably, the Agency seems to have developed a practice to allow recorders and to allow them to be deposited sealed with the Iraqi side. ElBaradei agreed with me that they must abandon this, but it does not seem they have done so yet ...

We had a session with all the staff at BOMVIC and I think such pep talks are desirable. We did not meet the diplomatic corps this time.

The press conference was well organized and lively. I was asked whether I thought we had made 'drastic' progress or a 'breakthrough' and answered in the negative to both. I said I had some cautious hope from a few of the developments: the papers delivered (more proactive), the idea of trying quantitative searches for VX, the Commissions ... As before, it was an advantage to have both Mohamed and me. You get some breathing space, and you can add to his answers and vice versa.

After the press conference came the more tedious and difficult, but important, sessions with various news channels, CNN, etc. I hate these pacifier-looking gadgets you put in your ear to hear what the hell they are saying in Atlanta or London, and which fall out of your ear in the most inconvenient moments.

Monday 10 February. Baghdad–Larnaca–Athens–New York

I got up shortly after 5, had breakfast and we went to the airport. Poor Bovallius lost the caravan and came after in a taxi. Al-Sa'adi was not there to say goodbye and I wholeheartedly approve of this. Meaningless to drag him out of bed that early in the morning. Bad enough that we did it. I was almost surprised that Mohamed went along with such an early departure. He does not like to get up that early. However, this was our chance to get early to Athens. For us going to New York it meant we could catch Delta direct Athens–New York. Great. Arrival NY around 4 in the afternoon (10 February). I slept a good deal but wrote also on my coming report to the Council. CNN and Fox were on board, but they had done their interviews on the plane from Larnaca so it was peaceful from Athens. Some people recognized me and the crew asked for photos to be taken together. Late in the day I was called to the cockpit. Condoleezza Rice was sending me a message. It was simple: could we meet the next day at the US mission. OK. Talked to the pilot who had been flying U2 planes and said the Iraqis could not reach it by anti-aircraft fire (contrary to what Dr al-Sa'adi claimed, that the planes were 'sitting ducks' for them). In New York, we were met by Delta and UN and quickly shepherded through immigration and avoiding media; on my way home with Torkel and Ewen we stopped at my Korean grocery, and I was able to stock up with the most necessary: pastrami, Swiss cheese, apples and other fruit, string beans, milk, etc.

Tuesday 11 February. New York

Arabic Eid holiday = UN closed: Australian Prime Minster, John Howard, at Hotel Pierre. Talk with Condoleezza Rice.

Having arrived the evening before after a long journey Baghdad–New York and waking up on a UN holiday it was a bit rough to get up as usual and walk over to Hotel Pierre, which (to its merit) is located on my street, E 61.

Journalists were crowding outside the hotel and squeezed some comments out of me. Torkel was with me as was Eric, my nice bodyguard.

Australia's conservative government has sided with the US in the Iraq affair and is ready to join in armed action. The decision is controversial in Australia and a substantial anti-war opinion exists.

The prime minister was courteous and did not demonstrate any hawkish convictions in our talk. Rather, he listened to my long explanations. I know I talk too much on these occasions, giving the other side little time and chance to come in with counter-arguments. However, in self-defence I might say I probably know more about the subject than he does . . .

TALK WITH CONDOLEEZZA RICE

From Prime Minister John Howard, I hurried down to the US mission to meet US national security adviser Condoleezza Rice and US permanent representative at the UN, John Negroponte, plus Assistant Secretary John Wolf and Mr Tobey, a young fellow, but head of the non-proliferation unit in the National Security Council. It was a nice, frank discussion as always with her. Very courteous. Very diplomatic. No pressure. However, I am sure she was worried about my presentation to the Council on the coming Friday 14 Feb. The day after our talk the NY *Times* had an article which was wildly misleading about what we had said. It alleged that she had 'admonished' me to say this or that . . . .

Actually the only point on which I have felt the US pressing hard has been for interviews outside Iraq. And last fall about doubling the number of inspectors, including an American as a deputy to Dimitri or in some other high position. On all these points – with the possible exception of the interviews – they have relented. Everybody seems to think that we are under awful pressures from all. That is not at all the case. All seem to be very courteous and restrained: from the US to the UK and France and Arabs.

One point I made to Condoleezza Rice clearly came to worry them. I did say that I planned to have some critical comments on the topic of the quality of intelligence that we see, including Colin Powell's presentation to the Security Council. The background was that our analysts felt they were not impressed by Powell's presentation and even less by the intelligence we have been acting on. We have acted on some twenty cases of sites given to us by intelligence. Only in three of these cases have we found something: in one case the pile of nuclear-related (not terribly interesting) documents, in a second case a number of non-declared Volga rocket engines (which may also have legitimate use) and in the third case a store of conventional ammunition in a chicken farm. Add to this the case of aluminium tubes alleged to be for centrifuges for the enrichment of uranium and the case of alleged attempt by Iraq to make contracts about the import of yellowcake from Niger. No one will give Iraq the benefit of doubt, but it is hard for any outsider to feel that the intelligence provided *has weighed heavily*.

The mild criticism of intelligence which I felt honesty required that I let surface surely had an echo in the so-called 'community'. When Jeremy Greenstock next came to *see* me, he had Eugene (his intelligence guy) with him and sometime thereafter (on Sunday) Mark Allan came over from London to have dinner with me, Eugene, Dimitri and Jim Corcoran to talk about the role of intelligence and to establish that despite shortcomings we all love intelligence ... It was an excellent meal at the Absinthe. Mark is very nice.

Wednesday 12 February 2003

We had an extra meeting of the College of Commissioners, so that I could report on the results of our Baghdad mission and have a discussion in the light of the various political winds. It was a lively discussion and easy as we did not have a need to summarize it or draw any conclusions from it.

SECURITY COUNCIL MEETING 14 FEBRUARY 2003

Friday 14 February 2003

Briefing of the Security Council in open meeting with foreign ministers. It was really tough to get enough time to draft this statement. I had Tuesday after lunch, quietly in the office. Most of Wednesday was taken for the College and on Thursday I had a group of British parliamentarians plus the Belgian Prime Minister. Nevertheless, I did write pieces on the Tuesday afternoon and placed orders for contributions to be written during Wednesday. I was not going to have many paragraphs about individual weapons issues, as I did on 17 Jan. On the Thursday morning I managed to get up an hour early and put together a plan for all the *inputs*. I brought it to the office and asked Surya and Torkel to be chief editors to stitch together the various parts. In the afternoon we sat together around my conference table (Torkel, Dimitri, Ewen, Surya, Sam) and we remained there until after 11 in the evening. This time I wanted to avoid any general judgement and rather to give short passages describing the positive and the negative. As it turned out, the speech was perceived as rather optimistic. France, Germany and Arabs were happy and the US and the UK were disappointed ...

Afterwards, commentators have asked how come I was so harsh in January and so mild in February. First, I fear they have not read the fine print. When I talk in somewhat hopeful terms about the Iraqi appointment of a Commission to look for documents or proscribed items I make the caveat that they may be helpful if they work fast and are 'serious' ... Secondly, the criticism is based on some simplistic notion that if you are harsh on one occasion you must continue that line. I have now tried to put out the line that these briefings should be snapshots of the reality which we see at any given time. When the reality changes, the snapshots will also change! Admittedly, it is not easy to get the right balance. You have to select your material – just as journalists do for their reports – and your selection is a matter of your judgement. I try to get an overall selection that has a balance that squares with my overall impression. By and large I think my judgement is realistic and reasonable.

Mohamed was pleased with my brief this time. Even the Iraqis said it was fair, though not sufficiently fair. These two comments should perhaps worry me ... I had no express criticism from the US and the UK; perhaps they were too courteous to do that ...

So, we had the foreign ministers of the US, UK, France, China and Russia, Spain, Chile, Mexico, Syria, and the German foreign minister, Joschka Fisher, acted as President.

Iraq's perm. rep. al-Douri, sat at the table like Mohamed and me. The room was packed with representatives of member states. After I and Mohamed had spoken, each of the others – including Iraq – were allowed seven minutes. Then the public part adjourned and we had sandwiches in the adjoining SC hall.

THE IDEA OF BENCHMARKS

I had a word both with Jack Straw, the UK foreign minister, and Colin Powell, about the idea of 'benchmarks' for Iraqi compliance, mentioning that we are about to finish our 'cluster document' in which each section will conclude with a section about what Iraq has to do to resolve the issue. They were both very interested and Powell asked me to phone him during the following weekend. Benchmarks for Iraqi compliance on matters of 'process' had also been in the air, focusing on acceptance of U2 and acceptable interviews.

The informal, unrecorded discussion that took place after the luncheon was an extraordinary affair, with the ministers speaking off the cuff, all trying to be a little funny. Villepin, the French foreign minister, had already in his public speech referred to France as an 'old country', alluding to Secretary of Defense Rumsfeld's discourteous references to 'old Europe' (France and Germany) and 'new Europe' (Bulgaria and Poland, supporting the US). Colin Powell then said in the informal session that he came from a young country but the oldest democracy in the room. Jack Straw said he, too, was from a very old country 'founded by the French in 1066 ... '. Mohamed and I got several questions from the ministers and we both spoke at length. I managed to comment that Iraq would not have accepted any inspection had it not been for the outside pressure – by the League of Arab States, the SG and, above all, the US military build-up.

Later in the afternoon I had a visit from the Finnish Commander in Chief, who had been visiting his American colleague and was quite convinced that the decision about armed action had been taken. But he also said the US military were very nervous about the whole project.

Saturday 15 February 2003

Condoleezza Rice phones. She is quite interested in what I have had to say about the cluster document and the idea of 'benchmarks'. I explain and promise that I could show the document to John Wolf to give them an idea, but I could not give it to him as others were not to have it. She promised that Wolf would come up on the following Tuesday.

Sunday 16 February 2003

I phone Colin Powell. John Wolf has talked to me during the day, and we have agreed on a meeting Tuesday. In the talk with Colin Powell, I explain that the cluster document could lend itself to setting 'benchmarks'. I say further that 15 April was a date that had been mentioned as a final date for checking whether Iraq had attained the benchmarks. He said this was too late.

Monday 17 February 2003

Meeting Sir Jeremy Greenstock in my office despite the fact that the UN was closed for President's Day. There had been a blizzard during the night.

Eva and I walked down to the UN on a Third Ave. that was closed to cars and full of snow. A lonely skier came up the avenue, presented himself as a member of the US delegation and asked if his girlfriend who was walking next to him could take picture of us (I am becoming a celebrity . . .). OK. She was kind to send the digital picture by email to me. They were excellent and I have had several colour print-outs. The city was unbearable for several days. Snow was not carted away. The mayor was lucky that the temperatures rose and much melted away.

Jack Straw had evidently alerted Jeremy and asked him to check my ideas about 'benchmarks'. At this stage I had worked out a memo and even a draft resolution (*see entry below for 2 March*). The latter included a last date (timeline) within which Iraq would have to have lived up to the benchmarks or else it would be open to members to take armed action. Thus, an ultimatum, a word not loved here. I gave Jeremy both – and he promptly gave both to the Americans, so that when I met John Wolf on the Tuesday he had both.

Tuesday 18 February 2003

I had invited John Wolf for lunch, and he came with Negroponte and Tobi. I had Dimitri with me. John then came over to the office and I showed the cluster document to him. He began immediately to look for pilotless vehicles (UAVs) and the treatment of 1998–2002. I sensed that he was not enthusiastic about the idea of benchmarks.

Later in the afternoon I gave a long interview to Dagens Nyheter. I also talked to Olof Skoog, my first special assistant (2000–2001) until the Swedish foreign minister stole him back to make him ambassador to Colombia. As Torkel Stiernlof's contract ends on 18 March I needed a successor and mentioned this to Anna Lindh, the Swedish Foreign Minister. She was enthusiastic and asked if I wanted anyone in particular and I said to her that Olof would be the only one. He knew the job; he was enthusiastic, and the Ministry fixed the conditions he wanted.

Thursday 20 February 2003. Telephone Talk with Tony Blair

Talk with British PM Tony Blair by secure phone at UK mission. It was a long talk. I pleaded somewhat for a resolution with a timeline, preferably a few months from now. He did not seem to think the US could wait longer than to the middle of March. (I have a transcript taken by the Brits in my office.)

Missile letter to Iraq was being prepared the whole day by Dimitri and his folks. At the end of the day, it is discussed with me Torkel and Surya. It is not finalized until Friday and delivered then. Important to make clear that we skip any technical discussions and tests. It is an order essentially. The expert panel we had was categorical and our College of Commissioners had also been very forceful when we met one week earlier. Any lengthy discussions or tests would have been very negative and shown us as soft at this time. The main difficulty related to the some 400 Volga rocket engines which had been imported illegally and could be used for the now-proscribed al-Samoud 2. Some of them might be for some permitted rocket (SA 2). We found a formulation which saved engines which the Iraqi could prove were for another programme. Dimitri was the soft one and Surya was the hawk. (I liked a formulation that I saw in the *New York Times* that 'scratch a little on a dove and you find a patient hawk ... ')

Friday 21 February 2003. Missile Letter Delivered to the Ambassador of Iraq. Condoleezza Phones

I forget what we spoke about. I certainly told her about the missile letter. I think she was eager to impress on me that whatever we say about cooperation from the Iraqi side, it has not been 'immediate'. This I can subscribe to, but it is the cooperation that shall be immediate, not the disarmament, sometimes contended by US spokesmen. She apologized for the misleading accounts of our previous meetings and says she will limit the attendance from their side (I suspect either John Wolf or Toby briefs the hawkish US mission spokesman, Grenell).

Later I had a talk with al-Douri the Iraqi ambassador. I told him that I understood that this (missile destruction) would be painful for them, but it was entirely in their interest at this juncture.

Saturday 22 February 2003

Kofi Annan phones from Paris. Kofi is very good at keeping track. He is on a long trip now. First to Brussels to the Europeans. I and Mohamed were also invited but felt it was not needed when Kofi was going.

Sunday 23 February 2003

Greek foreign minister George Papandreou phones. (He is chairman of European foreign ministers at present. He speaks good Swedish, but we talk in English.)

In my talk with Papandreou, I underline that the French said they did not think inspections were forever and that they did not rule out force. It was a question of time. Ergo: would it not be possible to set a timeline?

Monday 24 February 2003

College of Commissioners. We have a discussion about the current situation for a couple of hours. It becomes clear that the US is no longer interested in the solution of particular disarmament issues. All that matters is a 'change of heart' and this can be spotted in simpler ways than watching specific issues. Hence, the cluster document is not of any particular interest. Moreover, Wolf says the real problem is the period 1998–2002. Where are the UAVs? The mobile bioproduction units? I counter his views with some heat. Bryan Wells, UK, seeks to second Wolf but it is obvious that they are alone in their views. Wolf has also an ability to voice his line in a rather sarcastic, disdainful way. He is a good representative of what the Bush administration wants ... At lunchtime the members are given free time so that they can have time to study the document. Media are parked outside our conference room to catch me or Wolf or Fedotov ...

Tuesday 25 February 2003. College of Commissioners

Rather favourable reactions to the cluster document. They agree to send in their written comments before end of next Monday and also to pronounce themselves on priorities. This is important. We thus will know their views on the matter and will not need to submit our selection. It will be made in full awareness of theirs.

Thursday 27 February 2003

Visit by Angela Merkel, leader of CDU (*Christian Democratic Union, Germany*), and by Hans Dahlgren.

First, a talk with the ambassador of Bahrein. I have written a letter to him asking if Bahrein would allow us to take Iraqis to Bahrein for interviews – in the same manner and on the same conditions as with Cyprus. We still have office premises in Bahrein. It is Arab and conceivably it might be less difficult for Iraqis to allow themselves to go there than to Cyprus.

Hans Dahlgren said public opinion *in Sweden* was strongly engaged in the Iraqi issue. Anna Lindh was really rather hawkish compared to the public mood. He realizes that Iraq won't move a finger were it not for the outside pressure. He says that I have very high ratings at home.

Friday 28 February 2003

General staff meeting. Call from Condoleezza. Lunch with European Union.

We had an all-staff meeting and I described to them the political situation and where we find ourselves. I think it is good to pull them in so that they feel they are insiders in the great drama. Most of them, after all, do not see much of the play around us.

Condoleezza was probably interested in my next report to the Council. Not much she can do about it at this stage. I mildly prod her on the Canadian proposal for a timeline for Iraq. I remind her that 1441 is not only about disarmament (as held by White House spokesman) but it also establishes an enhanced inspection regime. And I remind her that it could not have been the intention to cut inspections early in Feb.

Indeed, something must have happened in Washington between my talk with Colin Powell about benchmarks on 16 Feb. and now. They evidently fear that they might be dragged into something that would take time. Better simply declare that Iraq is not cooperating as it should and say they could have done that; they missed the chance and now it is time for armed force.

Condoleezza also wanted to alert me to the noises they hear (through intelligence) that Iraqis talk about using human shields and that our inspectors might be used for this purpose. I said that if the implication of the US/UK resolution was that inspections were declared meaningless and over, there would be a moral political responsibility for the Council to withdraw the inspectors. I am responsible for the operational side, but the Council has the constitutional and political responsibility. It has created the Commission and sent it to Iraq.

Lunch with European Union at Lotos Club, invited by the Greek Ambassador.

Reception at the German Mission for the Security Council on the last day of the German presidency. Plenty of journalists. They congregate around me to hear the latest thoughts and because I always joke with them. I have good relations with the press.

Saturday 1 March 2003

Missile destruction has begun.

Tired and at half-speed.

Dimitri phones me twice. The Iraqis still try to drag their feet. Yet, as we remarked yesterday: never were some missiles put to better use than these which are destroyed in Iraq. They should have a big bonfire. I can see on US television that it has an impact even though the Bush administration says it is just a trick. Do they mean that Iraq should have refused . . . ?

I am a little encouraged. Everybody seems still to think that the US armed action is inevitable. However, the Turks have said no to having US troops and this delays the Americans. It is far from certain that they could get nine votes for the resolution. And the destruction of missiles is played up as a big thing. I am also on record as saying that this is a big chunk of real disarmament. Indeed, considering that there might be very little B and C perhaps this is the only significant disarmament one can do . . . ? It would be good if the Iraqis accelerated this destruction.

I am wondering about a point made by the Syrian foreign minister's adviser when they came to my office after the ministerial meeting. He said that the fact that Saddam had issued a decree in which he prohibited any private person from engaging in the production or import of weapons of mass destruction, was very significant. Mohamed – who has been insisting on internal legislation in our talks with Vice President Ramadan – now seemed inclined to think it was just a piece of paper. Well, who knows? Was it a signal to the Iraqi administration? All the frantic efforts have come after that decree. They could, of course, be due rather to the US build-up. But the decree could also be a signal prompted by the US build-up.

Sunday 2 March 2003

Article in NY *Times* reporting criticism of me in Washington. Kofi Annan phones. Dinner with Dick Gardner. Mårten phones. Six missiles destroyed in Iraq.

Reflections:
No missiles ever came to better use than those now blown up by Iraq.

(But al-Sa'adi appears to have said in an interview today that we should not publish pictures about it. Fine. We do not normally do that. They may feel humiliated by such pictures.)

Is it not preferable to see Iraq disarm as a result of threat than as a result of war?

Reply to NY *Times* quoted Washington critics that Blix is not coming out supporting war: 'Perhaps they should note that I have my mission from the Security Council and not from the US.'

NY *Times* quote people as saying that I try to please all by citing factors positive to armed action and other factors negative: 'I evidently succeed in displeasing all people . . . ' and: 'a state pushing for one kind of action does not like to see arguments that may speak against it. This is normal. However, I am asked to report all relevant facts and events. It is for the Council to assess and decide.'

Actually, I think the Pentagon and quite possibly some in the White House feel that all – including me – should join in pulling the war wagon. Once they have decided on a course, they want full support by all. However, others in the administration understand that I cannot and should not be pulling anybody's wagon. I may have credibility precisely because I am not seen as automatically supporting any party.

Some in Washington would object if I asked for more time for inspections. They say this is for the Council, not for Blix. OK, but the same people expect me to come out and say that inspections don't work.

Below is a memo and a skeleton resolution I wrote on 15 Feb. with the idea of benchmarks and a timeline after which armed action would be OK if disarmament had not occurred. I gave it to Sir Jeremy on Monday 17 Feb. Several got the memo but only he got the draft resolution. Through him the US also got it. By Tues 18 I think the US had turned against the idea of 'benchmarks' and concluded that this would drag them into a drawn-out procedure discussing whether the benchmarks had been attained. They seem to have settled in favour of simply asserting – whatever happened – that Iraq is not cooperating immediately. This is the Wolfowitz line. You recognize cooperation when you see it. South Africa was the example. However, if this was the line, why not have called it a day after we all agreed that the Iraqi declaration of 7 November was nearly devoid of new evidence? The reality, I think, is that President Bush (over the heads of Cheney, Rumsfeld and Wolfowitz) went for enhanced inspections and UN blessing. They could do nothing before the 'update' on 27 January. After that they got restless. The warmer weather as of March making military operations difficult, the problem of maintaining 200,000 men idle in the sun over a period of time, the risk that public opinion at home will slide. (Actually, it already has . . .) They really are in a dilemma. It will be increasingly difficult to argue for quick action when the inspections give increasing results – as they now do.

FEBRUARY 2003 RESOLUTION (BACKGROUND AND SKETCH)

Background: Resolution 1441 (2002) demands that Iraq shall cooperate immediately, unconditionally and actively with UNMOVIC and the IAEA – to bring to completion the disarmament process, in particular the actions required under paragraphs 8 to 13 of Resolution 687 (1991). This does not cover long-term monitoring, which is open-ended.

Resolution 1441 (2002) describes the cooperation required as a 'final opportunity'. However, among the various timelines it provides (for acceptance, for submission of the Declaration, etc.) the latest is the one, which requests the inspectors to 'update' the Council two months after the first inspection. This update took place on 27 January. There is no definition of 'active' and 'unconditional'. There are, accordingly, questions how long the 'final opportunity' for 'immediate' cooperation is to be open and whether the cooperation provided is, in fact, 'active' and 'unconditional'.

While Iraq has on some occasions tried to refer to its right to 'sovereignty and territorial integrity', recognized in Resolution 1441 (2002), against measures requested, e.g. air surveillance, it has generally steered clear of trying to set clear-cut conditions.

Can one say that the cooperation has been 'immediate'? On the whole, there has been great promptness of response. While unsatisfactory, the Declaration and the list of personnel requested were delivered within the timeline set. Cooperation on process, e.g. setting up the regional office in Mosul and other infrastructural measures, has been without delays or foot dragging.

It can hardly be said, on the other hand, that cooperation on substance, notably solving unresolved disarmament issues and questions so far has been 'active', or, as it is often termed in the Council, 'proactive'. A few recent measures could be seen as 'active', provided that their potential usefulness is borne out by real results. Two Commissions have been appointed, both on the initiative of the Iraqi side. One is to look for any remaining proscribed items, the other is to look for any relevant documentation. The first commission has so far come up with four empty chemical weapons warheads, not much. Will the Commission find more? Will it report all the finds it makes? It remains to be seen and assessed. The other Commission has not yet reported any result. Lack of documentary evidence supporting Iraqi declarations has been a key deficiency, causing many notes of 'unaccounted for'. Will the Commission make any important document finds that can help the accounting? Will it report all of them?

A third initiative from the Iraqi side has been recently to provide a list of personnel who took part in 1991 in the destruction of proscribed chemical items. Authentic documents contemporary with the action they refer to constitute the best evidence. However, if such documents were to remain unavailable, interviews with witnesses could provide important evidence, provided they can take place in circumstances that give credibility to the testimony. Witnesses can evidently be scripted. A list of persons who took part in the alleged destruction of biological items in 1991 would be of as great value as the one now received. So far no interviews have taken place. It is an urgent task.

The presentation by Iraq to the meeting on 8 and 9 February of papers on anthrax and growth media, VX and missiles was a spontaneous action, focused on central issues but without any new evidence attached.

While on the issue of interviews the Iraqi side claims to encourage persons to come for 'private' interviews in Baghdad, there is doubt that the persons really feel they can talk freely. Interviews out of Iraq are certainly an option that must be open, but it raises difficult questions.

If it seems clear that many governments feel that enough time has not yet been given for the option of disarmament through inspection. If so, how much further time would they ask for inspections under Resolution 1441 (2002) before they give up on this option and how 'active' should Iraq be required to be?

It does not seem unreasonable to hold that eleven weeks of inspections, which have barely come up to full strength, and which come after a period of eight years of inspections between 1991 and 1998 and four years of non-inspections between the end of 1998 and November 2002, is a rather short period to allow a final conclusion that the disarmament requirements cannot be fulfilled through this method. What is clear, on the other hand, is that the military and political pressure has been and remains indispensable to bringing about compliance. A slackening of it would, in all likelihood, result in less cooperation.

It would not seem unreasonable in the circumstances to provide an explicit timeline within which satisfactory cooperation and the required resolution of unresolved disarmament issues (or 'key remaining disarmament tasks') would be demanded. This, of course, would leave aside the monitoring, which has no timeline but requires continuing cooperation.

Dr ElBaradei has talked about needing a few further months. Dr Blix has said that a relatively short time could do if the required cooperation were to be provided. Under Resolution 1284 (1999), 120 days were thought to be a time frame within which 'progress' on key remaining disarmament tasks would be doable. It is evidently a question of political judgement how much time should now be given under Resolution 1441 (2002). However, a time frame should not be set without any regard as to what may be achievable in any given period of time. Even if very active and spontaneous cooperation were to come from the Iraqi side, notably in presenting proscribed items, or convincing evidence, the verification would take some time. (In South Africa it took two years! However, we have had inspections in Iraq since 1991 and the Iraqi side is thoroughly familiar with the questions.)

Another vital question relates to judging whether there has been cooperation and disarmament. And who provides this judgement. In the last resort the Security Council must provide the answer, but it seems likely that the Council would need to rely on a prior assessment by UNMOVIC and the IAEA. Both questions are, however, very broad. To make it easier to judge whether there has been cooperation, perhaps there could be some particular actions which one could look for (benchmarks) as indispensable but not conclusive. Similarly, the question whether there has been disarmament could perhaps be judged on the basis of progress noted on some key issues (as was specified in Resolution 1284 (1999)) rather than the whole catalogue of issues.

If the above reasoning were to be accepted, it would become important to define key points of cooperation and to have a precise list of unresolved disarmament issues from which key issues could be selected. In the latter respect UNMOVIC does have a document (the cluster document) that could be made available to the Security

Council rather soon, if requested (but not easily before 1 March, when the quarterly report is due anyway). This document seeks to define all unresolved issues and to indicate what Iraq would need to do to solve them. It is, of course, possible that some of the measures indicated for Iraq to take would turn out to be genuinely undoable and a risk that Iraq would claim that they are all undoable (no documents, no witnesses ...). Nevertheless, it would probably be possible to see whether Iraq provided active, genuine cooperation to solve the issues rather than dragging its feet and being evasive.

Below is an illustration of a draft resolution based on the reasoning and concepts given above.

Considering that Resolution 1441 (2002) gave Iraq a last opportunity to comply with its obligations to disarm and required Iraq to cooperate immediately, unconditionally and actively to do so; Iraq has not yet seized the opportunity; Iraq has shown cooperation on process but not, so far, on substance;

Iraq has not presented proscribed items, which may exist, or convincing evidence about their non-existence; and thus,

Iraq has not shown that it is free from weapons of mass destruction and other proscribed items and has not enabled UNMOVIC and the IAEA to examine relevant evidence,

Iraq has presented a Declaration of 12,000 pages without giving relevant new evidence;

Iraq has imported missile engines in contravention of UN resolutions and developed missiles which exceed the permitted range.

Iraq has not secured the private interviews to which UNMOVIC/IAEA are entitled.

The Security Council:

1. Requests UNMOVIC/IAEA to submit by *[1 March]* a list of currently remaining unresolved disarmament issues and questions, indicating which, in their view are key points, and what, in their view, Iraq should do to solve these issues and to answer these questions.
2. Demands that Iraq shall eliminate under UNMOVIC/IAEA supervision all missiles and other items identified by the organizations as proscribed under Resolutions 687 (1991) and 715 (1991).
3. Demands that Iraq shall present any and all other remaining proscribed items for elimination under supervision of UNMOVIC/IAEA and that such presentation by Iraq shall not constitute a material breach of its disarmament obligations.
4. Requests UNMOVI/IAEA to undertake private interviews at their discretion either inside or out of Iraq with scientists and other persons who can shed light on present and past proscribed activities and items; and demands that Iraq shall ensure that such persons called by UNMOVIC/IAEA will be made available for

the private interviews in Iraq or out of Iraq, as determined by UNMOVIC/IAEA; and requests UNMOVIC/IAEA to report to the Council any non-compliance with this requirement.

5. Demands that Iraq shall facilitate the establishment by UNMOVIC/IAEA of an effective system of checking that no proscribed items are being transported on the roads.

[6. *Oil pipeline to Syria?*]

[7. *No fly zones?*]

8. Requests UNMOVIC/IAEA to submit to the Security Council (*before*) a report whether, in their judgment, the disarmament issues and questions listed by them have been resolved and whether Iraq has fulfilled the obligations laid upon it in this resolution; and to report, at any time immediately to the Council any finding of proscribed items or programs and any impediments to the inspections process;

Decides that if the Council should conclude, on the basis of the reports by UNMOVIC and the IAEA, that Iraq has not fulfilled its disarmament obligations or provided the required cooperation, or both, and it thus must be taken that Iraq has not made use of the inspection process, which has been offered to convince the Council and the world that it is complying with its disarmament obligations, the inspections will be terminated and the Council will consider other measures to solve the disarmament issue.

Monday 3 March 2003

Visit by DG OPCW (Pfirter), Canad. amb., South African amb. (Kumalo), Kuwait amb. (Abdulhasan), UK amb. (Greenstock). Visit to President of SC (Guinea).

Talk to Kofi Annan and Assistant Secr. Wolf (Washington).

Insufficient work devoted to the preparation of my introduction to the quarterly report ... However, I now know for sure that it will be on Friday, which we had counted on.

I had spent time this weekend working on the introduction to the cluster document and the initial chapter on the period 1998 to 2002. This I gave to Surya (Sinha). I have the impression that the analysts are not keen to talk about this period. The texts we have seen seem to suggest that there was little change in the B and C industries during it and that everything happened in the missile sector. However, that they (*the Iraqis*) did not declare anything in B and C does not necessarily mean that nothing happened ... (They did not declare any B and Nuclear in 1991.) I have tried to sell the idea that the Iraqis should come up with ways in which they could convince us that no WMD are carted around on their highways. Some vehicle control. They all seem to find difficulties in that. So can I, but I think we could leave it to the Iraqis to argue the difficulties. We should argue that they need to find a way of convincing the world that no WMD are carted. We are at their disposal.

I have argued, with even less success, that the Iraqis should come up with some concept enabling them to counter the allegation that they use underground labs and stores. I realize that for them to present an inventory of all underground facilities would not be easy. Every basement in Iraq? Every ammunition store? Every shelter? Again, we could leave it to the Iraqis to find the objections... However, I conceded. We might say that we have many underground sites which we have learnt from intelligence and others. Dynamic use should be made of them. We might add that Iraq can help by facilitating the inspections of sites we identify.

Canada is still exploring a third option in the Iraq issue: a resolution which would give Iraq some time to comply fully with the inspectors to achieve disarmament. If it failed, that would be it. The ambassador visited me in my office this morning. We talked about our surfacing of the cluster document. A selection of key issues among the clusters could give benchmarks for substance fulfilment. He said that he saw no progress for the Canadian draft, but Chrétien (the Canadian prime minister) was still very actively exploring with heads of governments, including Tony Blair.

The South African, Kumalo, is chairman of the non-aligned and is trying to play a mediating role. He told me that the report of the SA group which had been in Iraq would soon go to Kofi Annan. Did I want a copy, too? Yes. Was there any special thing we thought they should push in Iraq? Yes, interviews abroad, road vehicle checking.

Mohamed Abdulhasan (amb. of Kuwait) reported that the Kuwaitis are just waiting for the war to come. The sooner the better so that *they get it over with*. Northern Kuwait is like a huge military camp: 150,000 men ...

President of the Security Council, Guinea. Good exercise in French. I went to the President's chamber and spoke in French for half an hour! I think he is attracted the Canadian line. The non-permanent members seek desperately to ask the P5 for a compromise so that they do not have to be torn between them.

UK ambassador. Sir Jeremy Greenstock. He really was concerned about British and American citizens among our inspectors. They might be particularly vulnerable to hostage taking ... Moral question: can we take them out early to protect them in case their countries launch aggression ... I asked whether US and UK did not have a political obligation to include an instruction to UNMOVIC to withdraw in case the SC were to authorize a military strike. Sir Jeremy thought that I and the SG had executive competence to act even before the resolution was adopted. I said that when one did not know whether the resolution would be adopted it might be seen as playing into the inevitability of war, if we were to assume war before it was authorized. I said I sympathized with the Canadian concept and thought one could have a near-consensus on it. I was interested to note that Sir Jeremy did not wave away the Canadian as sharply as he could have done. It is clear that there is no objection to our surfacing of the cluster document.

Friday 7 March 2003

Security Council at foreign minister level: UNMOVIC quarterly report. Long day.

End of a long day. It was billed as a decisive day in the Iraq affair. The papers have said that the US would first listen to the chief inspectors on 7 March. Thereafter it would move ahead with their military action in Iraq. What importance, if any, they would attach to Mohamed's and my report I do not know. But clearly, they were not going to put any second resolution to the vote until after our reports. We now know that it might be as of Tuesday that they will seek a vote on the resolution, which implies the right to use force.

So, where do I begin? We (Torkel, Dimitri. Jim and Surya) sat in my office until after 11 last night to finalize the speech introducing my twelfth quarterly report. Then I left. Got up today at the ordinary time and was driven down to the UN with bodyguard (Eric). The car took me right into the UN garage and walking past garbage cans and factory-like crates and what not I arrive at the basement level of elevators. In my corridor on the thirty-first floor lots of journalists and cameras. Joschka Fischer, the German foreign minister, was the first visitor...

Mohamed was there, too. Gustavo, his New York man, makes sure that Mohamed is there if I meet somebody. Fine. Mohamed was very anxious that I should somewhere in my speech have a line noting that inspections are going full swing and that they can bring results...

The Greek foreign minister, George Papandreou, called from a car on the way from the airport. He had been delayed so we talked to him on the phone. Greece has the Presidency of the European Union at this time. I told him that if the Europeans were ready to put a timeline on their delay and allow military action after that time they might have the US with them. Without a timeline I think there is no chance.

Monday 10 March 2003

I continue the tale from the memorable day (7 *March*) when we reported to the Security Council.

THE SECURITY COUNCIL MEETING. FRIDAY 7 MARCH 2003

Mohamed and I went up to the SG and talked a bit about the aim of the Arab League delegation headed by Amr Moussa to persuade Saddam. We then went down to the Security Council chamber. Packed with people. I walked up to the French foreign minister, Villepin, and gave him a chapter of Göran's thesis (as he had – perhaps out of sheer courtesy – once in Paris expressed interest ...). The Guinean foreign minister in African garb was the President of the Council. Almost all of the Council's members were represented by their foreign ministers. Colin Powell, Ana Palacio (Spain), China, Russia's Ivanov, Mexico, Chile, etc.

The President called on me and I read my statement, which I thought was balanced. I noted that the Iraqis were proactive – indeed, almost frantic – in cooperation, but was it all over the line or selectively? And the results of the active initiatives had to be measured soberly. I noted that we were now doing real disarmament, destroying al-Samoud missiles, and not breaking toothpicks. This had an edge against the White House spokesman, Ari Fischer, who had been saying that the missiles had been hidden (which was false, as they were declared) and that the whole thing was just a joke to throw dust in people's eyes. I honestly don't think the US gains by such a statement. Why not recognize that here big weapons are really destroyed and add that the motivation may well be that they want to throw dust in US eyes. Colin Powell spoke much later and answered, no, they were not toothpicks, but the aim was to create an illusion that Iraq is disarming. The US has not liked my toothpicks.

Generally, the US government has not been happy with my presentation. After my 27 January presentation, which suggested that Iraq had not taken a decision to disarm, the US has hoped that I would repeat this – regardless of what the situation looks like on the ground! They want to incorporate all either among their supporters or among their antagonists. They seem to have asked (Swedish ambassador Jan Eliasson in Washington) why I could not have given some general judgement (negative to the Iraqis ...), I bet that if they had feared that I would be positive to the doves, they would not have wanted me to give any general judgements! On two points they have gone public with insinuations that I have deliberately withheld information: a remotely piloted vehicle – a drone – with a wingspan of 7.40 m. The US says it strongly suggests that it is a means of delivering bioweapons. We are not so sure and want to explore more. The other case is an old cluster bomb, apparently a handmade copy of a South African one and possibly intended for use with chemicals. The latter seems to be more a scrap-heap item. However, the US, having got wind of it (I wonder if it is through some US inspector. Hope not ...), is now peddling it to media. I fear they are a bit frantic and jump at any item that can depict Iraq as particularly dangerous.

In my speech I took occasion to announce that the cluster document was now declassified. The US had not opposed this but had been lukewarm to this because they feared that it would provide an argument for those (like Germany) who want to have 'benchmarks' about issues of substance. Once the document was out the US realized that it contained a lot of material describing how Iraq had changed its declarations again and again and how UNSCOM had shown how they had been unreliable. So they have used this to their advantage. And now they are criticizing me for not highlighting these Iraqi faults. However, what they surely do not want me to say is that practically all unresolved issues are accountancy issues i.e. there are quantities not accounted for. They could be weapons or other prohibited items. Or they could be the result of poor book-keeping.

What was really new in my speech was the report on the many initiatives which Iraq has taken in the last ten days. They clearly mark an 'active', not to say 'proactive' or even 'hyperactive', attitude. However, I also said one would have soberly to assess how much mileage will be had through these initiatives. They could be dust thrown into our eyes. They could also have regard only to selected areas, deliberately ignoring others. However, I must note that they seem to have selected areas of high interest, like anthrax and VX.

In my statement I also noted that if Iraq were to fully cooperate, not weeks, nor years, but months would be required to verify disarmament. This does not square with US propaganda which portrays the alternative to armed action to be endless inspection.

The real objection in the US has come from the Pentagon side that has throughout maintained that inspection cannot complete the task of disarmament in Iraq. These groups were overruled when the US tabled Resolution 1441 but they had come back by the end of February and now have the upper hand ...

Evidently three factors are driving the US policy at present:

The weather in the Gulf region will not stay reasonable much beyond March. So, better have war before the hot weather comes.
The difficulty of having 200,000 men sitting on hot decks of aircraft carriers etc. week after week.
The concern that opinion polls may demonstrate that support in the US for war is dwindling.

Mohamed's speech was much more favourable than mine was to Iraq. It seems the Agency may have solved some of the remaining questions. On one point it was sensational: the allegation that Iraq had sought to import yellowcake (raw uranium) from Niger had been investigated and the Agency had established that there was a forged contract!

Mohamed pleaded for more months. I did not say so openly, but it could be gleaned from my statement that I wanted some more months. I said that if Iraq cooperated it would not take years, nor weeks. But months.

Jack Straw gave the most eloquent speech – without manuscript. He got applause for it despite the ban on applause in the Council. Colin Powell, too, spoke almost freely. Must be rare occasions in the Council when this happens.

The Council finished around 2 o'clock and we walked up for lunch in a room near the dining hall. I had to walk through the dining hall and some tables of lunching ladies recognized me. They rose and applauded! At the luncheon Ivanov said something regretting that some speakers had denigrated the inspectors ... I later commented that I was grateful to all for the kind comments they had made about the inspectors, and I suggested that Ivanov's comment really aimed at regretting that a war on Iraq will imply that the tool of inspections did not work. Villepin made another plea for a summit, though he now justified it by the need to heal wounds and get multilateral cooperation started again after the crisis. The Mexican foreign minister shot down the idea by saying that it was bad enough that the whole world could see that the foreign ministers could not agree. Would it not be even worse if the same disagreements were confirmed to exist at the level of heads of state or govt?

If the morning had been pressing, the afternoon and early evening became tougher. We were now reduced to ambassador level and met in the small consultation room (which really is not bad for talks because the small size gives an intimacy and directness to the discussions. This is never possible in the big chamber). Mohamed and I sat on the horrible audience chairs for two and a half hours. I bet the consultation meetings would be shorter if the ambassadors sat on such chairs ... A problem with the Council (as it was with the thirty-five members council of the IAEA) is that once a number of members have spoken, all the others feel obliged to take the floor.... What if the Council were to be expanded to thirty-five! When all ambassadors had spoken, some of them several times, I was given the floor and I used it to put several issues straight:

- It was not disarmament that had to be immediate (said by Bulgaria), but cooperation.
- Intelligence was important and we relied on it, but we had had no case in which it had enabled us to find WMD!

We went timewise by Resolution 1284 and recognized that Resolution 1441 had a higher degree of impatience. However, if we had made use of all the forty-five days before we undertook the first inspection, our 'update' would have been on 23 February. This could hardly suggest that time was up by 1 March.

When the Council was over Dimitri and I went to the Thai restaurant on Lexington and 65 for supper. We were taken by my bodyguard in the car. Rachel joined us after a little while. We were tired but relaxed.

Saturday 8 March 2003

US stopping US-contracted inspectors from joining us out of fear that they might be there during war (being taken hostage?). In the afternoon we met in the office (Sam, Dimitri, Torkel and Jim Corcoran) to discuss Sam's first draft of a Working Programme. It will not be very long. We have tentatively selected sixteen or seventeen issues as key tasks. By 6 o'clock I was at the Palace Hotel on 50 and Madison to see Amr Moussa, secretary-general of the Arab League. He had a nice suite that reeked of Amr's cigars ... We had a good discussion of what Saddam Hussein might say declaring how Iraq is determined to discontinue possession and production of WMD. Amr was to leave NY the same evening and to be in Baghdad by Wednesday.

Sunday 9 March: Visit by Chungling and Yvonne (*wife and daughter of my old Columbia University pal Jimmie Wang*), first meeting at my flat. Then we went to

ULRIKAs (*Swedish restaurant*). Chungling still does not really speak English, but she understands it. Yvonne is now twenty and she finishes college next year and would like to work on world problems, perhaps as a lawyer. She seemed sensible and balanced.

Monday 10 March: Phone with Tony Blair, Security Council consultations re our quarterly report. Press. Phone with President of Chile, Lagos.

Was roused by a call from Adam Bye from the UK mission. He asked if I could possibly come at 8.25 to take a call at the mission from Tony Blair. I did move fast and left the bed unmade and was at the mission in time. Blair wanted to check with me if their approach of listing a few items for Iraq to do to demonstrate that it was really intent on disarmament, was OK.

After the SC consultations the press was hungry and I was able to say that our cluster document nowhere held that Iraq actually had WMD but rather showed discrepancies and accountancy deficiencies. I talked about intelligence and said that we had the greatest respect and that it was necessary and difficult and that some of the people risked their lives. Yet we must soberly assess the results. The London *Times* correspondent, Bone, tried to corner me on the drones in Iraq; I did not go into polemics but noted that there was a lot about drop tanks in our reports.

At the end of the day in my office I had a talk with the President of Chile, Lagos. He began by telling me that he had talked to Mr Alfredo Echeverria, Professor at the University. He had reported that we were friends at Columbia University. Sure.

Lagos wanted to explore the benchmark approach, which I endorsed. I also made the point that a timeline was not so bad. There would be other constraints.

Wednesday 12 March: informal meeting on Iraq in Security Council regarding modified UK proposal. MTV television interview.

The UK/US/Spain draft resolution, which has been seen as a clear authorization of war, was supplemented today by a paper which would require Saddam Hussein to declare that Iraq had concealed WMD and violated resolutions, etc. and to order all citizens henceforth to be good, reveal what they know, etc. However, this declaration would not be enough to demonstrate a 'strategic decision' because who would believe a word of Saddam Hussein? So, in addition, Iraq was required to show through its performance on five different issues that it was seriously fulfilling its obligations. It was to accept that thirty Iraqi scientists (or similar) go to Larnaca with their families for interviews. This is a viable demand. Can be fulfilled – if the will is there. It can be messy to implement for us. Are we to force wives and children to go along? Or, if they have the option, will not the Iraqi regime engineer the wives to say no and keep them as hostages and pressures on their husbands to say only the right things abroad?

Another demand was to speed up implementation of the destruction program for the al-Samoud II missiles. This, too, is doable. In fact, about half of it is done, though we have not yet had any Volga engines destroyed (the Iraqis have been dragging their feet there, perhaps feeling that they should not be sacrificed until the last, useful as they are for more than the al-Samoud missiles). Other demands were more difficult. Iraq was to present all anthrax for destruction and all mobile production units for biological weapons. OK, if they have these things, as the US and the UK believe, it should not be difficult to present them. Could be done tomorrow! They would know where they are. But if they have neither anthrax nor mobile bioweapon factories, then it becomes more difficult ... For the anthrax they are exerting themselves (or are they creating the image of exerting themselves?) to prove that all (that was declared) was destroyed in the summer of 1991. It is unlikely that they will succeed. We have calculations showing that they had probably produced more than they declared. But if these calculations are wrong ... ? They claim they have no production records. Sorry, destroyed ... So, the matter may remain impossible to solve. I somewhat doubt, however, that all production records were destroyed. They seem to be able to dig up documents, whenever it is in their interest.

The mobile bioweapon production units have become a big ticket. I first heard about them from German intelligence rather long ago. Since then, it is more the US and the Brits who hammer the theme. No pictures, but Colin Powell showed drawings in the Security Council. Well, anyone can draw ... Some have told me that the information is not all that solid. Without evidence, how do we know? I was asked in the Council whether it was plausible, and I said yes. After all, we are told that the Russians did it in rail cars. Iraq could, of course, have destroyed any such units to avoid the risk that they be found. But it is strange that no satellite pictures or other pictures were taken. Only human stories.

The discussion was lively in the Council. Sir Jeremy was eloquent in selling the package as the last chance in town. He saved his most important move to last in his statement, namely, that the Brits were ready to drop the operative para. 3, *which*:

> *decides that Iraq will have failed to take the final opportunity afforded by resolution 1441 (2002) unless on or before 17 March 2003, the Council concludes that Iraq has demonstrated full, unconditional, immediate and active cooperation in accordance with its disarmament obligations ..... And is yielding possession to UNMOVIC and the IAEA of all weapons, weapons delivery and support systems ... and all information regarding prior destruction of such items.*

This was on condition, then, that Saddam would make the declaration and that Iraq would accept taking five actions in addition to the declaration. (interviews outside Iraq, clearing up the anthrax issue, finishing the destruction of the missiles, accounting for UAVs and RPVs, clearing up the mobile lab issue).

The French and the Germans were not impressed. The French whispered that this was a declaration of war 'by preamble'. I thought this was to exaggerate, because the remaining operative para simply 'calls on Iraq, immediately to take the decisions necessary in the interests of its people and the region'. That does not pronounce a threat of war – though it might be meant as one ... There was, however, a preambular para that I thought questionable:

> *Noting that Iraq has submitted a declaration pursuant to its resolution 1441 (2002) containing false statements and omissions and has failed to comply with, and cooperate fully in the implementation of, that resolution.*

This, of course, is tantamount to saying that there has been further 'material breach' since the resolution was adopted – justifying 'serious measures'. Of course, one must be aware that the French are understandably suspicious that the chief purpose is to get a second resolution that the UK needs to claim that the Council has blessed war, which would make it less difficult for Tony Blair to send in British troops. Much of the discussion in the Council was on the need or lack of need for a resolution authorizing the use of force. The French hold that 1441 requires such a resolution, while the US denies that. My recollection of the discussions about 1441 is that it was left moot, with the French declaring that there must be not only consideration but also decision of the Council and the US declaring that all that is needed is to bring the situation to the Council for consideration. Why not leave it moot this time too? Chileans and Mexicans and others seem inclined to the French view.

I said toward the end of the meeting that as I saw it the declaration demanded of Saddam was a bit like a demand for a commitment (contract) with some unreliable party. You want it but you need a solid fast down payment in the form of the five points ... I confirmed that all the points were found in our proposed list of key remaining disarmament tasks, though formulated a bit differently. We do not use language showing any assumption that Iraq has still anthrax or VX. My main advice to the Brits had been that the conditions should be 'doable'. They probably are – missile destruction OK, interviews OK though not so easy, UAVs and RPVs OK, for anthrax and mobile labs it would be easy if they have them ... just to surrender them. If they don't it is harder. Then they have to prove the absence ...

Thursday 13 March 2003

Meeting with SG, SC consultations, dinner with Australians.

Talk with SG about evacuations. The Brits and the Australians and – earlier – the US have urged us to take out their nationals early because they might be especially vulnerable to hostage taking. The Americans are actively in touch with the persons we have trained and offered contracts to and have warned them. Several have thereafter declined to sign contracts and go. One who had signed and was sitting in Larnaca was made to wait there and make up his mind. We do not order any of them to stay out of Iraq, nor do we prevent any one of them from doing so or even from leaving Baghdad. As of this weekend, we and the IAEA shall have about a dozen Brits and Amris in Baghdad. Several have gone to Larnaca on vacation. Of course, all this will be noticeable to the some 150 who remain in Baghdad. So far, we have no panic. Don McKay has expressed concern about the New Zealanders, too. I explained to him that if the medics and the communicators (all Kiwis) go, we will have to close the shop. He urged us to follow a precautionary principle: take all people out before the US issues the warning. Then it might be too late ... However, if we go out, that will be taken as a signal that war is coming. I have said to him that in any case I shall act in unison with the SG. And I told him that, for what it is worth, Ambassador Mussawi, head of the international organizations department in the Iraqi foreign ministry, has said that Iraq intended to protect the international staff. A second airplane is chartered to use for evacuation – mainly of UN people. It is sitting in Larnaca and would fly under our auspices but with Iraqi OK for us to take non-UNMOVIC people out.

Another consultation in the Security Council in the afternoon. It did not bring us forward, but I felt the French were a little less categorical. I informed the Council that our 'work programme' with the list of key remaining disarmament tasks would likely be ready Monday night.

Some media have been nasty, claiming that UNMOVIC is hiding evidence. The source of this, surely, is the US. Perhaps John Wolf or the National Security Council. Colin Powell has only said publicly that they think we could have done more to highlight all the cheating and contradictions by the Iraqis which are evident in the cluster document. However, we only declassified the document. Most of the cheating can be seen from older documents. Wolf barged into my office, I think it was on Thursday 6, the day before my report to the Council, and tossed pictures of a drone and of a cluster bomb on my table and asked why we did not let this surface. I said he could talk to our experts about it. Some media got the US line and began to criticize us. London *Times* (correspondent Bone) was very nasty. However, the *NY Times* correspondent in Baghdad went to a show of the drone and said it was farcical to describe this as something serious. I have further been assured by the inspectors that the cluster bomb is a dead monster from the past. The US is so anxious to depict the Iraqis as dangerous that they jump on any new thing they believe will convince the public.

After the Council discussion on Wednesday 12, Jack Straw made it known that the Brits could drop the formulation of the first condition, i.e. the rather humiliating declaration that they had prepared for Saddam to pronounce, provided that he declared that Iraq would comply ...

Friday 14 March 2003

Intermission! No formal meetings, but I did see SG about the problem with helicopter owners who plan to take out their machines. Kofi will give the signal when we should take inspectors out. It is certainly not yet. Nor do we think so. The initiative of the E6 (Chile, Mexico, Guinea, Cameroon, Angola, Pakistan) in the Council collapsed today after the US shot it down. One thing was that they wanted to give three weeks (in one place they said thirty days) to fulfil the five tasks. This was certainly too long for the US. The more important point, I suspect, was that they required a special decision of the Council afterwards to assess and decide if armed force was to be used. The US wants to assess alone and decide freely on the use of force.

The EU met on Friday but not surprisingly could not agree, as France and Germany and most of the others were of a different view from UK and Spain (and Italy?). The P5 were to have met but the meeting was cancelled.

Mohamed and I received an invitation from Baghdad today from Dr al-Sa'adi. He says we have agreed on monthly high-level meetings. (Not true.) Suggests we come as early as possible to accelerate inspection process and take note of the progress achieved through the various Iraqi initiatives (digging and taking soil samples to check if the quantity of anthrax poured into the ground in 1991 can be assessed now . . .). Talked to Mohamed, who was rather enthusiastic. I reminded him that we had agreed that if we were to go, we would need to have a prior declaration by Saddam committing himself to disarmament of WMD. We could then go to talk about the implementation. Mohamed has consistently wanted to meet Saddam and held that it would be a sign of his serious acceptance of disarmament that he meets us. I suspect he considers us to be some lowly mosquitos, not worthy of meeting a great ruler of Mesopotamia. He will hardly stoop to negotiate with us. The best that can be achieved would be if we could tell him some truths that his environment may not dare to say. With the Azores meeting coming up on Sunday we have to wait. On Saturday John Negroponte called to warn that the US was negative and added that Colin Powell had said 'I don't think Hans would want to do this these days . . . '

We had a senior staff meeting to bring all into the picture and went on with the work programme and the 'key remaining disarmament tasks'. We now began to get responses from our commissioners – Fedotov (in Moscow), Wolf (in Washington), Wells (in London).

Saturday 15 March 2003

Iraqi invitation to Mohamed and me to come to Baghdad. Finalize work programme.

Mohamed phoned me from Vienna about the invitation from al-Sa'adi . Mohamed translated. He is eager. I said we had agreed that we should hardly go unless Saddam first made a declaration about implementation of the resolutions. Mohamed would love for us to go there and have Saddam declare his adherence to the resolutions in our faces. I think this is unlikely. More likely he will make a statement out in the open. Then perhaps see us benevolently – like Bush ... I phoned Jeremy Greenstock to inform him of what had happened. He contacted London, as I wished, as this initiative should be before Bush, Blair and (*the Spanish PM*) Aznar when they meet tomorrow in the Azores. Jeremy called back after a while and said the FCO urged caution. One should not give Saddam huge room to play games. The bars should be set rather high for our going. Not only a declaration but also some of the down payment. I said I probably wanted some blessing from the

Council. It was now all so much high wire and high tension and we are a subsidiary organ of the Council. We cannot play it completely on our own. This was not just a monthly routine trip. Jeremy said he thought Azores was not about war but about further diplomacy ... Good, if it is right.

Then I talked to Kofi, who wisely said that we should not put conditions on coming but ask for clarifications about what could be attained to speed up the fulfilment of the 'key tasks'. We should wait with replying until we knew what had been done at the Azores. We should inform the President of the SC about the invitation. Part of the Council might wish us to go. Others may be reluctant. I also talked to (*Iqbal*) Riza and to Torkel and Olof Skoog, who is now succeeding Torkel.

Then Mohamed called again. He is very eager and would not mind now that the declaration be made by Saddam in our presence. I said that was risky and also more humiliating to Saddam. Besides the SC will probably want a declaration before we go. I told him about Kofi's advice on 'clarification'. We agreed that we would not make the invitation public, but it is quite likely that the Iraqis will. We agreed we should have no reply before the results of the Azores are there. However, the response might be that we are anxious to seek clarification that a meeting could speed up implementation of the key remaining disarmament issues, which they have now seen ... (sent to them on Saturday night). We would also like to be sure that we could get their prompt support and cooperation on the issue of interviews abroad.

Then John Negroponte called. He wanted to know what my reaction was to the invitation and I said we might ask for a clarification first and that I wanted to have contact with the President of the Security Council. On our earlier trips to Iraq, we had not had any authorizations from the Council, so this was not needed, but the situation was a bit different now. It was not a routine monthly visit. John said the US was discouraging a trip and Colin Powell had said 'I don't think Hans would want to do this these days ... '

How far away is the invasion and what is the Azores meeting about?

At the office today we decided not to send in any more people from Larnaca before we have seen the outcome of the Azores meeting. Sen Pang was dispatched to Larnaca to be on hand for receipt of the coffin of the Chinese chemistry inspector who died in a car accident. The brothers of the killed man are coming together with Chinese officials. There will be flags and solemnity. The Chinese asked if we could charter a plane to take the coffin to Beijing. We said we had to follow UN rules, and this was not within our mandates. The companies owning the helicopters we use in Baghdad have now all decided to withdraw their machines and people (UK, Canadian and Russian). We had a response from Syria that they will allow our machines to cross to Syria in emergency departures from Iraq.

Toil on the work programme. We had hoped to finish it Saturday evening and to send it to Baghdad. However, there is too much to go over. I knew it was not in very good shape. We had critical comments from Wolf, Fedotov and Thérèse Delpech. She was the most scathing – regrettably largely right. I spent from 2 to 10 p.m.

reworking the conceptual part. Torkel had some good ideas for changes but most of his reworking was a stirring of the soup. Olof Skoog contributed some thoughts and Sunday will have to be used for further revision. Kofi Annan phoned to tell me that the foreign ministers of Russia, France and Germany intend to come to the Council on Tuesday to be present when the document is presented. (I hope we shall be ready.) There is no way it will be a finished UN document at that time. Only a 'working paper' or draft ... The US and UK have said they do not want it on Monday. I wonder why. Invasion on Tuesday?

Sunday 16 March 2003 at 08.15

No newspaper yet. So, I watched TV and saw myself exiting from the UN building last night and talking about our work programme and the latest Iraqi letters and the invitation. Will be at the office by 10.30. A heavy day but I have some ideas for the working paper on a couple of crucial points. Also, Swedish TV around 2 o'clock. Worked in pyjamas two hours in the morning and managed to shuffle and rewrite to get the thing in reasonable shape. How often have I not had the feeling that a text is like lumps of clay that you form with your hands into something that takes a reasonable shape ... This time the central idea I had was that I should show that we have to implement all the resolutions directed to us and that, on analysis, they are not really incompatible. This is of particular importance for Resolution 1284 and 1441. The Russians are eager to place emphasis on 1284 and the US on 687. They want to battle each other with the texts. I will show that the texts are not inconsistent!

Went to the office and delivered my evening and morning work and discussed a couple of points on which Olof Skoog could work. Torkel Stiernlof was also there but he feels he is on the way out and is not eager to work.

Then I went to the CBS studios on the West Side for an interview with Lars Adaktusson in Swedish TV. Before going to the studio, I saw Bush and Blair on the screen giving press conferences at the Azores. Bush talked about the dictator and the cruel regime and what a bright future there would be if he was taken out. The US is not going to release the so-called roadmap for peace in the Middle East drawn up by the Quartet (US, Europe, Russia, UN). The purpose is no doubt to show to the Middle East that they are interested not only in Iraq but also in the Palestinians. Then came Blair, who talked mainly about going a last mile for peace on the Iraqi issue, but also about the necessity for the UN to stop a proliferator. Afterwards I said on Swedish TV that the parties at the Azores seemed to emphasize different things in their press statements. My comment was made by media here to mean that I had talked about a 'divide' at the Azores. There may well have been one, but that was not what I had said ... The Swedish interview was about twenty minutes long and apparently it went very well. I have received several compliments for it. At one point he asked if I longed for home and I responded that my sister had called earlier in the day and told me that the snowdrops had come up outside my house on the island.

Of course, I longed for home. I understand that this had appeal. On the way out from CBS I was 'stalked' as they say and answered a lot of questions in the street. I invited a fellow from Swedish Aftonbladet to join me in the car going to the UN and spoke to him during the ride.

In the afternoon we worked on with the working programme. Dimitri sat with the technical people and went through the annexes. I went through the conceptual part with Torkel, Olof, Sam, Surya and Ewen. Gradually the text emerged. It was sent to al-Sa'adi in Baghdad in the evening. We had promised him this. I had wanted to give him two days for reading, but it shrunk to one. We have said to the Council that it will be ready Monday evening.

By 18.45 Assistant Secretary John Wolf phones me to inform me that in the US view it is time to withdraw the UN inspectors. He will also inform ElBaradei. They suggest expeditious action. There will be no further notice. We discuss the matter in the office: Dimitri, Surya, Torkel, Olof, Sam and I. We are all anxious to get the order for withdrawal out to Baghdad already this Sunday night so that the operation can be undertaken Monday morning. We do not know when the US will start armed action and we worry a bit about hostage taking. Of course, the Iraqis can stop any plane or any car from leaving, but better be early ... I call Kofi Annan. Kofi, it turns out, does not want to hurry. I urge him and he tells me that Iqbal Riza, his chef de cabinet, will contact me. This was his way of keeping me at arm's-length and avoid having, himself, to say no to me ... OK. I talk to Riza several times. My team cannot quite understand Kofi. Mohamed on the line is even less keen than Kofi to go early. He wants us all to have permission from the Security Council to withdraw. I know that Kofi thinks he has authority to decide and then to notify the Council. We try to show Riza that if no decision is taken until Monday morning (Kofi wants to tell the Council in the morning) evacuation can hardly start until Tuesday, since Iraq is eight hours ahead of us. Eventually Kofi tells us that yes, he wants evacuation Tuesday morning. Reluctantly we go along. It is his responsibility. When Butler withdrew inspectors in December 1998, the UN stayed. Ewen maintains that Butler informed both Kofi and the President of the Security Council. Maybe so, but he did not seek Kofi's agreement. It was a bit odd to have only the inspectors leaving. They were not able to come back after the US/UK bombing.

Dimitri and I went to the little Thai restaurant on Lex. Ave. and had nice food. More and more people recognize me now after all the TV pictures. We were tired.

Monday 17 March 2003

Eva to Genoa for a cruise. Our forty-first wedding day and we both forgot it, only Mårten remembered! Meeting in Kofi's office on evacuation, meeting in Security Council on Iraq. Torkel's last day. Talk with Anna Lindh, the Swedish foreign minister. Talk with Carl Bildt. Distribution of working programme to members of the SC.

At nine in the morning meeting in Kofi's conference room. All engaged in Iraq: Benon Sevan for oil for food. Tim Miyat, security coordinator. Louise Frechette.

Ralph Zacklin for the lawyers, Iqbal Riza, Michael Moller et al. Mohamed ElBaradei is on a telephone line from Vienna. It begins with the SG and then with me and Mohamed, who suggests authorization by Council. He is a little out of touch with the atmosphere and cannot see us. Kofi is very clear that he has authority and does not need permission from the Council. This could result in paralysis if the Council is not agreed. He is responsible for life and has operative responsibility; we agree to talk about 'withdrawal', not evacuation. And about 'suspension'. But no action is to be taken until Kofi has actually told the Council. This has a negative consequence, because the Council begins with the long and painful debate about the British resolution on Iraq and Kofi does not get to make his announcement until around noon. We shall have lost two hours during which we could have sent the order to our people in Baghdad. They would have got it at 6 p.m. instead of 9 p.m.

The Council meeting was not acrimonious as one might have feared, but the UK and US try to put the blame on France for preventing the resolution with an ultimatum on Baghdad. And the French say that all the Brits and the US want is an authorization for them to go to war. For the US this is probably true. The French view is that the Brits and the US can jolly well simmer in their own stew. And the E10 on the whole feel that military action is not yet justified.

I also feel the military action is premature. The US speaks about twelve years of opportunity for Saddam. OK, but Resolution 1441 was adopted in November and the inspectors' update could have been 23 February. Did they really intend to give Iraq only four months altogether? Something must have happened at the end of January or early February to make the US lose its patience. I hope it was not my speech on 27 January ... Even during the latter part of that month, the US was eager to have participants in our inspector training course and a special employment contract was devised by the legal people for US service people to work for us (after attending our training course). I suspect the impatience came from the tremendous build-up of military strength. They cannot just sit and twiddle their thumbs. The weather getting hotter was another factor. And the aversion to move it all to the autumn, when the presidential campaign begins ...

I was invited to speak at the end of the meeting. I talked about the working programme and that the range of issues goes from the UDIs (unresolved disarmament issues) which are about 80–100. The cluster issues, about thirty, and the selected key remaining disarmament tasks: twelve. 'Benchmarks' are generally seen to be fewer. I have said that resolution of all issues (or clusters) or key tasks could be achieved in months if Iraq fully cooperates. If you select a lesser number of cases, you can perhaps give less time. Some issues are plausible for fast solutions (interviews in Larnaca, full destruction of all al-Samoud II missiles.) Other issues (anthrax) may take time if they do not have any and must present documents, witnesses, etc.

I think any initiatives are pretty hopeless at this time. The Russians, French and Germans wish to see the work programme on the table, because it will show that there is work to do. Inspectors are in full swing. One could try to tell Iraq to resolve three issues in a short time, or five or any number. It will be interesting to see if they still are interested in the programme on Wednesday ... It is ironical: our submission of the document is even a little ahead of time under Resolution 1284. So, we submit our work programme the same day that we order our inspectors out ...

A glass of wine for Torkel in the office at the end of the day. Short speech by me and response by Torkel. I had seen in a fresh interview with Colin Powell that he said that the 'time for diplomacy was over, now was the moment of truth ... '.

Tuesday 18 March 2003

All staff successfully withdrawn from Baghdad. Q&A at the UN Press Club. Drafting of introduction in SC of work programme.

Perricos phoned me at 7 a.m. to tell me that the first plane had arrived at Larnaca from Baghdad and that the second one was due a little later. All had gone well. Wonderful. Great relief.

Decided to work at home before lunch to get some peace to begin drafting the introduction of the work programme in the SC. Talked on the phone to Torkel Stiernlof who is leaving today. I asked him if the archive he left contained written notes of the conversations I had had (with him as note taker) with various political leaders. He said he had not had the time to write them but had them in his notebook. I said it was necessary to write them, which he promised.

I managed to write only half a page on the introduction at home.

At 14.00, I was briefed about various weapons issues that might come up in the SC. I was particularly interested in some issues, which had been controversial: the cluster bomb issue, the pilotless plane and the anthrax.

Press briefing. This is a practical way of meeting a lot of journalists, who otherwise get a no to individual interviews. What was new this time was, of course, that inspectors had been withdrawn. I was somewhat tired, but I think it went all right. There were probably a hundred journalists. I have begun now to answer fairly openly questions of why I thought the US abandoned the inspection line. I was asked whether I thought Iraq would use chemical weapons and I said Iraq certainly had the capability of making them and delivering them; it was a question of will. Personally, I doubted they would use them, because at present there is a strong public opinion against war, but if they used any C-weapon, public opinion would switch and say: OK, the US was right, they must be fought ... The follow-up question was: 'but what if they are in a lethal corner?' To this I successfully countered: 'Some people worry also about their reputation after death.'

Wednesday 19 March 2003

Security Council hears our working plan. Foreign ministers of Russia (Ivanov), France (Villepin) and Germany (Fischer) present.

I went (*first*) to the so-called Iraq group – a high-level coordinating (*Secretariat*) group for Iraq issues – led by the Deputy Secretary Louise Frechette first thing in the morning. Not much of use to me, but they all want to hear what we are up to. So, it is of importance to show our belonging to and solidarity with the system. In addition, questions like evacuation are in common. This morning one got the impression that the evacuation was all the work of Mr Ramirez, who is the Secretary-General's representative in Baghdad. Well, the two planes are in our name and fly under our rights. It was with Iraqi permission that we loaded UN people into them.

The Security Council was not quite as full as on the previous occasions. I said hello to Villepin, who claimed he had read Göran's opus Chapter III on architecture (I gave it to him last time). He said it was very serious work ...

My introduction to our work plan was short. Only two pages. Well, why should I spend more time on a programme that cannot be implemented. I noted that we had made it available to the members of the Council the same day that we ordered the inspectors to withdraw from Baghdad.

The reason why the Russians wanted the Security Council meeting to be there at ministerial level was to impress upon the world that here was a well-working authority at full speed implementing the resolutions; why intervene, why not let it continue? The tone was not very bitter, however. Rather they spoke about the necessity to come together on humanitarian assistance, etc. The UK spoke late in the debate and ended by referring to the need to make use again of UNMOVIC. I hear now that the UK is pressing hard among the P5 that UNMOVIC should be allowed to go in when the fighting is over and check for weapons of mass destruction. Some article today is also said to have reported that there were discussions in Washington earlier about calling on UNMOVIC from the beginning to check for WMD. It sounds a bit fantastic, and I am glad it did not come about. UNMOVIC as a trailer to the US war machine ... ! Our great value has been in our independence! Once the country is liberated it might possibly be another matter. The occupying power would then act as government, hopefully granting us freedom of access everywhere. Would Iraqis be more ready to be interviewed by us than by Americans? Questionable.

Before the Council I had a word with Mrs Negroponte, whom I think has had a very favourable opinion of my doings. She said we must talk again in due course. I said that at any rate we had tried to be honest in our pronouncements. She said something to show she was not quite convinced of that ... So, I can imagine that her husband, John, must be rather critical of us. It hurts me that they seem to believe in Condoleezza Rice's comments that the IAEA missed the Iraqi nuclear programmes in 1991, 1995 and 1998! I wonder if they have it from David Kay?

After the meeting we had a neutral chat with Jim Cunningham. I am a bit puzzled. Negroponte explicitly asked me some time ago if John Wolf had gone too far in polemics with me on 25 Feb. at the meeting of the College of Commissioners. I assured him that although it had been a 'lively' meeting it was all right. We can have some argument and cooperate well nevertheless. However, when Wolf came to my office on 6 March, one day before the Council's discussion of our cluster document, he tossed two documents on my table, one on the UAVs and one on the cluster bombs, and insinuated that these were clearly prohibited and that we should have highlighted it. I had not learnt much about these weapons at the time. Now I know that the bombs probably are out of the museum from the past and that the drones may or may not be illegal, depending upon their range, etc.

WAR HAS STARTED. 20 MARCH 2003

Thursday 20 March 2003

UK commercial television. ABC television with Peter Jennings. Japanese newspaper Yomiuri Shimbun.

Dimitri left for Vienna and Larnaca today. Yes, he needs to go home and see Regina and Alexandra.

Senior staff meeting today to put that group into the new picture; agreement we shall have a meeting of all staff tomorrow. Alice and Dimitri advocate that we should be very generous with people's contracts. Even prolonging some. It is not so easy for people to get new jobs.

The UK commercial TV was outside in the cold and the rain. Earplug and the questioner in Kuwait. Less than ideal conditions. He also insisted on asking me whether I thought the war was legal. Although as a lawyer I have thoughts on this, as chairman of UNMOVIC I should really not pronounce about it myself. Kofi Annan can do it and he did say that it was not consistent with the Charter. I limit myself to relating the arguments which are advanced and the counter-arguments without taking a stand of my own, except to say that I find the argument of the right to a pre-emptive strike the least convincing.

ABC with Peter Jennings was OK. He asked meaningful questions.

The interview with the Japanese newspaper was intrusive but OK. He asked how come we modified the cluster document between the College of Commissioners and the presentation to the Council. Easy! What do we have the College for if not to listen to its advice!

Friday 21 March 2003

Talk with Kofi Annan, all-staff meeting, TV Abu Dhabi and Middle East, TV CBC (?).

I brought Alice Hecht and Olof Skoog to Kofi Annan to discuss what we shall do with staff. We noted that the Security Council has by no means terminated our mandate and might, might ask us to do more. It is conceivable that international inspection may be desired after the war phase. I read in the press cuttings some speculation in that direction from Washington (but it doubts that Blix or ElBaradei would be involved. We have not been sufficiently on the US side ...). However, I wonder ... If there is little or nothing found, would they like us to come in and confirm that? If there is much found, it is more likely they would want to show it themselves.

In any case for some time UNMOVIC must be there. For the longer term there is the idea of having a roster of trained inspectors in the fields of biology and missiles (which have no specialized organization, like the IAEA and the OPCW) and having some multidisciplinary analytical capacity. Budget would be a difficulty. Another is that the analysis is so touchy. What does an international civil service say about Iran and non-proliferation? Or Syria? Or Libya? It is certainly much less difficult for SIPRI (*Stockholm International Peace Research Institute*) ...

How long should we keep people on board? Inspectors from the roster go back home. Those who were evacuated apparently get a terrific indemnity. We keep the offices in Larnaca and Bahrein for some time. Administrative staff is easily moved to other areas. (They know each other and help each other ...) Alice and Dimitri appear very generous. I feel that giving all people regardless of when their contracts end three to four months to look around for new jobs would be enough. I think Kofi is inclined to something like that too. However, they have to see what the other UN units do. We were told that the IAEA intended to prolong all their thirty people until the end of the year. Well, that sounds too much. We shall have to play it by ear. But there must be some consistency and people need learn rather soon.

Kofi asked me to stay alone with him after the meeting. He wanted to say that he felt I had managed the job very well and that he was happy that I had not left it.

We had an all-staff meeting in the afternoon and I tried to explain what had happened politically, why the US went ahead and what the UK had tried to do and what the French had been fighting about. I ended by saying that no one would need to worry for a few months about their job, regardless of what the contract said.

I had a long TV *interview* from the Middle East. I also talked to the Abu Dhabi TV. This was in the rain outside and barely hearing the lady at the other end. Moreover, she evidently gave consecutive translations so there was long waiting between the questions.

I had a long CBC (?) interview in my office. They had redone the whole office. I am told by Buchanan that the reason is that these anchors will sit in an environment that presents them in a good light ... When you get the big-shot anchors the interviews is more about their careers than what you say ...

I took farewell of Rod Barton, the Australian who was a biology inspector and who also writes well. We have had good use of him. But he was almost invariably conservative and negative in his conclusions. I wish he had been a bit more constructive ... He told me that he is now being sounded out from the US side if he wants to join Charles Duelfer in the US WMD inspection force to go with the US forces. It will be a COWBOY (Coalition of the Willing Brothers Observing One Year). I also took farewell of Ake Bovallius, who has been with us almost from the beginning and taken part in the UDI (*unresolved disarmament issues*) document, the cluster document and, lastly also the work programme.

Our weak side has been the analytical all the way through. The people who seek jobs with us are eager to go out in the field, see and report. They are not keen on reading through thousands of pages and sifting out data. It would have been a disaster if we were to have started inspections in the summer of 2000 ... We just barely managed to present the cluster document in time and to get a lot of credit for it and to use it as the basis for our work programme.

Saturday 22 March 2003. At Anchor ...

Tired. Did not go out at all.

I have begun to think about a book on my UNMOVIC saga. Went through my calendars to note the various more important occasions. I shall need to go through lots of documents.

Wednesday 26 March. Thoughts on the Security Council

It occurs to me that the US could be seen as prosecutor, judge and executor in the case of Iraq. Bringing all the charges. Stating that guilt is established, and that no SC resolution is needed. And starting and pursuing the war. What is UNMOVIC? A part of the court (SC) to explore and assess the evidence. The Security Council is not exactly an impartial court ... ? With Russia and Syria? Well, there is Chile, Mexico and others who are not that biased and who doubt the judgement reached by the US.

One experience is clear from the long discussions in the Council: an enlarged Security Council would be very cumbersome! As soon as five members have spoken on some item all feel obliged to declare their views. At the end of last year, I met a member (I think it was the ambassador of Mauritius) who confided that the day he longed for most was the end of the year, when his country would no longer sit on the Council! No doubt it is a terrible burden on the smaller countries to be members. Mexico, which came in this year, has really had to pay, as the US pressed it horribly to vote with the US on the Iraq resolutions. Had they not been members of the Council they would never have had any problem at all ...

Is there a political necessity for an expansion of the Council? Well, it might be desirable to have the heaviest economic states as members: Japan and Germany, India, Brazil ... But that leads to quite an expansion! And the Council is already heavy. Could not the Europeans have one seat together? Splendid but unlikely.

There are now four Europeans (Germany and Spain in addition to the UK and France). Without eternal seats and a veto, the Brits and the French would feel castrated! However, three seats vacated could give seats to Japan, India and Brazil without expansion of the Council. And the Europeans would be forced to harmonize their positions to one voice! Having seen the Brits and the French on different sides of the trench all through the Iraqi crisis I would not mind forcing them into a European consensus.

No, the issue is not ripe for solution. It may rot before it is ripe!

NO WEAPONS FOUND BY US IN IRAQ

There have been no inspection reports this week. But media are still interested, and I am seeing many, both press, radio and TV. It is tiring and a bit risky. Always something that comes out the wrong way. The big question now is: will they find some WMD? So far, none! There is much noise when they find some chemical factory that is heavily fenced ... Much noise when they find some missiles ... Much noise when they find some stock of atropin or chemical protection suits ... However, I am sure that when the real stuff is found, we shall hear it loud and clear! I doubt they will stumble upon it. They do not have more sites in their files than we do. However, as they control more of the population and as the Mukhabarat (*secret police*) is losing its terror grip on people, knowledgeable persons may come and speak and tell where stores are located – if they exist.

There has been some noise about the US setting up its own inspection force – with Charles Duelfer at the head. I told the Washington Post today that I knew some of our staff (from the Alliance states) had been approached about joining the US. I said we did not prevent anyone from terminating his or her contract. For the rest, I wish Duelfer good luck! Would UNMOVIC go in with the US, if invited? A theoretical question ... I would have to submit it to the Council if it came. Resolution 1441 does not fit an occupation authority ... Would we be entitled to immediate access to US headquarters? Could we ask General Tommy Frank for an interview in Larnaca?

THURSDAY 27 MARCH 2003. THE MAIN FACTORS LEADING TO THE WAR

I think one could point to three main factors as leading to the war:

- 9/11
- Saddam Hussein
- The rhythm of US elections

First, 9/11 convinced leading US politicians, especially on the right wing, that the US must root out any terrorist threat to the country, especially those that may be linked to a capacity for nuclear or other WMD. If this can be done together with other states and the UN, fine, if it cannot, the US will decide alone and do alone what it thinks needs to be done.

This view, sharpened in a revival of the Cold War concept of pre-emptive strike, has its immediate roots in what used to call 'counter-proliferation', a concept also championed by some in the US, urging that suspect production or stocking of WMD anywhere be 'taken out', by cloak-and-dagger operations or, if need be, military operations, regardless of any UN authorization. The most spectacular operation carried out in the name of counter-proliferation was not American, but the 1981 Israeli destruction of the Iraqi nuclear research reactor Osirak.

At least in two cases the US practised this idea: one was the bombing of a Libyan factory suspected of producing chemical weapons. The other case was after the terrorist destruction of the US embassies in Nairobi and Dar es Salaam. The Clinton administration, suspecting Al-Qaeda, shot cruise missiles at some targets in Afghanistan and others at a chemical factory outside Khartoum. The second attack, it was later understood, was based on faulty information. The case is troublesome. Does the concept of counter-proliferation, as enunciated by the US, license its author to attack any target it suspects might potentially produce or harbour WMD that could be directed against the US?

The war against Iraq may be seen as a huge counter-proliferation operation. The US is still convinced that the information on which the war is based is valid, and most intelligence services are of the same view. It remains to be seen whether they are right. If the intelligence should prove to be wrong, the war would appear to have been a costly miscalculation in terms of counter-proliferation. (I do not talk of other benefits, like human rights, that could be linked to it.)

UNMOVIC's inspection effort is at a cost of some 65 million dollars a year making use of some 200 people in Iraq and causing no casualties and destruction. The US/UK 'inspection effort' is at the cost of much more than 65 billion dollars a year, employing over 200,000 people and causing many deaths and injuries and much damage. At that price one would like to see the discovery and elimination of real weapons of mass destruction.

Monday 31 March 2003

I had an email today which read: 'If you do not see the smoking gun I advise you to go to an optician.' For once I answered: 'Thanks for the advice. I would like to have a pair of uncoloured lenses.'

Saturday 5 April 2003. London, Stockholm.

London: Arrived in the morning of Wednesday 2 April to London.

I was clearly recognized by some people in London. In the underground I sat next to a big African who was reading a tabloid proclaiming END OF

SADDAM. The African smiled at me and I smiled back. After a moment he said 'You look like Butler ... ' I shook my head. I was impressed, though. This guy had evidently followed the Iraq issue since 1998 when Butler was in focus! At Heathrow, waiting to be checked in, several teenagers, having recognized me, came up and told me that they were on their way to Sigtuna to take part in a UN GA mock session. I asked why not the SC. They were too many and needed the GA ... They were thrilled.

Friday 4 April 2003. Stockholm.

Lunch. The speaker of the Parliament (Björn von Sydow) was there and so was Katarina Englund and Lars Leijonborg, who had *delivered* a speech that was so pro-US and pro-NATO that I was amazed. I think he really saw the intervention as an upholding of democracy in some kind of Wilsonian-American tradition. While this is a twist that some have tried to give the affair rather lately in the US – a democratic renaissance for the Arab world – it is an idyllic belief. The US did not worry much about the Turkish democracy when it came to permission for US troops to move through Turkey into Iraq ...

After (*a visit to Prime Minister*) Persson I was invited to the Minister of Defence, Leni Björklund, and some of her advisers. All of the latter except a general were dressed in sweaters. Informality has advanced in the central government ...

Tuesday 8 April 2003. Back in New York. No WMD Found Yet

IRAQ. So far, no WMD have been found. With the US having said not only that these weapons exist but also that they threaten the US, a good deal of credibility is at stake. On the other hand, if the US knew where the things were, why did they not tell UNMOVIC? And if they were unsure, how could they start the war?

13 – 17 April

A main question in the past week and one that continues is are there any weapons of mass destruction in Iraq? The US seems to have three chains of searchers: first, the military who go in and fight look for any WMD that can hurt them; second, specialized military to identify and pick up and destroy any WMD-like ordnance: third, the Duelfer-led group of inspectors from former UNSCOM to go in with special equipment and expertise. It is amazing that this latest chain seems to have been organized late and that there seems to be a lot of turf fighting and improvisation. One might have thought that when they give the alleged possession by Iraq of WMD as a prime reason for going to war without UN authorization they would organize themselves early not only for the fight but for proving the point and the destruction of the weapons ... The fact that they did not could point to the conclusion that the 'taking out of Saddam' was at all times the focus. True, if they took him out, they might have expected to find the WMD easily and destroy them and with Saddam gone they would radically reduce the risk – which would otherwise have remained – that Iraq would any time soon turn to WMD.

Now, what happens if they simply declare they find nothing? They will not be suspected of cheating. They may say that in any case the invasion prevented Saddam from reviving a programme and that they could never have lived tranquil so long as he was there. They will point to having taken out a cruel and horrible regime, which would be perfectly true. I doubt that they will claim that WMD have been taken to Syria. Some in media have tried that, but the US military have not subscribed to the thesis.

Tuesday 22 April 2003. Security Council Briefing

In the afternoon (21 April) I received Mohamed Abdulhasan, the Ambassador of Kuwait. He was pleased with the US invasion of Iraq, but remained friendly with me and told me I would always be welcome as his guest in Kuwait. He did not think that Saddam Hussein would ever allow himself to be taken prisoner or go into exile.

After Abdulhasan came the representative of the Arab League, the Lebanese. He foresaw terrible things in Iraq. The Shias who are in majority would dominate and they would lean to fundamentalism. It would be worse than in Iran. Today we watch on TV how hundreds of thousands of Shias for the first time in twenty-five years are allowed to pilgrimage to Karbala. There is a political message in this, too, He believed that Saddam had escaped. He thought that a deal had been struck when Condoleezza Rice was in Moscow. The Russians would take Saddam and there would be no resistance in Baghdad ... I wonder. I am inclined to think that he is dead.

The informal meeting of the Council was a mild affair. All were anxious not to get back to the acrimony of the past month. All but the US seemed to be in favour of getting the UN inspectors back. Negroponte repeated in several turns that the US inspection people were still in the early phase, they had just begun, they would have to examine a lot, there was still insecurity ... They would practise transparency ... Not a word about the UN inspections ... I talked a fair amount about long term monitoring and a zone free from weapons of mass destruction.

Friday 25 April 2003

To Washington. Dinner with Walter Pincus and his wife, Ann.

The Pincuses have excellent taste. Lots of well-known people: Strobe Talbot, nowadays head of the Brookings Institution, earlier Deputy Secretary under Madeleine Albright. There was Jim Wolfinson, the head of the World Bank, jovial appearance, telling me that the US now tries to squeeze him to follow their tune on

Iraq. Stephen Briar is a Judge on the Supreme Court and, apparently, he and Walter and I were all in Vienna for the Youth Festival in 1959 (?) trying to spread Liberal thoughts in the minds of lots of Africans who had been invited. Henry Cato, Republican, former Ambassador in London and now chairman of the NATO Council. Jan and Kerstin Eliasson were also invited. Kerry, Presidential candidate? Ann, our hostess. Walter gave a very kind welcome speech, applauding my independence. I responded by citing the two 'gruks' (*a kind of comical verses*) by Piet Hein, the Danish poet:

> The noble art of losing face,
> May
> One day
> Save the Human race!

I explained that it was still relevant.

I also cited a 'gruk' that applied more to my own situation, which read:

> Little cat, little cat
> Walking so alone
> Whose are you?
> Whose are you?
> I am goddam my own!

Saturday 26 April 2003

Lunch with Schwebels. Other guests: Bob and Jessica Einhorn, the former Assistant Secretary for Non-proliferation. He doubted that the current administration would be minded to let UNMOVIC in to verify what the US identifies. There was a young deputy assistant secretary named Matheson, an excellent lawyer according to Steve. He told me that he was dealing with the drafting of the next US resolution on Iraq. He seemed to think that the US probably would continue to wish Iraq to be submitted to long-term monitoring of their missile and biological sectors.

White House correspondents' dinner at the Hilton. 2,000 guests.

Walter picked me up. It was black tie. We went first to a pre-dinner cocktail given by Newsweek. Had a long chat with Brezhinsky (former national security adviser), Democrat and friend of Dick Gardner. He claimed that when Wolfowitz said early in 2002 that it was necessary to turn to Iraq and Powell had said that he only spoke for himself and not for the administration (I remember the incident), President Bush had said to Wolfowitz: keep it up . . . Query whether it is true. Brezhinsky did not say whether he had heard it himself. He thought my theory about Saddam feeling like an emperor of Mesopotamia and would not tolerate any intrusion he could avoid had some plausibility. (It squares rather well with the special sensitivity about no-fly zones and the U2 flights.) I met Madeleine Albright, who gave me her cheek to kiss.

I talked a little while with Kissinger, who seemed a bit distracted and old. I shook hands with Alan Greenspan, who looked aged and thin. I talked at length with a Congresswoman from California, Ellen Tauscher, who had Lawrence Livermore in her district and gave me her compliments and agreed with me about nuclear power. She would welcome me any day to California for speaking. I met John Negroponte, the US UN ambassador and we agreed that we should have coffee one day next week in New York. His wife hugged me and said that we must remain friends. A lot of people, especially the young, took pictures of themselves with me. On the way out I had a few words with Richard Perle, who still insisted that interviewing Iraqi scientists outside Iraq would have been important ... I countered by saying that there would always be the problem in a totalitarian state that it would have influence over the interviewees, even if they were abroad.

The dinner hall was huge and we sat at a table for the Washington Post right in front of the speaker's place at the head table on the dais. So we saw well.

At a table near us was Colin Powell and he spotted me and came up and hugged me warmly. It was nice of him to do it so publicly. It could have been a spontaneous act or a demonstration or both. I think both. We chatted a little. I said that maybe we could come back to international inspection when we think of the long-term monitoring. He seemed to agree with that. Condoleezza Rice sat at the table next to ours and we shook hands and exchanged a few words during the dinner. It was all friendly. Wolfowitz sailed in early and out early. I saw Maureen Dowd. I would have liked to tell her that reading the *New York Times* and her columns and those of N. Kristof are among my greatest joys.

All in all, quite an experience and I am grateful to Walter Pincus who arranged it all. He had, moreover, written a piece the same day in which he went through what the administration had said about weapons of mass destruction and how this contrasted with findings so far.

Sunday 27 *April*. We were picked up by Eva's friend Ray and his wife Rose Gottemoeller. He is in the State Department in the division of oceans and fisheries – a scientist originally. She is also from the state department and has dealt with non-proliferation both there and in the Department of Energy. She is a Democrat and now works with the Carnegie Endowment.

Tuesday 13 May 2003

Iraq. The UK/US/Spain draft resolution on the lifting of sanctions was tabled on Friday. It establishes an Authority (dominated by the above) to run the place and establishes a Fund into which all income from oil is to flow. A letter attached informs that the Authority will be in charge of disarmament and disposal of proscribed items. Funds may be used to pay for the disarmament work. There is nothing about inspection and long-term monitoring.

Friday 23 May 2003. New Resolution Adopted

Yesterday the new resolution was adopted by 14–1, with Syria absent. Sir Jeremy Greenstock visited me in the afternoon yesterday and explained that in the British view UNMOVIC ought to be used both to confirm the disarmament and to perform the long-term monitoring.

We had an interesting discussion about what led to the souring of the US attitude to me and UNMOVIC. I have begun to understand it by various things I have read during the last few days: Blair saying to me over the phone that the US was terribly disappointed that my early February speech sounded somewhat hopeful about Iraqi compliance compared to what I had said 27 January; German former inspectors transiting in Larnaca said to some journal that the German government's soft line had undermined the US effort to 'crack' Saddam. So here is my reading and my reply:

The US was making itself ready for war. Cheney's target date was 1 February (according to Greenstock). My 27 January speech fitted perfectly, gave them legitimacy and should have influenced the UN members. Came the 14 Feb. They had hoped that I would continue on the January line. This would have 'put increased pressure upon Saddam' and he might crack. Instead, they found that I registered a somewhat more helpful Iraq, which encouraged France, Germany, Russia and China to oppose military action. This, in turn, encouraged Saddam not to crack but to ride it out. A similar line of reasoning came from the German inspectors in Larnaca. It may be that Saddam was encouraged by my statement and these states' support and became more resistant – to what? But what should I have done? I saw my duty as pursuing effective verification and honest reporting to the Council. I had certainly hoped that my January speech should rattle the Iraqis from an attitude of almost arrogance. But above all it was an honest description of the Iraqi conduct. When the Iraqis, in fact, became rattled and began to cooperate much more 'proactively' with us, following our talks in Baghdad and following the US accelerating military build-up, I simply reported this. I am not sure that Saddam thereafter became any stiffer but certainly France, Germany and Russia became strengthened in their opposition to war. The US would have wanted me to testify that the Iraqis were as bad now as we had seen them in January to bolster their position. Blair said that my speech had made the use of force inevitable. Well, it might have made it impossible for the US to get an authorization for the war, but that was not the aim of the speech. Suppose I had reported very negatively about Iraq. Would this have prevented war?

Thursday 5 June 2003

Today I presented the thirteenth quarterly report of UNMOVIC to the Security Council. We had made it rather detailed and solid. I did not want to call it a 'testament' but making my exit I felt it was good to have a document showing that we did a good many things and that we were highly professional.

I learned yesterday afternoon that the meeting would be public during my presentation. This was clearly a compliment to me. I was to appear one last time in public in the Security Council Chamber. Thereafter, the President of the Council, this month Russia (Ambassador Sergei Lavrov), thanked me on behalf of the whole Council.

Monday 16 June 2003

Back from a great farewell dinner (perhaps sixty people) organized for me by Edith Lederer (AP) and other journalists at the UN. Kofi Annan and Nane came for the drinks. That was a very kind gesture, seen by fifty journalists and five ambassadors! I understood that he had had a thought to come to the Security Council for my presentation of UNMOVIC's thirteenth report at the open meeting. He did not and I think he was right. It might have been seen by the US as a demonstration against them.

At the journalists' dinner reception Kofi gave a short speech for me, in which he revealed that I had wanted to end my contract in the summer 2002 and not found it possible At the 1st of March this year it had been out of question. He is kind and praising but there is some restraint in what he says. With all Kofi's attentiveness, kindness he nevertheless keeps a certain distance. He does not get buddy. Perhaps wisely so. I mostly acted the same way – learnt to do it. Getting too close has its risks. I genuinely like him and admire him for several things. First of all, I admire his presence of mind during diplomatic talks. He is not to be taken by surprise and he is the supreme diplomat to avoid getting stuck on controversy or unpleasantness unnecessarily. Like me he is not conflict-prone. He also keeps remarkably much in his head. He has all the UN agenda. I only have one point. Yet I must say he is very well briefed on it. Thirdly, I think he is superb in responding to media. Very precise and circumspect. I have been more in demand in the past half year. There were 1,500 journalists accredited to the Security Council meetings at which I spoke! The journalists said that Iraq was the greatest media event in a number of years – some thought for all times – of the UN. It also occurred to me – but I did not say it – that I hardly ever run into trouble because of diplomatic mistakes I make, but not so rarely because I have been misunderstood by media or have spoken too freely with them.

The Security Council, after the end of the Cold War, became an interesting body – after having been so static through the Cold War. However, after the US disenchantment with it after the Iraq affair, it is damaged. Not that it does not have a lot of business to transact, mainly in African matters, but the US does not see it as a central natural mechanism for multilateral security action. Does the US care only about à la carte multilateralism, which it can, itself, dominate? I am not certain that the question of membership and composition is so vital as what issues are brought there and the way of working. Since members of the Council represent not only themselves but also the region they come from perhaps one could require that they should all consult the group that has nominated them to gauge the view of the group. It will then also be less painful not to be on the Council. Of course, the Europeans are doing this through the

EU – not always with the result of unity. Yet, there is an attempt made. It would be a good if states in other regions – Africans, Latinos, South Asians, tried the same. They could perhaps be better informed and act on a stronger footing.

Thursday 19 June 2003

I saw Kofi Annan in his office and officially said goodbye in front of cameras. Lunch the same day at the Russian mission for departing dignitaries, among whom I was included. There was Jeremy Greenstock, departing UK ambassador, who should have gone into retirement but whom Tony Blair has appointed highest Brit in Baghdad. He tries to look cheerful. As our Russian host said, Sir Jeremy will now have to implement all the resolutions he has drafted! Lavrov asked me to take the floor, which I did.

Epilogue

In the preface to the diary, I have explained what I believe led to the Iraq war in 2003 and the sequence of events. In this epilogue, I conclude with two broad reflections.

The first has regard to the motivation for war. The invasion of Iraq in March 2003 is generally termed the 'Iraq war', but it did not have the aims that we often associate with 'wars' – to grab territory or move borders. Its aim was 'regime change', and such armed actions have commonly been termed 'interventions'. In the history of interventions, what is the place and significance of the 2003 invasion?

Before the twentieth century, 'intervention' – like 'war' – was not subject to any prohibitory norm, and it was frequently practised. The term was used for armed territorial incursions with other aims than that of permanent acquisition of territory.

After the Napoleonic wars, the group of powers that formed the so-called European Concert and Holy Alliance famously agreed on and performed many armed interventions to uphold monarchic regimes and to prevent liberal regime change in various regions. There were also military actions for many other purposes, including 'humanitarian interventions' to protect threatened Christian groups.

A modest reaction to the not uncommon practice of sending warships and threatening bombardment to recover contract debts was a convention adopted at the second Hague Peace Conference in 1907. It can perhaps be seen as an early legal straw in the wind against powerful states' excessive uses of armed interventions. Art. 10 of the Covenant of the League of Nations (1920) outlawed aggression but may not have covered interventions. By contrast, Art. 2:4 of the UN Charter (1945) clearly prohibits what in descriptive terms is called 'threat or use of force' against the 'territorial integrity or political independence' of states. It does not prevent a state from using force at the request of another state's government, for instance to help suppress internal rebellion, but it clearly outlaws interventions for 'humanitarian' reasons or for 'regime change'.

During the Cold War, the main protagonists used both legal means of influence and subversion and illegal armed interventions to maintain their domination or influence – for instance, in Czechoslovakia, Nicaragua, Dominican Republic and

Grenada. With the end of the Cold War, armed interventions for bloc competition seem to have largely disappeared. However, several large invited or uninvited armed interventions have occurred – in Afghanistan, Syria and Libya. They have proved to be both singularly destructive and unsuccessful. The same is true of the armed intervention in Iraq in 2003.

We should note that in none of the post–Cold War cases has it proved possible for outside powers through their armed actions to secure the kind of regimes they wanted to see. Nor does it seem likely that the Russian full-scale invasion of Ukraine will result in the pro-Russian regime that was declared to be the objective of the 'special military operation'. One would hope that the recent cases will impress on all powers the experience that attempting regime changes from the outside – whether by intervention or war – is fraught with dangers, is likely to end in disaster and tragedy and should only be undertaken with UN authorization under the R2P (responsibility to protect) doctrine to prevent humanitarian catastrophes.

A second reflection concerns the role of truth. While for good reason it is often said that in war truth is the first casualty, exceptionally it was the 2003 war in Iraq that brought conclusive moments of truth about the country's weapons of mass destruction (WMD).

Following the 1991 Gulf war and until 1998, UNSCOM and the IAEA had looked for WMD in Iraq, but while they identified facilities and methods that had been used in past WMD production, they found no weapons. Iraq's explanation that it had itself ensured the destruction of WMD already in 1991 was probably correct – but it was not believed by the major powers. As Iraq had no credibility and as proving the negative (that nothing exists) is difficult, it was hard for inspection teams to conclude with 100 per cent certainty that no WMD remained hidden somewhere. In 1997, the US warned the IAEA against coming even close to such a conclusion. The US government wanted to be able to point to possibly retained WMD as grounds for renewed armed action.

By the end of 1999, however, the Security Council had come to feel that only a residue of unresolved disarmament issues could remain. It adopted a resolution – with the US concurring – that foresaw the suspension of sanctions when 'unresolved disarmament issues' had been resolved through full Iraqi cooperation.

In the aftermath of the 9/11 terrorist attack, this softer outlook – that could have left a complying Saddam 'on parole' – waned. The Bush government now discerned an 'axis of evil' that included Iraq. In 2002, British and US intelligence published dossiers alleging continued presence of WMD in Iraq, and, in well-published statements, US Vice President Cheney and US Defense Secretary Rumsfeld as well as UK Prime Minister Blair asserted the same as facts. However, despite some 700 inspections by UNMOVIC, including several dozen that went to sites recommended by Western intelligence, no hidden weapons were found. It was the war, occupation and especially access to Iraqis who now dared speak freely, that led to the moment of truth for all – that there were no hidden WMD.

It is understandable, and perhaps even inevitable, that governments may take important actions based on incomplete or uncertain information. Inaction may have grave consequences. However, the launching of the Iraq war in 2003 was no such case. The armed action could without great inconvenience have been deferred many months to allow more inspections, as was suggested by many states. The residue of uncertainty would have shrunk to levels that would not possibly have sufficed to justify war.

Could I, as head of the UN inspections, have done more to impede the armed action? I have asked myself the question, and it has been put to me. I have not ventured an answer. Only a few weeks before the war, UNMOVIC circulated a paper listing what it saw as remaining 'unresolved disarmament issues', and we were on track to continue inspections as mandated in the 1999 Security Council resolution. Could we have ordered our inspectors to stay in Iraq despite the US warnings of imminent armed attack – and risk their lives? No. The inspectors' task was to inspect – not to be human shields against invasion.

Theoretically, the many states that wanted to stave off invasion could have tabled a resolution urging no national intervention and demanding continued UN inspections. Although it could have been vetoed, it would have manifested the resistance to invasion and confirmed support for the UN path to an adequate assurance of the absence of Iraqi WMD. No such resolution was tabled, inspectors were withdrawn in face of US warnings and on the very day the invasion was launched I had the strange task under SC Res. 1284 of presenting to the Security Council our programme for the future work.

The fact-finding inspections that were mandated by the UN Security Council and that had been working well were overrun by national action. They were not reaching 100 per cent certain conclusions but provided far more reliable observations than did government intelligence. The rash action that scoffed at impartial and credible UN inspection affected the respectability of the US and undermined the authority of the UN.

Fact-finding through impartial international verification or bilateral mutual inspection has become of increasing use and acceptance to create confidence that arms control agreements are respected. Examples are IAEA safeguards verification under the NPT (Treaty of nuclear non-proliferation) and under the JCPOA (Joint Comprehensive Plan of Action) with Iran, the monitoring by the CTBTO (Comprehensive Test Ban Treaty Organization) of the absence of weapons testing and the verification by the OPCW (Organization for the Prohibition of Chemical Weapons) of the ban on chemical weapons.

In a world where communications and media enable governments and other actors freely to disseminate biased, misleading or false information, there is also more generally a need for impartial mechanisms seeking, compiling and presenting truthful information. The scientific IPCC (International Program on Climate Change) and UNSCEAR (UN Scientific Committee on the Effects of Atomic

Radiation) and many international inquiries into war crimes are examples of such bodies. Art. 100 of the UN Charter reflects the same vital public interest in truthful documentation and service when it requires that international civil servants shall act without bias and that governments shall respect their impartial role.

Hans Blix, former diplomat and writer of non-fiction

For EU product safety concerns, contact us at Calle de José Abascal, 56–1º, 28003 Madrid, Spain or eugpsr@cambridge.org.

www.ingramcontent.com/pod-product-compliance
Ingram Content Group UK Ltd.
Pitfield, Milton Keynes, MK11 3LW, UK
UKHW021539130825
461759UK00021B/516